Valuation of Interest Rate Swaps and Swaptions

Gerald W. Buetow, Jr., Ph.D., CFA

Frank J. Fabozzi, Ph.D., CFA

Published by Frank J. Fabozzi Associates

Web Site

While the authors have made every effort to produce an error-free book, it is highly likely that there will be errors in this book. If you find an error, please send an email identifying the error. The email should be sent to: info@frankfabozzi.com.

All corrections will be posted on http://www.frankfabozzi.com/9899corrections.htm. In addition to any corrections, there may be some comments the authors may make to clarify the explanation of a topic. Please note that the web site is *not* a vehicle for asking questions about topics or for assistance in explaining topics.

© 2001 By Frank J. Fabozzi Associates
New Hope, Pennsylvania

This publication is designed to provide accurate and authoritative information in regard to the subject matter covered. It is sold with the understanding that the publisher is not engaged in rendering legal, accounting, or other professional services.

ISBN: 1-883249-89-9

Dedication

GWB
To my extraordinary wife, Tricia, and my amazing children, James Ward and Mary Elizabeth — for giving my life meaning and value.

FJF
To the memory of my father, Alfonso Fabozzi (4/1/16 – 11/23/00)

Acknowledgments

The authors would like to thank Dr. James Sochacki of James Madison University's Applied Mathematics Department and Bernd Hanke a doctoral candidate in finance at the London Business School for their invaluable assistance in the development of the software used to produce the many examples throughout the book.

About the Authors

Gerald W. Buetow, Jr., Ph.D., CFA, is currently President and Founder of BFRC Services, LLC, a Quantitative Financial Consulting firm in Charlottesville, Virginia. Prior to that he was Vice President of Curriculum Development for the Association for Investment Management and Research (AIMR). Formerly, Dr. Buetow was the Wheat First Professor of Finance and Director of the Quantitative Finance program at James Madison University. He was also lead quantitative researcher for Prudential Investment's Quantitative Investment Management Group where he managed an enhanced index fund and developed structured securities. Dr. Buetow has spent most of the last few years developing advanced term structure modeling software and other financial software. Dr. Buetow also has numerous publications in various academic and practitioner journals as well as in various edited works. Dr. Buetow has a B.S. in Electrical Engineering and a Ph.D. in Finance and Econometrics from Lehigh University. He also has an M.S. in Finance from the University of Texas-Dallas and holds the Chartered Financial Analyst designation. He can be contacted via his website: www.BFRCServices.com.

Frank J. Fabozzi, Ph.D., CFA, is editor of the *Journal of Portfolio Management* and an Adjunct Professor of Finance at Yale University's School of Management. Prior to joining Yale's faculty, he was a Visiting Professor of Finance at MIT's Sloan School of Management. He is a Chartered Financial Analyst and Certified Public Accountant. Dr. Fabozzi is on the board of directors of the Guardian Life family of funds and the BlackRock complex of funds. He earned a doctorate in economics from the City University of New York in 1972 and in 1994 received an honorary doctorate of Humane Letters from Nova Southeastern University. Dr. Fabozzi is a Fellow of the International Center for Finance at Yale University.

Table of Contents

About the Authors   iv

1. Introduction   1
2. Calculating Swap Payments   17
3. Computing the Present Value of Swap Payments and   33
    Determining the Swap Fixed Rate
4. Traditional Approach to the Valuation of a Plain Vanilla Swap   49
5. Lattice Approach to Valuation   65
6. Swap Valuation Using the Lattice Approach   77
7. Valuation of Forward Start Swaps   95
8. Valuing a Swaption   111
9. Factors that Affect the Value of a Swaption   129
10. Valuing Non-LIBOR Based Swaps and Basis Swaps   145
11. Controlling Interest Rate Risk with Swaps   165

    Appendix A   Theoretical Spot and Forward Rates   195
    Appendix B   Binomial Interest Rate Model   215
    Appendix C   Valuation of Swaps Using the Trinomial Approach   219

    Index   241

Chapter 1

Introduction

One of the major innovations in the financial markets has been the interest rate swap. This instrument has allowed portfolio and risk managers and corporate treasurers with a better tool for controlling interest rate risk. Our objective in this book is to explain how interest rate swaps are valued and the factors that affect their value. This will allow the user of interest rate swaps to better understand how swaps can be used for managing interest rate risk.

Our purpose in this chapter is to explain the basic features of an interest rate swap and their economic interpretation. At the end of the chapter we provide an overview of the chapters to follow.

THE PLAIN VANILLA SWAP

In an interest rate swap, two parties agree to exchange interest payments at specified future dates. The dollar amount of the interest payments exchanged is based on some predetermined dollar principal, which is called the *notional principal* or *notional amount*. The payment each party pays to the other is the agreed-upon periodic interest rate times the notional principal. The only dollars that are exchanged between the parties are the interest payments, not the notional principal.

In the most common type of swap, one party agrees to pay the other party fixed interest payments at designated dates for the life of the contract. This party is referred to as the *fixed-rate payer*. The fixed rate that the fixed-rate payer must make is called the *swap fixed rate* or *swap rate*. The other party, who agrees to make payments that float with some reference rate, is referred to as the *fixed-rate receiver*. The fixed-rate payer is also referred to as the *floating-rate receiver* and the floating-rate receiver is also called the *floating-rate payer*. The type of swap that we have just described is called a *plain vanilla swap*.

The reference rates that have been used for the floating rate in an interest rate swap are those on various money market instruments: the London interbank offered rate, Treasury bills, commercial paper, bankers acceptances, certificates of deposit, the federal funds rate, a constant maturity Treasury rate, and the prime rate. The most common is the London interbank offered rate (LIBOR). LIBOR is the rate at which prime banks offer to pay on Eurodollar deposits available to other prime banks for a given maturity. Basically, it is viewed as the global cost of bank borrowing. There is not just one rate but a rate for different maturities. For example, there is a 1-month LIBOR, 3-month LIBOR, 6-month LIBOR, and so on.

To illustrate a plain vanilla interest rate swap, suppose that for the next five years party X agrees to pay party Y 6% per year (the swap fixed rate), while party Y agrees to pay party X 3-month LIBOR (the reference rate). Party X is the fixed-rate payer, while party Y is the fixed-rate receiver. Assume that the notional principal is $100 million, and that payments are exchanged every three months for the next five years. This means that every three months, party X (the fixed-rate payer) will pay party Y $1.5 million (6% times $100 million divided by 4). The amount that party Y (the fixed-rate receiver) will pay party X will be 3-month LIBOR times $100 million divided by 4. If 3-month LIBOR is 5%, party Y will pay party X $1.25 million (5% times $100 million divided by 4). Note that we divide by four because one-quarter of a year's interest is being paid. (We will be more precise about the days in the period for determining the payments in the next chapter.) This is illustrated in panel a of Exhibit 1.

Swap Payments versus Cash Flows

The payments between the parties are usually netted. In our illustration, if the fixed-rate payer must pay $1.5 million and the fixed-rate receiver must pay $1.25 million, than rather than writing checks for the respective amounts, the fixed-rate party can just make a payment of $0.25 million (= $1.5 million − $1.25 million) to the fixed-rate receiver. We shall refer to this netted payment between the two parties as the *cash flow for the swap* for the period. We note that throughout the literature the terms "swap payments" and "cash flows" are used interchangeably. However, in this book we will use the term swap payments to mean the payment made by a counterparty before any netting and cash flow to mean the netted amount.

Exhibit 1: Summary of How the Value of a Swap to Each Counterparty Changes when Interest Rates Change
a. Initial position

Swap fixed rate	=	6%
Payment frequency	=	quarterly
Reference rate	=	3-month LIBOR
Term of swap	=	5 years
Notional principal	=	$100 million
Payment by fixed-rate payer	=	$1.5 million

Every quarter

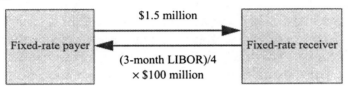

b. Interest rates increase such that swap fixed spread is 7%

Fixed-rate payer pays initial swap fixed rate of 6% to obtain 3-month LIBOR
    Advantage to fixed-rate payer: pays only 6% not 7% to obtain 3-month LIBOR

Fixed-rate receiver pays 3-month LIBOR
    Disadvantage to fixed-rate receiver: receives only 6% in exchange for 3-month LIBOR, not 7%

Results of a rise in interest rates:

Party	Value of swap
Fixed-rate payer	Increases
Fixed-rate receiver	Decreases

c. Interest rates decrease such that swap fixed spread is 5%

Fixed-rate payer pays initial swap fixed rate of 6% to obtain 6-month LIBOR
    Disadvantage to fixed-rate payer: must pay 6% not 5% to obtain 3-month LIBOR

Fixed-rate receiver pays 3-month LIBOR
    Advantage to fixed-rate receiver: receives 6% in exchange for 3-month LIBOR, not 5%

Results of a rise in interest rates:

Party	Value of swap
Fixed-rate payer	Decreases
Fixed-rate receiver	Increases

Swap Quote Conventions

The convention that has evolved for quoting a swap fixed rate is that a dealer sets the floating rate equal to the reference rate and then quotes the swap fixed rate that will apply. The swap fixed rate is some "spread" above the Treasury yield curve with the same term to maturity as the swap. This spread is called the *swap spread*.

Entering Into a Swap and Counterparty Risk

Interest rate swaps are over-the-counter (OTC) instruments. This means that they are not traded on an exchange. A party wishing to enter into a swap transaction can do so through either a securities firm or a commercial bank that transacts in swaps. These entities can do one of the following. First, they can arrange or broker a swap between two parties that want to enter into an interest rate swap. In this case, the securities firm or commercial bank is acting in a brokerage capacity. The broker is *not* a party to the swap.

The second way in which a securities firm or commercial bank can get a party into a swap position is by taking the other side of the swap. This means that the securities firm or the commercial bank is acting as a dealer rather than a broker in the transaction. Acting as a dealer, the securities firm or the commercial bank must hedge its swap position in the same way that it hedges its position in other securities that it holds. Also it means that the dealer (which we refer to as a *swap dealer*) is the counterparty to the transaction. If a party entered into a swap with a swap dealer, the party will look to the swap dealer to satisfy the obligations of the swap; similarly, that same swap dealer looks to the counterparty to fulfill its obligations as set forth in the swap agreement.

The risk that the two parties take on when they enter into a swap is that the other party will fail to fulfill its obligations as set forth in the swap agreement. That is, each party faces default risk and therefore there is bilateral *counterparty risk*.

RISK/RETURN CHARACTERISTICS OF AN INTEREST RATE SWAP

The value of an interest rate swap will fluctuate with market interest rates. To see how, let's consider our hypothetical swap. Suppose that interest rates change immediately after parties X and Y enter into the swap. Panel a in Exhibit 1 shows the transaction. First, consider what would happen if the market required that in any 5-year swap the fixed-rate payer must pay a swap fixed rate of 7% in order to receive 3-month LIBOR. If party X (the fixed-rate payer) wants to sell its position to party A, then party A will benefit by having to pay only 6% (the original swap fixed rate agreed upon) rather than 7% (the current swap fixed rate) to receive 3-month LIBOR. Party X will want compensation for this benefit. Consequently, the value of party X's position has increased. Thus, if interest rates increase, the fixed-rate payer will realize a profit and the fixed-rate receiver will realize a loss. Panel b in Exhibit 1 summarizes the results of a rise in interest rates.

Next, consider what would happen if interest rates decline to, say, 5%. Now a 5-year swap would require the fixed-rate payer to pay 5% rather than 6% to receive 3-month LIBOR. If party X wants to sell its position to party B, the latter would demand compensation to take over the position. In other words, if interest rates decline, the fixed-rate payer will realize a loss, while the fixed-rate receiver will realize a profit. Panel c in Exhibit 1 summarizes the results of a decline in interest rates.

While we know in what direction the change in the value of a swap will be for the counterparties when interest rates change, the question is how much will the value of the swap change. We show how to compute the change in the value of a swap in later chapters in this book.

INTERPRETING A SWAP POSITION

There are two ways that a swap position can be interpreted: (1) a package of futures (forward) contracts and (2) a package of cash flows from buying and selling cash market instruments.[1] These interpretations will help us understand how to value swaps and how to assess the sensitivity of a swap's value to changes in interest rates.

---

[1] Swaps can also be replicated using caps and floors. Specifically, a portfolio consisting of a long cap and a short floor struck such that the net cost is zero is equivalent to a plain vanilla swap. We do not discuss this interpretation because of the complex nature of interest rate options.

Package of Futures (Forward) Contracts

Contrast the position of the counterparties in an interest rate swap to the position of a long and short interest rate futures (forward) position. The long futures position gains if interest rates decline and loses if interest rates rise; this is similar to the risk/return profile for a fixed-rate receiver. The risk/return profile for a fixed-rate payer is similar to that of short futures position: there is a gain if interest rates increase and a loss if interest rates decrease. By taking a closer look at the interest rate swap we can understand why the risk/return profile are similar.

Consider party X's position in our swap illustration. Party X has agreed to pay 6% and receive 3-month LIBOR. More specifically, assuming a $100 million notional principal, party X has agreed to buy a commodity called "3-month LIBOR" for $1.5 million. This is effectively a 3-month forward contract where party X agrees to pay $1.5 million in exchange for delivery of 3-month LIBOR. If interest rates increase to 7%, the price of that commodity (3-month LIBOR) in the market is higher, resulting in a gain for the fixed-rate payer, who is effectively long a 3-month forward contract on 3-month LIBOR. The fixed-rate receiver is effectively short a 3-month forward contract on 3-month LIBOR. There is therefore an implicit forward contract corresponding to each exchange date.

Now we can see why there is a similarity between the risk/return profile for an interest rate swap and a forward contract. If interest rates increase to, say, 7%, the price of that commodity (3-month LIBOR) increases to $1.75 million (7% times $100 million divided by 4). The long forward position (the fixed-rate payer) gains, and the short forward position (the fixed-rate receiver) loses. If interest rates decline to, say, 5%, the price of our commodity decreases to $1.25 million (5% times $100 million divided by 4). The short forward position (the fixed-rate receiver) gains, and the long forward position (the fixed-rate payer) loses.

Consequently, interest rate swaps can be viewed as a package of more basic interest rate derivatives such as forward contracts. The pricing of an interest rate swap will then depend on the price of a package of forward contracts with the same settlement dates in which the underlying for the forward contract is the same reference rate. We will make use of this principle in later chapters when we explain how to value swaps.

While an interest rate swap may be nothing more than a package of forward contracts, it is not a redundant contract for several reasons. First, maturities for forward or futures contracts do not extend out as far as those of an interest rate swap; for example, an interest rate swap with a term of 10 years or longer can be obtained. Second, an interest rate swap is a more transactionally efficient instrument. By this we mean that in one transaction an entity can effectively establish a payoff equivalent to a package of forward contracts. Third, the interest rate swap market has grown in liquidity since its introduction in 1981; interest rate swaps now provide more liquidity than forward contracts, particularly long-dated (i.e., long-term) forward contracts.

Package of Cash Market Instruments

To understand why a swap can also be interpreted as a package of cash market instruments, consider an investor who enters into the transaction below:

- buy $100 million par of a 5-year floating-rate bond that pays 3-month LIBOR every three months
- finance the purchase by borrowing $100 million for five years on terms requiring a 6% annual interest rate paid every three months

As a result of this transaction, the investor

- receives a floating rate every three months for the next five years
- pays a fixed rate every three months for the next five years

The cash flows for this transaction are set forth in Exhibit 2. The second column of the exhibit shows the cash flows from purchasing the 5-year floating-rate bond. There is a $100 million cash outlay and then 20 cash inflows. The amount of the cash inflows is uncertain because they depend on future LIBOR. The next column shows the cash flows from borrowing $100 million on a fixed-rate basis. The last column shows the net cash flows from the transaction. As the last column indicates, there is no initial cash flow (no cash inflow or cash outlay). In all 20 of the 3-month periods, the net position results in a cash inflow of LIBOR and a cash outlay of $1.5 million. This net position is identical to the position of a fixed-rate payer.

It can be seen from the net cash flow in Exhibit 2 that a fixed-rate payer has a cash market position that is equivalent to a long position in a floating-rate bond and a short position in a fixed-rate bond — the short position being the equivalent of borrowing by issuing a fixed-rate bond.

What about the position of a fixed-rate receiver? It can be easily demonstrated that the position of a fixed-rate receiver is equivalent to purchasing a fixed-rate bond and financing that purchase at a floating rate, where the floating rate is the reference rate for the swap. That is, the position of a fixed-rate receiver is equivalent to a long position in a fixed-rate bond and a short position in a floating-rate bond.[2]

Exhibit 2: Cash Flows for the Purchase of a 5-Year Floating-Rate Bond Financed by Borrowing on a Fixed-Rate Basis

Transaction:
- Purchase for $100 million a 5-year floating-rate bond:
  floating rate = LIBOR, quarterly pay
- Borrow $100 million for five years:
  fixed rate = 6%, semiannual payments

3-Month Period	Cash Flow (In Millions of Dollars) From Floating-Rate Bond*	Borrowing Cost	Net cash flow = Same as swap's cash flow
0	−100	+100.0	0
1	+(LIBOR1/4) × 100	−1.5	+(LIBOR1/4) × 100 − 1.5
2	+(LIBOR2/4) × 100	−1.5	+(LIBOR2/4) × 100 − 1.5
3	+(LIBOR3/4) × 100	−1.5	+(LIBOR3/4) × 100 − 1.5
...	....	....	....
...	....	....	....
...	....	....	....
19	+(LIBOR19/4) × 100	−1.5	+(LIBOR19/4) × 100 − 1.5
20	+(LIBOR20/4) × 100 + 100	−100 − 1.5	+(LIBOR20/4) × 100 − 1.5

* The subscript for LIBOR indicates the 3-month LIBOR as per the terms of the floating-rate bond at time t.

---

[2] See footnote 1 for a brief description of how caps and floors can be used to replicate a swap.

Exhibit 3: Describing the Parties to a Swap Agreement

Fixed-rate payer	Fixed-rate receiver
• pays fixed rate in the swap	• pays floating rate in the swap
• receives floating in the swap	• receives fixed in the swap
• is short the bond market	• is long the bond market
• has bought a swap	• has sold a swap
• is long a swap	• is short a swap
• has established the price sensitivities of a longer-term liability and a floating-rate asset	• has established the price sensitivities of a longer-term asset and a floating-rate liability

Source: Robert F. Kopprasch, John Macfarlane, Daniel R. Ross, and Janet Showers, "The Interest Rate Swap Market: Yield Mathematics, Terminology, and Conventions," Chapter 58 in Frank J. Fabozzi and Irving Pollack (eds.), *The Handbook of Fixed Income Securities* (Homewood, IL: Dow Jones-Irwin, 1987).

DESCRIBING THE COUNTERPARTIES TO A SWAP

The terminology used to describe the position of a party in the swap market combines cash market jargon and futures market jargon. This is not surprising given that a swap position can be interpreted as a position in a package of cash market instruments or a package of futures/forward positions. As we have said, the counterparty to an interest rate swap is either a fixed-rate payer or fixed-rate receiver.

Exhibit 3 lists how the counterparties to an interest rate swap agreement are described. To understand why the fixed-rate payer is viewed as "short the bond market," and the fixed-rate receiver is viewed as "long the bond market," consider what happens when interest rates change. Those who borrow on a fixed-rate basis will benefit if interest rates rise because they have locked in a lower interest rate. But those who have a short bond position will also benefit if interest rates rise. Thus, a fixed-rate payer can be said to be short the bond market. A fixed-rate receiver benefits if interest rates fall. A long position in a bond also benefits if interest rates fall, so terminology describing a fixed-rate receiver as long the bond market is not surprising. From our discussion of the interpretation of a swap as a package of cash market instruments, describing a swap in terms of the sensitivities of long and short cash positions follows naturally.

BEYOND THE PLAIN VANILLA SWAP

Thus far we have provided a description of a plain vanilla swap. There are other types of swap structures — simple extensions and complex structures. We describe these in this section.

A simple extension of the plain vanilla swap is one in which the notional principal changes based on a specified schedule. A plain vanilla swap in which the notional principal decreases over time is called an *amortizing swap*. When the notional principal increases over time, the swap is referred to as an *accreting swap*. As we will see, once we know how to value a plain vanilla swap where the notional principal is constant over the life of the swap, it is a simple matter to value one with a varying notional principal.

There are swaps where both parties pay a floating rate based on two reference rates. For example, one party can make payments based on the 3-month Treasury bill rate plus some spread and the other party make payments based on 3-month LIBOR. Swaps where both parties make floating payments are called *basis swaps*. These are swaps where the floating leg is based on a reference rate other than LIBOR. For example, the floating leg might be based on the 2-year U.S. Treasury note yield. Swaps tied to U.S. Treasuries are referred to as *Constant Maturity Treasury* (CMT) swaps. An example of this swap is provided in Chapter 10. Other intermediate-term floating reference rates are called *constant maturity swaps* (CMS).

Two complex swap structures are (1) a swap that starts at some future date and (2) an option on a swap. A swap that starts at some future date is called a *forward start swap*. An example of a forward start swap would be one where the swap starts two years from now and matures three years later. The swap fixed rate for determining the fixed payments is specified.[3]

An option on a swap gives the owner of the option the right to enter into a swap at some future date. An option on a swap is called a *swaption*. A *payer's swaption* is one in which the owner of the option has the right to enter into a swap to pay a fixed rate and receive a floating rate. A *receiver's swaption* is one in which the owner of the option has the right to enter into a swap to receive a

---

[3] Swaps that combine some or all of these characteristics are also possible.

fixed rate and pay a floating rate. The swap fixed rate is the strike rate of the swaption.

OVERVIEW OF BOOK

In the balance of this book, we will see how to value a swap and investigate the factors that affect a swap's value. In Chapter 2 we explain how to compute the swap payments taking into account the number of days in a payment period based on day count conventions used in the bond market. In Chapter 3 will see how to compute the present value of the swap payments and how to compute the swap fixed rate.

There are two approaches that are used to value a plain vanilla swap — the *traditional approach* and the *lattice approach*. In Chapter 4, we explain the traditional approach. The reason for introducing the lattice approach is that it can handle the valuation of complex swap structures. The framework for the lattice approach is provided in Chapter 5 and applied in Chapter 6 to value the same plain vanilla swap that is valued in Chapter 4 using the traditional approach. The particular lattice approach used is the binomial lattice.

In Chapters 7 and 8 we show how to use the binomial lattice approach to value a forward start swap and a swaption. In Chapter 9 we investigate how various factors affect the value of a swaption. The valuation of both a basis swap and a non-LIBOR-based swap are covered in Chapter 10.

To use swaps in portfolio and risk management, it is necessary to understand how the value of a swap changes when interest rates change. We investigate this in Chapter 11 where we discuss how a swap can be used to provide a better matching of the cash flows of an institution and how to compute the dollar duration of a swap position.

Appendix A reviews some basic fixed income analytics. Specifically, the derivation of spot rates and forward rates are reviewed. Appendix B describes the binomial interest rate model used in this book and how the binomial rate lattice is constructed. Appendix C explains the trinomial interest rate model and how the trinomial lattice approach is used to value various swap structures.

QUESTIONS

1. Suppose that party G and party H enter into a 4-year interest rate swap. The notional principal for the swap is $100 million and the reference rate is 3-month LIBOR. Suppose that the payments are made quarterly by both the fixed-rate payer and the fixed-rate receiver. Also assume that the swap fixed rate is 4.4%.

   a. What are the payments that must be made by the fixed-rate payer every quarter?

   b. Suppose for the first floating-rate payment 3-month LIBOR is 7.2%. What is the amount of the first floating-rate payment that must be made by the fixed-rate receiver?

2. In an interest rate swap what is meant by the swap fixed rate and the swap spread?

3. Suppose that Jane Collins, a portfolio manager, enters into a 3-year interest rate swap with a commercial bank that is a swap dealer. The notional principal for the swap is $40 million and the reference rate is 3-month LIBOR. Suppose that the payments are made quarterly. The swap fixed rate that Ms. Collins agrees to pay is 5.6%.

   a. Who is the fixed-rate payer and who is the fixed-rate receiver in this swap?

   b. What are the payments that must be made by the fixed-rate payer every quarter?

   c. Suppose for the first floating-rate payment 3-month LIBOR is 3.6%. What is the amount of the first floating-rate payment that must be made by the fixed-rate receiver?

4. Give two interpretations of an interest rate swap and explain why an interest rate swap can be interpreted in each way.

5. Suppose that interest rates decrease subsequent to the inception of an interest rate swap.

   a. What is the effect on the value of the swap from the perspective of the fixed-rate payer?

b. What is the effect on the value of the swap from the perspective of the fixed-rate receiver?

6. Why is the fixed-rate payer in an interest rate swap said to be "short the bond market"?

7. Briefly describe each of the following swap structures:

   a. an amortizing swap.
   b. an accreting swap.
   c. a basis swap.
   d. a forward start swap.
   e. a payer's swaption.

SOLUTIONS TO QUESTIONS

1. a. Since the swap rate is 4.4%, the fixed-rate payment each quarter will be:

   $100 million × (0.044/4) = $1.1 million

   (In the next chapter, this number will be fine tuned to allow for the fact that not every quarter has the same number of days.)

   b. Since 3-month LIBOR is 7.2%, the first quarterly payment will be:

   $100 million × (0.072/4) = $1.8 million

2. The swap fixed rate is the fixed rate that the fixed-rate payer agrees to pay over the life of the swap. The swap spread is the spread that is added to a benchmark Treasury security (from the Treasury yield curve) to obtain the swap fixed rate.

3. a. The fixed-rate payer agrees to pay the swap fixed rate (i.e., the fixed rate). Since Ms. Collins has agreed to pay the swap fixed rate, she is the fixed-rate payer.

   b. Since the swap fixed rate is 5.6%, the fixed-rate payment each quarter will be:

   $40,000,000 × (0.056/4) = $560,000

   (In the next chapter, this number will be fine tuned to allow for the fact that not every quarter has the same number of days.)

   c. Since 3-month LIBOR is 3.6%, the first quarterly payment will be:

   $40,000,000 × (0.036/4) = $360,000

4. A swap can be interpreted in the following two ways: (i) as a package of forward contracts and (ii) as a package of cash market instruments. It is a package of forward contracts because basically the fixed-rate payer is agreeing to pay a fixed amount for

"something." That something is the reference rate and therefore the value of what the fixed-rate receiver is receiving in exchange for the fixed-rate payment at an exchange date will vary. This is equivalent to a forward contract where the underlying is the reference rate. There is not just one forward contract but one for each date at which an exchange of payments will be made over the life of the swap. Thus, it is a package of forward contracts.

The second interpretation is that an interest rate swap is a package of cash market instruments. Specifically, from the perspective of the fixed-rate payer — the party paying fixed and receiving floating — it is equivalent to buying a floating-rate note (with the reference rate for the note being the reference rate for the swap) and funding (i.e., obtaining the funds to buy the floating-rate note) by issuing a fixed-rate bond (with the coupon rate for the bond being the swap fixed rate). The par value of the floating-rate note and the fixed-rate bond is the notional principal of the swap. For the fixed-rate receiver, a swap is equivalent to purchasing a fixed-rate bond and funding it by issuing a floating-rate note.

5. a. If interest rates decrease, the fixed-rate payer will realize a decline in the value of the swap. This is because the swap fixed rate is being paid but that rate is above the prevailing market rate necessary to receive the reference rate.

   b. If interest rates increase, the fixed-rate receiver will realize a decline in the value of the swap. This is because the fixed-rate receiver is being paid a lower rate (i.e., the swap fixed rate) than prevailing in the market in exchange for the reference rate.

6. An investor who is short the bond market benefits if interest rates increase. The party to an interest rate swap that benefits if interest rates increase is the fixed-rate payer. Thus, a fixed-rate payer is said to be short the bond market.

7. a. A swap where the notional principal decreases over the life of the swap.
   b. A swap where the notional principal increases over the life of the swap.

c. A swap where both parties agree to swap make floating payments and the floating payments are based on different reference rates.

d. A swap that begins at a designated date in the future with the swap fixed rate specified.

e. A payer's swaption (i.e., option on a swap) where the owner of the swaption has the right to enter into a swap to pay a fixed rate. The fixed rate or swap fixed rate is the strike rate for the swaption.

Chapter 2

Calculating Swap Payments

In an interest rate swap, the counterparties agree to exchange periodic interest payments. The dollar amount of the interest payments exchanged is based on the notional principal. In the most common type of swap, there is a fixed-rate payer and a fixed-rate receiver. In this chapter we will explain how to compute the payments for both parties to a plain vanilla swap in which the reference rate is 3-month LIBOR.

CALCULATING THE FLOATING PAYMENTS

Since the floating rate is set at the beginning of the period, the first floating payment is known. For all subsequent payments, the floating payments depend on the value of the reference rate when the floating rate is determined. To illustrate the issues associated with calculating the floating payment, we will assume that

- a swap starts today, January 1 of year 1(swap settlement date)
- the floating payments are made quarterly based on "actual/360"
- the reference rate is 3-month LIBOR
- the notional principal of the swap is $100
- the term of the swap is five years (20 payments)

The quarterly floating payments are based on an "actual/360" day count convention. This convention means that 360 days are assumed in a year and that in computing the interest for the quarter the actual number of days in the quarter are used. The floating payment is set at the beginning of the quarter but paid at the end of the quarter — that is, the floating payments are made in arrears.

Suppose that today 3-month LIBOR is 6.99%. Let's look at what the fixed-rate payer will receive on March 31 of year 1 — the

17

date when the first quarterly swap payment is made. There is no uncertainty about what the floating payment will be. In general, the floating payment is determined as follows:

$$\text{notional principal} \times (3\text{-month LIBOR}) \times \frac{\text{number of days in period}}{360}$$

In our illustration, assuming a non-Leap year, the number of days from January 1 of year 1 to March 31 of year 1 (the first quarter) is 90. If 3-month LIBOR is 6.99%, then the fixed-rate payer will receive a floating payment on March 31 of year 1 equal to:

$$\$100 \times 0.0699 \times \frac{90}{360} = \$1.74625$$

Now the difficulty is in determining the floating payments after the first quarterly payment. That is, for the 3-year swap there will be 12 quarterly floating payments. So, while the first quarterly payment is known, the next 11 are not. However, there is a way to hedge the next 11 floating payments by using a futures contract. Specifically, the futures contract used to hedge the future floating payments in a swap whose reference rate is 3-month LIBOR is the Eurodollar CD futures contract. We will digress to discuss this contract.

The Eurodollar CD Futures Contract

As explained in the previous chapter, a swap position can be interpreted as a package of forward/futures contracts or a package of cash flows from buying and selling cash market instruments. It is the former interpretation that will be used as the basis for valuing a swap. In the case of a LIBOR-based swap, the appropriate futures contract is the Eurodollar CD futures contract. For this reason, we will describe this important contract.

Eurodollar certificates of deposit (CDs) are denominated in dollars but represent the liabilities of banks outside the United States. The contracts are traded on both the International Monetary Market of the Chicago Mercantile Exchange and the London International Financial Futures Exchange. The rate paid on Eurodollar CDs is the London interbank offered rate (LIBOR).

The 3-month Eurodollar CD is the underlying instrument for the Eurodollar CD futures contract. The contract is for $1 million of face value and is traded on an index price basis. The index price basis in which the contract is quoted is equal to 100 minus the annualized LIBOR futures rate. For example, a Eurodollar CD futures price of 93.00 means a 3-month LIBOR futures rate of 7% (100 minus 93.00 divided by 100).

The Eurodollar CD futures contract is a cash settlement contract. That is, the parties settle in cash for the value of a Eurodollar CD based on LIBOR at the settlement date.

The Eurodollar CD futures contract allows the buyer of the contract to lock in the rate on 3-month LIBOR today for a future 3-month period. For example, suppose that on February 1 an investor purchases a Eurodollar CD futures contract that settles in March of the same year. Assume that the LIBOR futures rate for this contract is 7%. This means that the investor has agreed to invest in a 3-month Eurodollar CD that pays a rate of 7%. Specifically, the investor has locked in a rate for a 3-month investment of 7% beginning in March. If the investor on February 1 purchased a contract that settles in September of the *following* year and the LIBOR futures rate is 7.4%, the investor has locked in the rate on a 3-month investment beginning September of the following year.

From the perspective of the seller of a Eurodollar CD futures contract, the seller is agreeing to lend funds for three months at some future date at the LIBOR futures rate. For example, suppose on February 1 a bank sells a Eurodollar CD futures contract that settles in March of the same year and the LIBOR futures rate is 7%. The bank locks in a borrowing rate of 7% for three months beginning in March of that year. If the settlement date is September of the *following* year and the LIBOR futures rate is 7.4%, the bank is locking in a borrowing rate of 7.4% for the 3-month period beginning September of the following year.

The key point here is that the Eurodollar CD futures contract allows a participant in the financial market to lock in a 3-month rate on an investment or a 3-month borrowing rate. The 3-month period begins in the month that the contract settles.

Determining Future Floating Payments

Now let's return to our objective of determining the future floating payments. These payments can be locked in over the life of the swap using the Eurodollar CD futures contract. We will show how these floating payments are computed using this contract.

We will begin with the next quarterly payment — from April 1 of year 1 to June 30 of year 1. This quarter has 91 days. The floating payment will be determined by 3-month LIBOR on April 1 of year 1 and paid on June 30 of year 1. There is a 3-month Eurodollar CD futures contract for settlement on June 30 of year 1. That futures contract will have the market's expectation of what 3-month LIBOR on April 1 of year 1 is. For example, if the futures price for the 3-month Eurodollar CD futures contract that settles on June 30 of year 1 is 95.055, then as explained above, the 3-month Eurodollar futures rate is 6.945%. We will refer to that rate for 3-month LIBOR as the "forward rate." Therefore, if the fixed-rate payer bought one of these 3-month Eurodollar CD futures contracts on January 1 of year 1 (the inception of the swap) that settles on June 30 of year 1, then the payment that will be locked in for the quarter (April 1 to June 30 of year 1) is

$$\$1{,}000{,}000 \times 0.06945 \times \frac{91}{360}$$

Similarly, the Eurodollar CD futures contract can be used to lock in a floating payment for each of the next 10 quarters. It is important to remember that the reference rate at the beginning of period t determines the floating-rate that will be paid for the period. However, the floating payment is not made until the end of period t, denoted $t + 1$.

Exhibit 1 shows this for the 3-year swap. Shown in Column (1) is when the quarter begins and in Column (2) when the quarter ends. The payment will be received at the end of the first quarter (March 31 of year 1) and is \$1,012,500. That is the known floating payment as explained earlier. It is the only payment that is known. The information used to compute the first payment is in Column (4) which shows the current 3-month LIBOR (6.99%). The payment is shown in the last column, Column (8).

Exhibit 1: Floating Payments Based on Initial LIBOR and Euro CD Futures

(1) Quarter Starts	(2) Quarter Ends	(3) Number of Days in Quarter	(4) Current 3-Month LIBOR	(5) Eurodollar CD Futures Price	(6) For-ward Rate	(7) End of Qua-rter	(8) Floating Payment at End of Quarter
1/1/YR1	3/31/YR1	90	6.99%			1	1.74625
4/1/YR1	6/30/YR1	90		93.055	6.945%	2	1.73625
7/1/YR1	9/30/YR1	91		93.035	6.965%	3	1.76059
10/1/YR1	12/31/YR1	91		93.030	6.970%	4	1.76186
1/1/YR2	3/31/YR2	89		92.975	7.025%	5	1.73673
4/1/YR2	6/30/YR2	90		93.025	6.975%	6	1.74375
7/1/YR2	9/30/YR2	91		93.015	6.985%	7	1.76565
10/1/YR2	12/31/YR2	91		93.015	6.985%	8	1.76565
1/1/YR3	3/31/YR3	89		92.950	7.050%	9	1.74291
4/1/YR3	6/30/YR3	90		92.995	7.005%	10	1.75125
7/1/YR3	9/30/YR3	91		92.975	7.025%	11	1.77576
10/1/YR3	12/31/YR3	91		92.965	7.035%	12	1.77829
1/1/YR4	3/31/YR4	89		92.895	7.105%	13	1.75651
4/1/YR4	6/30/YR4	90		92.930	7.070%	14	1.76750
7/1/YR4	9/30/YR4	91		92.900	7.100%	15	1.79472
10/1/YR4	12/31/YR4	91		92.875	7.125%	16	1.80104
1/1/YR5	3/31/YR5	90		92.790	7.210%	17	1.80250
4/1/YR5	6/30/YR5	90		92.825	7.175%	18	1.79375
7/1/YR5	9/30/YR5	91		92.790	7.210%	19	1.82252
10/1/YR5	12/31/YR5	91		92.755	7.245%	20	1.83137

Notice that Column (7) numbers the quarters from 1 through 20. Look at the heading for Column (7). It identifies each quarter in terms of the end of the quarter. This is important because we will eventually be discounting the payments. We must take care to understand when each payment is to be exchanged in order to properly discount. So, for the first payment of $1.74625 it is going to be received at the end of quarter 1. When we refer to the time period for any payment, the reference is to the end of quarter. So, the fifth payment of $1.7367 would be identified as the payment for period 5, where period 5 means that it will be exchanged at the end of the fifth quarter.

CALCULATING THE FIXED PAYMENTS

The swap will specify the frequency of settlement for the fixed payments. The frequency need not be the same as the floating payments. For example, in the 3-year swap we have been using to illustrate the calculation of the floating payments, the frequency is quarterly. The frequency of the fixed payments could be semiannual rather than quarterly.

In our illustration we will assume that the frequency of settlement is quarterly for the fixed payments, the same as with the floating payments. The day count convention is the same as for the floating payment, "actual/360." The equation for determining the dollar amount of the fixed payment for the period is:

$$\text{notional principal} \times (\text{swap fixed rate}) \times \frac{\text{number of days in period}}{360}$$

It is the same equation as for determining the floating payment except that the swap fixed rate is used instead of the reference rate (3-month LIBOR in our illustration).

For example, suppose that the swap fixed rate is 7.0513% and the quarter has 90 days. Then the fixed payment for the quarter is:

$$\$100 \times 0.070513 \times \frac{90}{360} = \$1.762825$$

If there are 91 days in a quarter, the fixed payment for the quarter is:

$$\$100 \times 0.070513 \times \frac{91}{360} = \$1.782412$$

Note that the rate is fixed for each quarter but the dollar amount of the payment depends on the number of days in the period.

Exhibit 2 shows the fixed payments based on an assumed swap fixed rate (SFR) of 7.0513%. (Later we will see how the swap rate is determined in the next chapter.) The first three columns of the exhibit show the same information as in Exhibit 1 — the beginning and end of the quarter and the number of days in the quarter. Column (4) simply uses the notation for the period. That is, period 1 means the end of the first quarter, period 2 means the end of the second quarter, and so on. Column (5) shows the fixed payments for each period based on a swap fixed rate of 7.0513%.

DEALING WITH SWAPS WITH A VARYING NOTIONAL PRINCIPAL

There are swaps where the notional principal changes in a predetermined way over the life of the swap. For such swaps, the swap payments are adjusted for the notional principal for the period as follows:

floating payment for period t

$$= NP_t \times (\text{3-month LIBOR}_{t-1}) \times \frac{\text{number of days in period } t}{360}$$

Exhibit 2: Fixed Payments Assuming a Swap Fixed Rate of 7.0513%

(1) Quarter Starts	(2) Quarter Ends	(3) Number of Days in Quarter	(4) End of Quarter	(5) Fixed Payment
1/1/YR1	3/31/YR1	90	1	1.762825
4/1/YR1	6/30/YR1	90	2	1.762825
7/1/YR1	9/30/YR1	91	3	1.782412
10/1/YR1	12/31/YR1	91	4	1.782412
1/1/YR2	3/31/YR2	89	5	1.743238
4/1/YR2	6/30/YR2	90	6	1.762825
7/1/YR2	9/30/YR2	91	7	1.782412
10/1/YR2	12/31/YR2	91	8	1.782412
1/1/YR3	3/31/YR3	89	9	1.743238
4/1/YR3	6/30/YR3	90	10	1.762825
7/1/YR3	9/30/YR3	91	11	1.782412
10/1/YR3	12/31/YR3	91	12	1.782412
1/1/YR4	3/31/YR4	89	13	1.743238
4/1/YR4	6/30/YR4	90	14	1.762825
7/1/YR4	9/30/YR4	91	15	1.782412
10/1/YR4	12/31/YR4	91	16	1.782412
1/1/YR5	3/31/YR5	90	17	1.762825
4/1/YR5	6/30/YR5	90	18	1.762825
7/1/YR5	9/30/YR5	91	19	1.782412
10/1/YR5	12/31/YR5	91	20	1.782412

Exhibit 3: Floating Payments for an Amortizing Swap

(1)	(2)	(3)	(4)	(5)	(6)	(7)	(8)	(9)
Quarter Starts	Quarter Ends	Number of Days in Quarter	Current 3- Month LIBOR	Eurodollar CD Futures Price	Forward Rate (%)	End of Quarter	Varying Notional Principal	Floating Payment
1/1/YR1	3/31/YR1	90	6.985%			1	100	1.746250
4/1/YR1	6/30/YR1	90		93.055	6.945%	2	95	1.649438
7/1/YR1	9/30/YR1	91		93.035	6.965%	3	90	1.584538
10/1/YR1	12/31/YR1	91		93.030	6.970%	4	85	1.497582
1/1/YR2	3/31/YR2	89		92.975	7.025%	5	80	1.389389
4/1/YR2	6/30/YR2	90		93.025	6.975%	6	75	1.307813
7/1/YR2	9/30/YR2	91		93.015	6.985%	7	70	1.235957
10/1/YR2	12/31/YR2	91		93.015	6.985%	8	65	1.147674
1/1/YR3	3/31/YR3	89		92.950	7.050%	9	60	1.045750
4/1/YR3	6/30/YR3	90		92.995	7.005%	10	55	0.963187
7/1/YR3	9/30/YR3	91		92.975	7.025%	11	50	0.887882
10/1/YR3	12/31/YR3	91		92.965	7.035%	12	45	0.800231
1/1/YR4	3/31/YR4	89		92.895	7.105%	13	40	0.702606
4/1/YR4	6/30/YR4	90		92.930	7.070%	14	35	0.618625
7/1/YR4	9/30/YR4	91		92.900	7.100%	15	30	0.538417
10/1/YR4	12/31/YR4	91		92.875	7.125%	16	25	0.450260
1/1/YR5	3/31/YR5	90		92.790	7.210%	17	20	0.36050
4/1/YR5	6/30/YR5	90		92.825	7.175%	18	15	0.269063
7/1/YR5	9/30/YR5	91		92.790	7.210%	19	10	0.182253
10/1/YR5	12/31/YR5	91		92.755	7.245%	20	5	0.091569

fixed payment for period t

$$= NP_t \times (\text{swap fixed rate}) \times \frac{\text{number of days in period } t}{360}$$

where NP_t = notional principal for period t.

A swap in which the notional principal declines over the life of the swap is called an *amortizing swap*. A swap in which the notional principal increases over the life of the swap is called an *accreting swap*. A *roller coaster swap* is a swap where the notional principal can increase or decrease from the previous period.

To illustrate the calculations of the payments for a swap that has a changing notional principal, we will use the 5-year quarterly pay swap in Exhibit 3. The notional principal is shown in Column (8). Since the notional principal declines over the life of the swap, this is an example of an amortizing swap. The Eurodollar CD futures prices in Exhibit 1 are used to compute the floating payments. For example, consider quarter 9 ($t = 9$). The information for calculating the floating payment is as follows:

NP_9 = $60
3-month LIBOR   = 7.050%
number of days in period 9 = 89

then,

floating payment for period 9

$$= \$60 \times (0.07050) \times \frac{89}{360} = \$1.04575$$

Exhibit 4 shows the fixed payments assuming a swap fixed rate of 7.0095%. The fixed payment for period 9 is found as follows:

NP_9 = $60
swap fixed rate   = 7.0095%
number of days in period 9 = 89

fixed payment for period 9

$$= \$60 \times (0.070095) \times \frac{89}{360} = \$1.039743$$

Exhibit 4: Fixed Payments for an Amortizing Swap
(Assuming a Swap Fixed Rate = 7.0095%)

(1)	(2)	(3)	(4)	(5)	(6)
Quarter Starts	Quarter Ends	Number of Days in Quarter	End of Quarter	Varying Notional Principal	Fixed Payment
1/1/YR1	3/31/YR1	90	1	100	1.752375
4/1/YR1	6/30/YR1	90	2	95	1.664756
7/1/YR1	9/30/YR1	91	3	90	1.594661
10/1/YR1	12/31/YR1	91	4	85	1.506069
1/1/YR2	3/31/YR2	89	5	80	1.386323
4/1/YR2	6/30/YR2	90	6	75	1.314281
7/1/YR2	9/30/YR2	91	7	70	1.240292
10/1/YR2	12/31/YR2	91	8	65	1.151700
1/1/YR3	3/31/YR3	89	9	60	1.039743
4/1/YR3	6/30/YR3	90	10	55	0.963806
7/1/YR3	9/30/YR3	91	11	50	0.885923
10/1/YR3	12/31/YR3	91	12	45	0.797331
1/1/YR4	3/31/YR4	89	13	40	0.693162
4/1/YR4	6/30/YR4	90	14	35	0.613331
7/1/YR4	9/30/YR4	91	15	30	0.531554
10/1/YR4	12/31/YR4	91	16	25	0.442961
1/1/YR5	3/31/YR5	90	17	20	0.350475
4/1/YR5	6/30/YR5	90	18	15	0.262856
7/1/YR5	9/30/YR5	91	19	10	0.177185
10/1/YR5	12/31/YR5	91	20	5	0.088592

QUESTIONS

1. Assume a 3-year swap beginning on January 1 of year 1. The reference rate for the swap is 3-month LIBOR and the notional amount is $100 million. The floating and fixed payments are based on the "actual/360" day count convention. Below is the current 3-month LIBOR and the Eurodollar CD futures price for each quarter. Determine the futures rate for each quarter and the floating payment at the end of each quarter.

Quarter starts	Quarter ends	Number of Days in Quarter	Current 3-Month LIBOR	Eurodollar CD Futures Price	Forward Rate	End of Quarter	Floating Payment at End of Quarter
Jan 1 year 1	Mar 31 year 1	90	7.30%		—	1	
Apr 1 year 1	June 30 year 1	91		92.60		2	
July 1 year 1	Sept 30 year 1	92		92.10		3	
Oct 1 year 1	Dec 31 year 1	92		92.05		4	
Jan 1 year 2	Mar 31 year 2	90		92.00		5	
Apr 1 year 2	June 30 year 2	91		91.85		6	
July 1 year 2	Sept 30 year 2	92		91.75		7	
Oct 1 year 2	Dec 31 year 2	92		91.70		8	
Jan 1 year 3	Mar 31 year 3	90		91.55		9	
Apr 1 year 3	June 30 year 3	91		91.40		10	
July 1 year 3	Sept 30 year 3	92		91.25		11	
Oct 1 year 3	Dec 31 year 3	92		91.10		12	

2. Complete the following table for the fixed payments for the 3-year swap in Question 1 assuming a swap rate of 8.1313%:

Quarter Starts	Quarter Ends	Number of Days in Quarter	End of Quarter	Fixed Payment if Swap Fixed Rate is 8.1313%
Jan 1 year 1	Mar 31 year 1	90	1	
Apr 1 year 1	June 30 year 1	91	2	
July 1 year 1	Sept 30 year 1	92	3	
Oct 1 year 1	Dec 31 year 1	92	4	
Jan 1 year 2	Mar 31 year 2	90	5	
Apr 1 year 2	June 30 year 2	91	6	
July 1 year 2	Sept 30 year 2	92	7	
Oct 1 year 2	Dec 31 year 2	92	8	
Jan 1 year 3	Mar 31 year 3	90	9	
Apr 1 year 3	June 30 year 3	91	10	
July 1 year 3	Sept 30 year 3	92	11	
Oct 1 year 3	Dec 31 year 3	92	12	

3. Assume a 5-year swap beginning on January 1 of year 1. The reference rate for the swap is 3-month LIBOR and the notional principal varies as shown in the table below. The floating and fixed payments are based on the "actual/360" day count convention. Using the table below determine the forward rate and the floating payment at the end of each quarter.

Quarter Starts	Quarter Ends	Number of Days	Current 3-Month LIBOR	Eurodollar CD Price	End of Quarter	Varying NP ($ millions)	Forward Rate	Floating Payment
1/1/YR1	3/31/YR1	90	6.985%		1	50		
4/1/YR1	6/30/YR1	90		94.055	2	100		
7/1/YR1	9/30/YR1	91		93.985	3	60		
10/1/YR1	12/31/YR1	91		93.93	4	120		
1/1/YR2	3/31/YR2	89		93.825	5	70		
4/1/YR2	6/30/YR2	90		93.825	6	140		
7/1/YR2	9/30/YR2	91		93.765	7	80		
10/1/YR2	12/31/YR2	91		93.715	8	160		
1/1/YR3	3/31/YR3	89		93.6	9	90		
4/1/YR3	6/30/YR3	90		93.595	10	180		
7/1/YR3	9/30/YR3	91		93.525	11	100		
10/1/YR3	12/31/YR3	91		93.465	12	200		
1/1/YR4	3/31/YR4	89		93.345	13	110		
4/1/YR4	6/30/YR4	90		93.33	14	220		
7/1/YR4	9/30/YR4	91		93.25	15	120		
10/1/YR4	12/31/YR4	91		93.175	16	240		
1/1/YR5	3/31/YR5	90		93.04	17	130		
4/1/YR5	6/30/YR5	90		93.025	18	260		
7/1/YR5	9/30/YR5	91		92.94	19	140		
10/1/YR5	12/31/YR5	91		92.855	20	280		

4. Complete the following table for the fixed payments for the 5-year swap in Question 3 assuming a swap rate of 6.6223%.

Quarter Starts	Quarter Ends	Number of Days	End of Quarter	Varying NP	Fixed Payment
1/1/YR1	3/31/YR1	90	1	50	
4/1/YR1	6/30/YR1	90	2	100	
7/1/YR1	9/30/YR1	91	3	60	
10/1/YR1	12/31/YR1	91	4	120	
1/1/YR2	3/31/YR2	89	5	70	
4/1/YR2	6/30/YR2	90	6	140	
7/1/YR2	9/30/YR2	91	7	80	
10/1/YR2	12/31/YR2	91	8	160	
1/1/YR3	3/31/YR3	89	9	90	
4/1/YR3	6/30/YR3	90	10	180	
7/1/YR3	9/30/YR3	91	11	100	
10/1/YR3	12/31/YR3	91	12	200	
1/1/YR4	3/31/YR4	89	13	110	
4/1/YR4	6/30/YR4	90	14	220	
7/1/YR4	9/30/YR4	91	15	120	
10/1/YR4	12/31/YR4	91	16	240	
1/1/YR5	3/31/YR5	90	17	130	
4/1/YR5	6/30/YR5	90	18	260	
7/1/YR5	9/30/YR5	91	19	140	
10/1/YR5	12/31/YR5	91	20	280	

SOLUTIONS TO QUESTIONS

1.

Quarter Starts	Quarter Ends	Number of Days in Quarter	Current 3-Month LIBOR	Eurodollar CD Futures Price	Forward Rate	End of Quarter	Floating Payment at End of Quarter
Jan 1 year 1	Mar 31 year 1	90	7.30%		—	1	1,825,000
Apr 1 year 1	June 30 year 1	91		92.60	7.40%	2	1,870,556
July 1 year 1	Sept 30 year 1	92		92.10	7.90%	3	2,018,889
Oct 1 year 1	Dec 31 year 1	92		92.05	7.95%	4	2,031,667
Jan 1 year 2	Mar 31 year 2	90		92.00	8.00%	5	2,000,000
Apr 1 year 2	June 30 year 2	91		91.85	8.15%	6	2,060,139
July 1 year 2	Sept 30 year 2	92		91.75	8.25%	7	2,108,333
Oct 1 year 2	Dec 31 year 2	92		91.70	8.30%	8	2,121,111
Jan 1 year 3	Mar 31 year 3	90		91.55	8.45%	9	2,112,500
Apr 1 year 3	June 30 year 3	91		91.40	8.60%	10	2,173,889
July 1 year 3	Sept 30 year 3	92		91.25	8.75%	11	2,236,111
Oct 1 year 3	Dec 31 year 3	92		91.10	8.90%	12	2,274,444

2.

Quarter Starts	Quarter Ends	Number of Days in Quarter	End of Quarter	Fixed Payment if Swap Fixed Rate is 8.1313%
Jan 1 year 1	Mar 31 year 1	90	1	2,032,825
Apr 1 year 1	June 30 year 1	91	2	2,055,412
July 1 year 1	Sept 30 year 1	92	3	2,077,999
Oct 1 year 1	Dec 31 year 1	92	4	2,077,999
Jan 1 year 2	Mar 31 year 2	90	5	2,032,825
Apr 1 year 2	June 30 year 2	91	6	2,055,412
July 1 year 2	Sept 30 year 2	92	7	2,077,999
Oct 1 year 2	Dec 31 year 2	92	8	2,077,999
Jan 1 year 3	Mar 31 year 3	90	9	2,032,825
Apr 1 year 3	June 30 year 3	91	10	2,055,412
July 1 year 3	Sept 30 year 3	92	11	2,077,999
Oct 1 year 3	Dec 31 year 3	92	12	2,077,999

3.

Quarter Starts	Quarter Ends	Number of Days	Current 3-Month LIBOR	Eurodollar CD Price	End of quarter	Varying NP	Forward Rate	Floating Payment
1/1/YR1	3/31/YR1	90	6.985%		1	50		$873,125.00
4/1/YR1	6/30/YR1	90		94.055	2	100	5.94%	$1,486,250.00
7/1/YR1	9/30/YR1	91		93.985	3	60	6.02%	$912,275.00
10/1/YR1	12/31/YR1	91		93.93	4	120	6.07%	$1,841,233.33
1/1/YR2	3/31/YR2	89		93.825	5	70	6.18%	$1,068,618.06
4/1/YR2	6/30/YR2	90		93.825	6	140	6.17%	$2,161,250.00
7/1/YR2	9/30/YR2	91		93.765	7	80	6.24%	$1,260,855.56
10/1/YR2	12/31/YR2	91		93.715	8	160	6.29%	$2,541,933.33
1/1/YR3	3/31/YR3	89		93.6	9	90	6.40%	$1,424,000.00
4/1/YR3	6/30/YR3	90		93.595	10	180	6.41%	$2,882,250.00
7/1/YR3	9/30/YR3	91		93.525	11	100	6.48%	$1,636,736.11
10/1/YR3	12/31/YR3	91		93.465	12	200	6.54%	$3,303,805.56
1/1/YR4	3/31/YR4	89		93.345	13	110	6.66%	$1,809,790.28
4/1/YR4	6/30/YR4	90		93.33	14	220	6.67%	$3,668,500.00
7/1/YR4	9/30/YR4	91		93.25	15	120	6.75%	$2,047,500.00
10/1/YR4	12/31/YR4	91		93.175	16	240	6.83%	$4,140,500.00
1/1/YR5	3/31/YR5	90		93.04	17	130	6.96%	$2,262,000.00
4/1/YR5	6/30/YR5	90		93.025	18	260	6.98%	$4,533,750.00
7/1/YR5	9/30/YR5	91		92.94	19	140	7.06%	$2,498,455.56
10/1/YR5	12/31/YR5	91		92.855	20	280	7.15%	$5,057,072.22

4.

Quarter Starts	Quarter Ends	Number of Days	End of Quarter	Varying NP	Fixed Payment
1/1/YR1	3/31/YR1	90	1	50	$827,783.15
4/1/YR1	6/30/YR1	90	2	100	$1,655,566.29
7/1/YR1	9/30/YR1	91	3	60	$1,004,376.88
10/1/YR1	12/31/YR1	91	4	120	$2,008,753.77
1/1/YR2	3/31/YR2	89	5	70	$1,146,019.78
4/1/YR2	6/30/YR2	90	6	140	$2,317,792.81
7/1/YR2	9/30/YR2	91	7	80	$1,339,169.18
10/1/YR2	12/31/YR2	91	8	160	$2,678,338.35
1/1/YR3	3/31/YR3	89	9	90	$1,473,454.00
4/1/YR3	6/30/YR3	90	10	180	$2,980,019.32
7/1/YR3	9/30/YR3	91	11	100	$1,673,961.47
10/1/YR3	12/31/YR3	91	12	200	$3,347,922.94
1/1/YR4	3/31/YR4	89	13	110	$1,800,888.22
4/1/YR4	6/30/YR4	90	14	220	$3,642,245.84
7/1/YR4	9/30/YR4	91	15	120	$2,008,753.77
10/1/YR4	12/31/YR4	91	16	240	$4,017,507.53
1/1/YR5	3/31/YR5	90	17	130	$2,152,236.18
4/1/YR5	6/30/YR5	90	18	260	$4,304,472.35
7/1/YR5	9/30/YR5	91	19	140	$2,343,546.06
10/1/YR5	12/31/YR5	91	20	280	$4,687,092.12

Chapter 3

Computing the Present Value of Swap Payments and Determining the Swap Fixed Rate

At the initiation of an interest rate swap, the counterparties are agreeing to exchange future payments and no upfront payments by either party are made. This means that the swap terms must be such that the present value of the payments to be made by the counterparties must be at least equal to the present value of the payments that will be received. In fact, to eliminate arbitrage opportunities, the present value of the payments made by a party must be equal to the present value of the payments received by that same party. The equivalence (or no arbitrage) of the present value of the payments is the key principle in calculating the swap rate. In this chapter we will demonstrate how to compute the present value of the fixed and floating payments for a swap and how to determine the determine the swap rate.

CALCULATING THE PRESENT VALUE OF THE FLOATING PAYMENTS

We must be careful about how we compute the present value of the swap payments. In particular, we must carefully specify (1) the timing of the payment and (2) the interest rates that should be used to discount the payments. We already addressed the first issue in the previous chapter. In constructing the exhibit for the payments, we indicated that the payments are at the end of the quarter. So, we denoted the timing of the payments with respect to the end of the quarter.

Let's look at the interest rates that should be used for discounting. To do so we draw on two important principles from financial theory. First, every cash flow should be discounted at its own discount rate using a spot rate. So, if we discounted a cash flow of $1 using the spot rate for period t, the present value would be:

present value of $1 to be received in period t

$$= \frac{\$1}{(1 + \text{spot rate for period } t)^t}$$

The second principle is that forward rates are derived from spot rates so that if we discounted a cash flow using forward rates rather than a spot rate, we would come up with the same value. That is, the present value of $1 to be received in period t can be rewritten as:

present value of $1 to be received in period t =

$$\frac{\$1}{(1 + \text{forward rate for period } 1)(1 + \text{forward rate for period } 2)\cdots}$$

$$\times \frac{\$1}{(1 + \text{forward rate for period } t)}$$

We will refer to the present value of $1 to be received in period t as the *forward discount factor*. In our calculations involving swaps, we will compute the forward discount factor for a period using the forward rates. These are the same forward rates that are used to compute the floating payments — those obtained from the Eurodollar CD futures contract.

We must make just one more adjustment. We must adjust the forward rates used in the formula for the number of days in the period (i.e., the quarter in our illustrations) in the same way that we made this adjustment to obtain the payments. Specifically, the forward rate for a period, which we will refer to as the *period forward rate*, is computed using the following equation:

$$\text{period forward rate} = \text{annual forward rate} \times \left(\frac{\text{number of days in period}}{360} \right)$$

Exhibit 1: Calculating the Forward Discount Factor

(1) Quarter Starts	(2) Quarter Ends	(3) Number of Days in Quarter	(4) End of Quarter	(5) Forward Rate	(6) Period Forward Rate	(7) Forward Discount Factor
1/1/YR1	3/31/YR1	90	1	6.99%	1.7463%	0.98284
4/1/YR1	6/30/YR1	90	2	6.94%	1.7363%	0.96606
7/1/YR1	9/30/YR1	91	3	6.97%	1.7606%	0.94935
10/1/YR1	12/31/YR1	91	4	6.97%	1.7619%	0.93291
1/1/YR2	3/31/YR2	89	5	7.03%	1.7367%	0.91699
4/1/YR2	6/30/YR2	90	6	6.97%	1.7438%	0.90127
7/1/YR2	9/30/YR2	91	7	6.99%	1.7657%	0.88563
10/1/YR2	12/31/YR2	91	8	6.99%	1.7657%	0.87027
1/1/YR3	3/31/YR3	89	9	7.05%	1.7429%	0.85536
4/1/YR3	6/30/YR3	90	10	7.01%	1.7513%	0.84064
7/1/YR3	9/30/YR3	91	11	7.03%	1.7758%	0.82597
10/1/YR3	12/31/YR3	91	12	7.04%	1.7783%	0.81154
1/1/YR4	3/31/YR4	89	13	7.11%	1.7565%	0.79753
4/1/YR4	6/30/YR4	90	14	7.07%	1.7675%	0.78368
7/1/YR4	9/30/YR4	91	15	7.10%	1.7947%	0.76986
10/1/YR4	12/31/YR4	91	16	7.13%	1.8010%	0.75624
1/1/YR5	3/31/YR5	90	17	7.21%	1.8025%	0.74285
4/1/YR5	6/30/YR5	90	18	7.18%	1.7938%	0.72976
7/1/YR5	9/30/YR5	91	19	7.21%	1.8225%	0.71670
10/1/YR5	12/31/YR5	91	20	7.25%	1.8314%	0.70381

For example, look at Exhibit 1 of the previous chapter. The annual forward rate for period 4 is 6.970%. The period forward rate for period 4 is:

$$\text{period forward rate} = 0.06970 \times \left(\frac{91}{360}\right) = 1.7619\%$$

Column (5) in Exhibit 1 shows the annual forward rate for all 20 periods and Column (6) shows the period forward rate for all 20 periods. Note that the period forward rate for period 1 is 90/360 of 6.99%, which is 90/360 of the known rate for 3-month LIBOR.

Also shown in Exhibit 1 is the forward discount factor for all 20 periods. These values are shown in the last column. Let's show how the forward discount factor is computed for periods 1, 2, and 3. For period 1, the forward discount factor is:

Exhibit 2: Present Value of the Floating Payments

(1) Quarter Starts	(2) Quarter Ends	(3) End of Quarter	(4) Forward Discount Factor	(5) Floating Payment at End of Quarter	(6) PV of Floating Payments
1/1/YR1	3/31/YR1	1	0.982837	1.746250	1.716279
4/1/YR1	6/30/YR1	2	0.966064	1.736250	1.677328
7/1/YR1	9/30/YR1	3	0.949350	1.760597	1.671422
10/1/YR1	12/31/YR1	4	0.932913	1.761861	1.643663
1/1/YR2	3/31/YR2	5	0.916987	1.736736	1.592565
4/1/YR2	6/30/YR2	6	0.901271	1.743750	1.571592
7/1/YR2	9/30/YR2	7	0.885634	1.765653	1.563723
10/1/YR2	12/31/YR2	8	0.870268	1.765653	1.536592
1/1/YR3	3/31/YR3	9	0.855360	1.742917	1.490821
4/1/YR3	6/30/YR3	10	0.840638	1.751250	1.472168
7/1/YR3	9/30/YR3	11	0.825971	1.775764	1.466730
10/1/YR3	12/31/YR3	12	0.811540	1.778292	1.443154
1/1/YR4	3/31/YR4	13	0.797531	1.756514	1.400874
4/1/YR4	6/30/YR4	14	0.783679	1.767500	1.385153
7/1/YR4	9/30/YR4	15	0.769862	1.794722	1.381689
10/1/YR4	12/31/YR4	16	0.756242	1.801042	1.362024
1/1/YR5	3/31/YR5	17	0.742852	1.802500	1.338991
4/1/YR5	6/30/YR5	18	0.729762	1.793750	1.309011
7/1/YR5	9/30/YR5	19	0.716700	1.822528	1.306206
10/1/YR5	12/31/YR5	20	0.703811	1.831375	1.288941
				Total	29.61893

$$\text{forward discount rate for period 1} = \frac{1}{1.017463} = 0.98284$$

$$\text{forward discount rate for period 2} = \frac{1}{(1.017463)(1.017363)}$$

$$= 0.96606$$

forward discount rate for period 3

$$= \frac{1}{(1.017463)(1.017363)(1.017606)} = 0.94935$$

Given the floating payment for a period and the forward discount factor for the period, the present value of the payment can be computed. For example, from Exhibit 1 in the previous (reproduced in Column (5) of Exhibit 2) we see that the *floating payment* for period 4 is $1.761861111. From Exhibit 1, the forward discount factor for period 4 is 0.93291. Therefore, the present value of the payment is:

present value of period 4 payment
= $1.761861111 × 0.93291 = $1.643663

Exhibit 2 shows the present value for each payment. The total present value of the 20 floating payments is $29.61893. Thus, the present value of the payments that the fixed-rate payer will receive is $29.61893 and the present value of the payments that the fixed-rate receiver will make is $29.61893.

DETERMINATION OF THE SWAP FIXED RATE

The fixed-rate payer will require that the present value of the fixed payments that must be made based on the swap fixed rate not exceed the $29.61893 to be received from the floating payments. The fixed-rate receiver will require that the present value of the fixed payments to received be at least as great as the $29.61893 that must be paid. This means that both parties will require a present value for the fixed payments to be $29.61893.

If that is the case, the present value of the fixed payments is equal to the present value of the floating payments and therefore the value of the swap is zero for both parties at the inception of the swap. The interest rates that should be used to compute the present value of the fixed payments are the same interest rates as those used to discount the floating payments.

Beginning with the basic relationship for no arbitrage to exist:

PV of floating payments = PV of fixed payments

it can be shown that the formula for the swap fixed rate is:[1]

$$SFR = \frac{PV \text{ of floating payments}}{\sum_{t=1}^{N} \text{notional principal} \times \dfrac{\text{Days}_t}{360} \times FDF_t}$$

where

$$SFR = \text{swap fixed rate}$$
$$\text{Days}_t = \text{number of days in period } t$$
$$FDF_t = \text{forward discount rate for period } t$$

Note that all the values to compute the swap fixed rate are known.

Let's apply the formula to determine the swap fixed rate for our 5-year swap. Exhibit 3 shows the calculation of the denominator of the formula. The forward discount factor for each period shown in Column (5) is obtained from Column (4) of Exhibit 2. The sum of the last column in Exhibit 3 shows that the denominator of the swap fixed rate formula is $420.052. We know from Exhibit 2 that the present value of the floating payments is $29.61893. Therefore, the swap rate is

$$SFR = \frac{\$29.61893}{\$420.052} = 0.070513 = 7.0513\%$$

---

[1] The formula is derived as follows. The fixed payment for period t is equal to:

$$\text{notional principal} \times SFR \times \frac{\text{Days}_t}{360}$$

The present value of the fixed payment for period t is found by multiplying the previous expression by the forward discount factor for period t (FDF$_t$). That is, the present value of the fixed payment for period t is equal to:

$$\text{notional principal} \times SFR \times \frac{\text{Days}_t}{360} \times FDF_t$$

Summing up the present value of the fixed payment for each period gives the present value of the fixed payments. Letting N be the number of periods in the swap, then the present value of the fixed payments can be expressed as:

$$SFR \sum_{t=1}^{N} \text{notional principal} \times \frac{\text{Days}_t}{360} \times FDF_t$$

The condition for no arbitrage is that the present value of the fixed payments as given by the expression above is equal to the present value of the floating payments. That is,

$$SFR \sum_{t=1}^{N} \text{notional principal} \times \frac{\text{Days}_t}{360} \times FDF_t = PV \text{ of floating payments}$$

Solving for the swap fixed rate gives the formula in the text.

Exhibit 3: Calculating the Denominator for the Swap Fixed Rate Formula

(1) Quarter Starts	(2) Quarter Ends	(3) Number of Days in Quarter	(4) End of quarter	(5) Forward Discount Factor	(6) Forward Discount Factor × Days/360 × 100
1/1/YR1	3/31/YR1	90	1	0.982837	24.57093
4/1/YR1	6/30/YR1	90	2	0.966064	24.15160
7/1/YR1	9/30/YR1	91	3	0.949350	23.99745
10/1/YR1	12/31/YR1	91	4	0.932913	23.58197
1/1/YR2	3/31/YR2	89	5	0.916987	22.66997
4/1/YR2	6/30/YR2	90	6	0.901271	22.53179
7/1/YR2	9/30/YR2	91	7	0.885634	22.38687
10/1/YR2	12/31/YR2	91	8	0.870268	21.99845
1/1/YR3	3/31/YR3	89	9	0.855360	21.14640
4/1/YR3	6/30/YR3	90	10	0.840638	21.01596
7/1/YR3	9/30/YR3	91	11	0.825971	20.87872
10/1/YR3	12/31/YR3	91	12	0.811540	20.51392
1/1/YR4	3/31/YR4	89	13	0.797531	19.71674
4/1/YR4	6/30/YR4	90	14	0.783679	19.59198
7/1/YR4	9/30/YR4	91	15	0.769862	19.46041
10/1/YR4	12/31/YR4	91	16	0.756242	19.11612
1/1/YR5	3/31/YR5	90	17	0.742852	18.57131
4/1/YR5	6/30/YR5	90	18	0.729762	18.24405
7/1/YR5	9/30/YR5	91	19	0.716700	18.11659
10/1/YR5	12/31/YR5	91	20	0.703811	17.79077
				Total	420.052

Given the swap rate, the swap spread can be determined. For example, since this is a 5-year swap, the convention is to use the 5-year on-the-run Treasury rate as the benchmark. If the yield on that issue is 6.8513%, the swap spread is 20 basis points (7.0513% − 6.8513%).

The calculation of the swap fixed rate for all swaps follows the same principle: equating the present value of the fixed payments to that of the floating payments.

APPLICATION TO AMORTIZING SWAP

The application to an amortizing swap is straightforward. To illustrate the calculations, we will use the amortizing swap shown in Exhibit 3 of the previous chapter and the fixed payments based on a swap fixed rate of 7.0095% shown in Exhibit 4 of the previous chapter. The forward discount factor for each quarter is the same as in Exhibit 1 and is reproduced in Column (4) of Exhibit 4. Column (5) of Exhibit 4 shows the floating payment at the end of each quarter for the amortizing swap and the forward discount rate. The last column in the exhibit shows the present value of the each floating payment. The present value of the floating payments is $16.30363.

Exhibit 5 shows the calculations for the denominator of the formula for the swap fixed rate. The value is $232.5923. Since the present value of the floating payments is $16.30363, the swap fixed rate is 7.0095% as shown below:

$$SFR = \frac{\$16.30363}{\$232.5923} = 0.070095 = 7.0095\%$$

Exhibit 4: Calculating the Present Value of the Floating Payments for an Amortizing Swap

(1) Quarter Starts	(2) Quarter Ends	(3) End of Days in Quarter	(4) Forward Discount Factor	(5) Floating Payment	(6) PV of Floating Payment
1/1/YR1	3/31/YR1	1	0.982837	1.746250	1.716279
4/1/YR1	6/30/YR1	2	0.966064	1.649438	1.593462
7/1/YR1	9/30/YR1	3	0.949350	1.584538	1.504280
10/1/YR1	12/31/YR1	4	0.932913	1.497582	1.397114
1/1/YR2	3/31/YR2	5	0.916987	1.389389	1.274052
4/1/YR2	6/30/YR2	6	0.901271	1.307813	1.178694
7/1/YR2	9/30/YR2	7	0.885634	1.235957	1.094606
10/1/YR2	12/31/YR2	8	0.870268	1.147674	0.998785
1/1/YR3	3/31/YR3	9	0.855360	1.045750	0.894493
4/1/YR3	6/30/YR3	10	0.840638	0.963187	0.809692
7/1/YR3	9/30/YR3	11	0.825971	0.887882	0.733365
10/1/YR3	12/31/YR3	12	0.811540	0.800231	0.649419
1/1/YR4	3/31/YR4	13	0.797531	0.702606	0.560350
4/1/YR4	6/30/YR4	14	0.783679	0.618625	0.484804
7/1/YR4	9/30/YR4	15	0.769862	0.538417	0.414507
10/1/YR4	12/31/YR4	16	0.756242	0.450260	0.340506
1/1/YR5	3/31/YR5	17	0.742852	0.360500	0.267798
4/1/YR5	6/30/YR5	18	0.729762	0.269063	0.196352
7/1/YR5	9/30/YR5	19	0.716700	0.182253	0.130621
10/1/YR5	12/31/YR5	20	0.703811	0.091569	0.064447
				Total	16.30363

Exhibit 5: Calculating the Denominator for the Swap Rate Formula

Quarter Starts	Quarter Ends	Number of Days in Quarter	End of Quarter	Forward Discount Factor	Varying Notional Principal	Forward Discount Factor × Days/360 × 100
1/1/YR1	3/31/YR1	90	1	0.982837	100	24.57093
4/1/YR1	6/30/YR1	90	2	0.966064	95	22.94402
7/1/YR1	9/30/YR1	91	3	0.949350	90	21.59771
10/1/YR1	12/31/YR1	91	4	0.932913	85	20.04467
1/1/YR2	3/31/YR2	89	5	0.916987	80	18.13597
4/1/YR2	6/30/YR2	90	6	0.901271	75	16.89884
7/1/YR2	9/30/YR2	91	7	0.885634	70	15.67081
10/1/YR2	12/31/YR2	91	8	0.870268	65	14.29899
1/1/YR3	3/31/YR3	89	9	0.855360	60	12.68784
4/1/YR3	6/30/YR3	90	10	0.840638	55	11.55878
7/1/YR3	9/30/YR3	91	11	0.825971	50	10.43936
10/1/YR3	12/31/YR3	91	12	0.811540	45	9.231263
1/1/YR4	3/31/YR4	89	13	0.797531	40	7.886694
4/1/YR4	6/30/YR4	90	14	0.783679	35	6.857194
7/1/YR4	9/30/YR4	91	15	0.769862	30	5.838124
10/1/YR4	12/31/YR4	91	16	0.756242	25	4.779031
1/1/YR5	3/31/YR5	90	17	0.742852	20	3.714261
4/1/YR5	6/30/YR5	90	18	0.729762	15	2.736608
7/1/YR5	9/30/YR5	91	19	0.716700	10	1.811659
10/1/YR5	12/31/YR5	91	20	0.703811	5	0.889539
				Total		232.5923

QUESTIONS

1. a. For the 3-year swap in Question 1 in the previous chapter, compute the forward discount factor for each period.

b. Compute the present value of the floating payments given the forward discount factors found in (a) and the floating payments found in Question 1 in the previous chapter.

c. What is the swap fixed rate for the swap in Question 1 of the previous chapter?

2. a. For the 5-year swap in Question 3 in the previous chapter, compute the forward discount factor for each period.

b. Compute the present value of the floating payments given the forward discount factors found in (a) and the floating payments found in Question 3 in the previous chapter.

c. What is the swap fixed rate for the swap in Question 3 of the previous chapter?

SOLUTIONS TO QUESTIONS

1. a. The forward discount factors are shown below.

Quarter Starts	Quarter Ends	Number of Days in Quarter	End of Quarter	Forward Rate	Period Forward Rate	Forward Discount Factor
Jan 1 year 1	Mar 31 year 1	90	1	7.30%	1.8250%	0.98207709
Apr 1 year 1	June 30 year 1	91	2	7.40%	1.8706%	0.96404411
July 1 year 1	Sept 30 year 1	92	3	7.90%	2.0189%	0.94496629
Oct 1 year 1	Dec 31 year 1	92	4	7.95%	2.0317%	0.92615001
Jan 1 year 2	Mar 31 year 2	90	5	8.00%	2.0000%	0.90799021
Apr 1 year 2	June 30 year 2	91	6	8.15%	2.0601%	0.88966194
July 1 year 2	Sept 30 year 2	92	7	8.25%	2.1083%	0.87129219
Oct 1 year 2	Dec 31 year 2	92	8	8.30%	2.1211%	0.85319498
Jan 1 year 3	Mar 31 year 3	90	9	8.45%	2.1125%	0.83554411
Apr 1 year 3	June 30 year 3	91	10	8.60%	2.1739%	0.81776677
July 1 year 3	Sept 30 year 3	92	11	8.75%	2.2361%	0.79988055
Oct 1 year 3	Dec 31 year 3	92	12	8.90%	2.2744%	0.7820923

We will use the forward discount factor for period 5 to illustrate the computation. The period forward rates are shown in the sixth column of the table above. The forward discount factor is

$$\frac{\$1}{(1.018250)(1.018706)(1.020189)(1.020317)(1.02)} = 0.90799$$

b. The present value of the floating payments is \$21,790,770 as shown below:

Quarter Starts	Quarter Ends	End of Quarter	Forward Discount Factor	Floating Payment at End of Quarter	PV of Floating Payment
Jan 1 year 1	Mar 31 year 1	1	0.98207709	1,825,000	1,792,291
Apr 1 year 1	June 30 year 1	2	0.96404411	1,870,556	1,803,298
July 1 year 1	Sept 30 year 1	3	0.94496629	2,018,889	1,907,782
Oct 1 year 1	Dec 31 year 1	4	0.92615001	2,031,667	1,881,628
Jan 1 year 2	Mar 31 year 2	5	0.90799021	2,000,000	1,815,980
Apr 1 year 2	June 30 year 2	6	0.88966194	2,060,139	1,832,827
July 1 year 2	Sept 30 year 2	7	0.87129219	2,108,333	1,836,974
Oct 1 year 2	Dec 31 year 2	8	0.85319498	2,121,111	1,809,721
Jan 1 year 3	Mar 31 year 3	9	0.83554411	2,112,500	1,765,087
Apr 1 year 3	June 30 year 3	10	0.81776677	2,173,889	1,777,734
July 1 year 3	Sept 30 year 3	11	0.79988055	2,236,111	1,788,622
Oct 1 year 3	Dec 31 year 3	12	0.7820923	2,274,444	1,778,825
				Total	21,790,770

c. The denominator for the swap fixed rate formula is computed in the following table:

(1)	(2)	(3)	(4)	(5)	(6)	(7)
Quarter Starts	Quarter Ends	Number of Days in Quarter	End of Quarter	Forward Discount Rate	Days/360	Fwd. disc. factor × Days/360 × Notional
Jan 1 year 1	Mar 31 year 1	90	1	0.98207709	0.25000000	24,551,927
Apr 1 year 1	June 30 year 1	91	2	0.96404411	0.25277778	24,368,893
July 1 year 1	Sept 30 year 1	92	3	0.94496629	0.25555556	24,149,139
Oct 1 year 1	Dec 31 year 1	92	4	0.92615001	0.25555556	23,668,278
Jan 1 year 2	Mar 31 year 2	90	5	0.90799021	0.25000000	22,699,755
Apr 1 year 2	June 30 year 2	91	6	0.88966194	0.25277778	22,488,677
July 1 year 2	Sept 30 year 2	92	7	0.87129219	0.25555556	22,266,356
Oct 1 year 2	Dec 31 year 2	92	8	0.85319498	0.25555556	21,803,872
Jan 1 year 3	Mar 31 year 3	90	9	0.83554411	0.25000000	20,888,603
Apr 1 year 3	June 30 year 3	91	10	0.81776677	0.25277778	20,671,327
July 1 year 3	Sept 30 year 3	92	11	0.79988055	0.25555556	20,441,392
Oct 1 year 3	Dec 31 year 3	92	12	0.78209230	0.25555556	19,986,803
					Total	267,985,021

The present value of the floating payments is $21,790,770. Therefore, the swap fixed rate is

$$SFR = \frac{\$21,790,770}{\$267,985,021} = 0.081313 = 8.1313\%$$

2a.

Quarter Starts	Quarter Ends	Number of Days	Forward Rate	Period Forward Rate	Forward Discount Factor
1/1/YR1	3/31/YR1	90	6.9850%	1.7463%	0.9828
4/1/YR1	6/30/YR1	90	5.9450%	1.4863%	0.9684
7/1/YR1	9/30/YR1	91	6.0150%	1.5205%	0.9539
10/1/YR1	12/31/YR1	91	6.0700%	1.5344%	0.9395
1/1/YR2	3/31/YR2	89	6.1750%	1.5266%	0.9254
4/1/YR2	6/30/YR2	90	6.1750%	1.5438%	0.9113
7/1/YR2	9/30/YR2	91	6.2350%	1.5761%	0.8972
10/1/YR2	12/31/YR2	91	6.2850%	1.5887%	0.8832
1/1/YR3	3/31/YR3	89	6.4000%	1.5822%	0.8694
4/1/YR3	6/30/YR3	90	6.4050%	1.6013%	0.8557
7/1/YR3	9/30/YR3	91	6.4750%	1.6367%	0.8419
10/1/YR3	12/31/YR3	91	6.5350%	1.6519%	0.8282
1/1/YR4	3/31/YR4	89	6.6550%	1.6453%	0.8148
4/1/YR4	6/30/YR4	90	6.6700%	1.6675%	0.8015
7/1/YR4	9/30/YR4	91	6.7500%	1.7063%	0.7880
10/1/YR4	12/31/YR4	91	6.8250%	1.7252%	0.7747
1/1/YR5	3/31/YR5	90	6.9600%	1.7400%	0.7614
4/1/YR5	6/30/YR5	90	6.9750%	1.7438%	0.7484
7/1/YR5	9/30/YR5	91	7.0600%	1.7846%	0.7352
10/1/YR5	12/31/YR5	91	7.1450%	1.8061%	0.7222

We will use the forward discount factor for period 3 to illustrate the computation. The period forward rates are shown in the fourth column and the corresponding period forward rates in the fifth column. The period forward rates are found by multiplying the forward rates by the actual/360 day count fraction. The forward discount factor for period 3 is found as follows:

$$\frac{1}{(1.017463)(1.014863)(1.015205)} = 0.9539$$

b. The present value of the floating payments is $38,891,103.66 as shown below:

Quarter Starts	Quarter Ends	Number of Days	Forward Rate	Period Forward Rate	Forward Discount Factor	PV of Floating Payment
1/1/YR1	3/31/YR1	90	6.9850%	1.7463%	0.9828	$858,139.73
4/1/YR1	6/30/YR1	90	5.9450%	1.4863%	0.9684	$1,439,349.46
7/1/YR1	9/30/YR1	91	6.0150%	1.5205%	0.9539	$870,255.12
10/1/YR1	12/31/YR1	91	6.0700%	1.5344%	0.9395	$1,729,882.49
1/1/YR2	3/31/YR2	89	6.1750%	1.5266%	0.9254	$988,895.61
4/1/YR2	6/30/YR2	90	6.1750%	1.5438%	0.9113	$1,969,607.78
7/1/YR2	9/30/YR2	91	6.2350%	1.5761%	0.8972	$1,131,224.17
10/1/YR2	12/31/YR2	91	6.2850%	1.5887%	0.8832	$2,244,926.15
1/1/YR3	3/31/YR3	89	6.4000%	1.5822%	0.8694	$1,238,027.19
4/1/YR3	6/30/YR3	90	6.4050%	1.6013%	0.8557	$2,466,339.11
7/1/YR3	9/30/YR3	91	6.4750%	1.6367%	0.8419	$1,377,999.62
10/1/YR3	12/31/YR3	91	6.5350%	1.6519%	0.8282	$2,736,335.84
1/1/YR4	3/31/YR4	89	6.6550%	1.6453%	0.8148	$1,474,674.00
4/1/YR4	6/30/YR4	90	6.6700%	1.6675%	0.8015	$2,940,181.57
7/1/YR4	9/30/YR4	91	6.7500%	1.7063%	0.7880	$1,613,473.72
10/1/YR4	12/31/YR4	91	6.8250%	1.7252%	0.7747	$3,207,466.93
1/1/YR5	3/31/YR5	90	6.9600%	1.7400%	0.7614	$1,722,305.80
4/1/YR5	6/30/YR5	90	6.9750%	1.7438%	0.7484	$3,392,872.13
7/1/YR5	9/30/YR5	91	7.0600%	1.7846%	0.7352	$1,836,958.86
10/1/YR5	12/31/YR5	91	7.1450%	1.8061%	0.7222	$3,652,188.37
					Total	$38,891,103.66

c. The denominator for the swap fixed rate formula is computed in the following table:

Quarter Starts	Quarter Ends	Number of Days	Forward Rate	Forward Discount Factor	Varying NP	Forward Discount Factor × Days/ 360 × Notional
1/1/YR1	3/31/YR1	90	6.9850%	0.9828	50	$12,285,465.07
4/1/YR1	6/30/YR1	90	5.9450%	0.9684	100	$24,211,092.77
7/1/YR1	9/30/YR1	91	6.0150%	0.9539	60	$14,468,081.79
10/1/YR1	12/31/YR1	91	6.0700%	0.9395	120	$28,498,887.73
1/1/YR2	3/31/YR2	89	6.1750%	0.9254	70	$16,014,503.85
4/1/YR2	6/30/YR2	90	6.1750%	0.9113	140	$31,896,482.24
7/1/YR2	9/30/YR2	91	6.2350%	0.8972	80	$18,143,130.30
10/1/YR2	12/31/YR2	91	6.2850%	0.8832	160	$35,718,793.15
1/1/YR3	3/31/YR3	89	6.4000%	0.8694	90	$19,344,174.83
4/1/YR3	6/30/YR3	90	6.4050%	0.8557	180	$38,506,465.44
7/1/YR3	9/30/YR3	91	6.4750%	0.8419	100	$21,281,847.35
10/1/YR3	12/31/YR3	91	6.5350%	0.8282	200	$41,872,009.80
1/1/YR4	3/31/YR4	89	6.6550%	0.8148	110	$22,158,888.03
4/1/YR4	6/30/YR4	90	6.6700%	0.8015	220	$44,080,683.22
7/1/YR4	9/30/YR4	91	6.7500%	0.7880	120	$23,903,314.38
10/1/YR4	12/31/YR4	91	6.8250%	0.7747	240	$46,995,852.40
1/1/YR5	3/31/YR5	90	6.9600%	0.7614	130	$24,745,773.05
4/1/YR5	6/30/YR5	90	6.9750%	0.7484	260	$48,643,328.07
7/1/YR5	9/30/YR5	91	7.0600%	0.7352	140	$26,019,247.35
10/1/YR5	12/31/YR5	91	7.1450%	0.7222	280	$51,115,302.63
					Total	$589,903,323.43

The present value of the floating payments is $38,891,103.66. Therefore, the swap fixed rate is:

$$SFR = \frac{\$38,891,103.66}{\$589,903,323.43} = 0.065928 = 6.5928\%$$

Chapter 4

Traditional Approach to the Valuation of a Plain Vanilla Swap

To value a swap it is necessary to determine the present value of the fixed payments and the present value of the floating payments. The difference between these two present values is the value of a swap. Whether the value is positive (i.e., an asset) or negative (i.e., a liability) will depend on whether the party is the fixed-rate payer or the fixed-rate receiver.

We already know how to determine the present value of the counterparty swap payments. Our illustrations in the previous chapter showed how this is done for a swap at its inception. In this chapter we will see how the value of a swap changes after its inception as market interest rates change. We will use the same 5-year swap that we used in the previous two chapter.

SWAP FLOATING PAYMENTS WHEN RATES CHANGE

Once the swap transaction is completed, changes in market interest rates will change the payments of the floating-rate side of the swap. The value of an interest rate swap is the difference between the present value of the payments of the two sides of the swap. The 3-month LIBOR forward rates from the current Eurodollar CD futures contracts are used to:

- calculate the floating payments and
- determine the discount factors at which to calculate the present value of the payments

Exhibit 1: Rates and Floating Payments Two Years Later

(1)	(2)	(3)	(4)	(5)	(6)	(7)	(8)
Quarter Starts	Quarter Ends	Number of Days in Quarter	Current 3- Month LIBOR	Eurodollar CD Futures Price	Forward Rate	End of Quarter	Floating Payment at End of Quarter
1/1/YR3	3/31/YR3	89	7.05%	92.950		1	1.7429
4/1/YR3	6/30/YR3	90		92.995	7.01%	2	1.7512
7/1/YR3	9/30/YR3	91		92.975	7.03%	3	1.7757
10/1/YR3	12/31/YR3	91		92.965	7.04%	4	1.7782
1/1/YR4	3/31/YR4	89		92.895	7.11%	5	1.7565
4/1/YR4	6/30/YR4	90		92.930	7.07%	6	1.7675
7/1/YR4	9/30/YR4	91		92.900	7.10%	7	1.7947
10/1/YR4	12/31/YR4	91		92.875	7.13%	8	1.8010
1/1/YR5	3/31/YR5	90		92.790	7.21%	9	1.8025
4/1/YR5	6/30/YR5	90		92.825	7.18%	10	1.7937
7/1/YR5	9/30/YR5	91		92.790	7.21%	11	1.8225
10/1/YR5	12/31/YR5	91		92.755	7.25%	12	1.8313

To illustrate this, consider the 5-year swap. Suppose that two years later, interest rates change as shown in Columns (4) and (6) in Exhibit 1. Column (4) shows the current 3-month LIBOR. In Column (5) are the Eurodollar CD futures prices for each period. These rates are used to compute the forward rates in Column (6). Note that the interest rates have increased one year later since the rates in Exhibit 1 are greater than those in Exhibit 1 in Chapter 2. The current 3-month LIBOR and the forward rates are used to compute the floating-rate payments.

PERIOD FORWARD RATES AND FORWARD DISCOUNT FACTORS AFTER RATES CHANGE

In addition to using the new forward rate to obtain the floating payments, the new forward rates in Exhibit 1 are used to compute the period forward rates. These are shown in Column (6) of Exhibit 2. In the last column of Exhibit 2, the forward discount factor is computed for each period. The calculation is the same as in Exhibit 1 of Chapter 3.

Exhibit 2: Period Forward Rates and Forward Discount Factors Two Years Later

(1)	(2)	(3)	(4)	(5)	(6)	(7)
Quarter Starts	Quarter Ends	Number of Days in Quarter	End of Quarter	Forward Rate	Period Forward Rate	Forward Discount Factor
1/1/YR3	3/31/YR3	89	1	7.05%	1.7429%	0.98287
4/1/YR3	6/30/YR3	90	2	7.01%	1.7513%	0.96595
7/1/YR3	9/30/YR3	91	3	7.03%	1.7758%	0.94910
10/1/YR3	12/31/YR3	91	4	7.04%	1.7783%	0.93252
1/1/YR4	3/31/YR4	89	5	7.11%	1.7565%	0.91642
4/1/YR4	6/30/YR4	90	6	7.07%	1.7675%	0.90050
7/1/YR4	9/30/YR4	91	7	7.10%	1.7947%	0.88463
10/1/YR4	12/31/YR4	91	8	7.13%	1.8010%	0.86898
1/1/YR5	3/31/YR5	90	9	7.21%	1.8025%	0.85359
4/1/YR5	6/30/YR5	90	10	7.18%	1.7938%	0.83855
7/1/YR5	9/30/YR5	91	11	7.21%	1.8225%	0.82354
10/1/YR5	12/31/YR5	91	12	7.25%	1.8314%	0.80873

VALUING A SWAP AFTER RATES CHANGE

We now have all the information needed to calculate the value of the swap. In Exhibit 3 the forward discount factor (from Exhibit 2) and the floating payments (from Exhibit 1) are shown. The fixed payments need not be recomputed. They are the payments shown in Column (8) of Exhibit 2 in Chapter 2. These are the fixed payments based on the initial swap rate of 7.0513% and are reproduced in Exhibit 3.

Now the two payment streams must be discounted using the new forward discount factors. As shown at the bottom of Exhibit 3, the two present values are as follows:

Present value of floating payments $19.12716
Present value of fixed payments $18.97279

The two present values are not equal and therefore for one party the value of the swap increased and for the other party the value of the swap decreased. Let's look at which party gained and which party lost.

Exhibit 3: Valuing the Swap Two Years Later

(1)	(2)	(3)	(4)	(5)	(6)	(7)
Quarter Starts	Quarter Ends	Forward Discount Factor	Floating Payment at End of Quarter	PV of Floating Payment	Fixed Payment at End of Quarter	PV of Fixed Payment
1/1/YR3	3/31/YR3	0.9829	1.742916667	1.713059	1.743226	1.713363
4/1/YR3	6/30/YR3	0.9660	1.751250000	1.691625	1.762813	1.702794
7/1/YR3	9/30/YR3	0.9491	1.775763889	1.685376	1.782399	1.691674
10/1/YR3	12/31/YR3	0.9325	1.778291667	1.658286	1.782399	1.662117
1/1/YR4	3/31/YR4	0.9164	1.756513889	1.609704	1.743226	1.597526
4/1/YR4	6/30/YR4	0.9005	1.767500000	1.591639	1.762813	1.587418
7/1/YR4	9/30/YR4	0.8846	1.794722222	1.587659	1.782399	1.576758
10/1/YR4	12/31/YR4	0.8690	1.801041667	1.565062	1.782399	1.548862
1/1/YR5	3/31/YR5	0.8536	1.802500000	1.538596	1.762813	1.504719
4/1/YR5	6/30/YR5	0.8385	1.793750000	1.504146	1.762813	1.478204
7/1/YR5	9/30/YR5	0.8235	1.822527778	1.500923	1.782399	1.467876
10/1/YR5	12/31/YR5	0.8087	1.831375000	1.481085	1.782399	1.441477
			Total	19.12716	Total	18.97279

Summary	Fixed-rate payer	Fixed-rate receiver
PV of payments received	$19.12716	$18.97279
PV of payments made	18.97279	19.12716
Value of swap	$0.15437	−$0.15437

The fixed-rate payer will receive the floating payments. And these payments have a present value of $19.12716. The present value of the payments that must be made by the fixed-rate payer is $18.97279. Thus, the swap has a positive value for the fixed-rate payer equal to the difference in the two present values of $0.15437. This is the value of the swap to the fixed-rate payer. Notice, consistent with what we said in the Chapter 1, when interest rates increase (as they did in the illustration analyzed), the fixed-rate payer benefits because the value of the swap increases.

In contrast, the fixed-rate receiver must make payments with a present value of $19.12716 but will only receive fixed payments with a present value equal to $18.97279 Thus, the value of the swap for the fixed-rate receiver is −$0.15437. Again, as explained in Chapter 1, the fixed-rate receiver is adversely affected by a rise in interest rates because it results in a decline in the value of a swap.

VALUING SWAPS WITH A CHANGING NOTIONAL PRINCIPAL

The same valuation principle applies to more complicated swaps. For example, there are swaps whose notional amount changes in a predetermined way over the life of the swap. These include amortizing swaps, accreting swaps, and roller coaster swaps. Once the payments are specified, the present value is calculated as described above by simply adjusting the payment amounts by the changing notional amounts — the methodology does not change.

Exhibit 4 illustrates this for the amortizing swap whose swap payments were computed in the two previous chapters. The amortizing swap is valued two years later after rates rise. The rates are the same as shown in Column (5) in Exhibit 1. Column (9) of panel a in Exhibit 4 shows the floating payment for each period. The period forward rates and the forward discount factors are the same as in Exhibit 2. These values are shown in panel b of Exhibit 4. Using the new floating payments and forward discount factors, the present value of the amortizing swap's floating and fixed payments are computed in panel b of Exhibit 4. The present value of the floating payment is \$5.546353; the present value of the fixed payments is \$6.317104. The value of the amortizing swap is in panel c of Exhibit 4. For the fixed-rate payer the swap's value is \$0.770751; for the fixed-rate receiver the swap's value is −\$0.770751.

REWORKED ILLUSTRATION USING SEMIANNUAL PAYMENTS AND ROUNDED DAY COUNT

Thus far in this book, we used quarterly payments and the exact daycount in determining the payments by the counterparties to the swap. As will become evident when we present the lattice approach in the next two chapters, the exhibits get rather large if we allow for quarterly cash flows. So, we will be simplifying the illustrations going forward by assuming semiannual payments. Moreover, rather than using the exact daycount in the payment period, we will assume that each 6-month period is one half of a year (0.5 years).

Exhibit 4: Valuing an Amortizing Swap Two Years Later After Rates Rise

a. Forward Rates and Floating Payments Two Years Later

(1)	(2)	(3)	(4)	(5)	(6)	(7)	(8)	(9)
Quarter Starts	Quarter Ends	Number of Days in Quarter	Current 3-Month LIBOR	Eurodollar CD Futures Price	Forward Rate	End of Quarter	Varying Notional Principal	Floating Payment at End of Quarter
1/1/YR3	3/31/YR3	89	7.05%	92.950		1	60	1.045750
4/1/YR3	6/30/YR3	90		92.995	7.01%	2	55	0.963187
7/1/YR3	9/30/YR3	91		92.975	7.03%	3	50	0.887882
10/1/YR3	12/31/YR3	91		92.965	7.04%	4	45	0.800231
1/1/YR4	3/31/YR4	89		92.895	7.11%	5	40	0.702606
4/1/YR4	6/30/YR4	90		92.930	7.07%	6	35	0.618625
7/1/YR4	9/30/YR4	91		92.900	7.10%	7	30	0.538417
10/1/YR4	12/31/YR4	91		92.875	7.13%	8	25	0.450260
1/1/YR5	3/31/YR5	90		92.790	7.21%	9	20	0.360500
4/1/YR5	6/30/YR5	90		92.825	7.18%	10	15	0.269063
7/1/YR5	9/30/YR5	91		92.790	7.21%	11	10	0.182253
10/1/YR5	12/31/YR5	91		92.755	7.25%	12	5	0.091569

b. Present Value of Floating and Fixed Swaps

(1)	(2)	(3)	(4)	(5)	(6)	(7)
Quarter Starts	Quarter Ends	Forward Discount Factor	Floating Payment at End of Quarter	PV of Floating Payments	Fixed Payment	PV of Fixed Payment
1/1/YR3	3/31/YR3	0.982869	1.045750	0.894493	1.039743	1.021931
4/1/YR3	6/30/YR3	0.965953	0.963187	0.809692	0.963806	0.930992
7/1/YR3	9/30/YR3	0.949099	0.887882	0.733365	0.885923	0.840829
10/1/YR3	12/31/YR3	0.932517	0.800231	0.649419	0.797331	0.743524
1/1/YR4	3/31/YR4	0.916419	0.702606	0.560350	0.693162	0.635227
4/1/YR4	6/30/YR4	0.900503	0.618625	0.484804	0.613331	0.552307
7/1/YR4	9/30/YR4	0.884627	0.538417	0.414507	0.531554	0.470227
10/1/YR4	12/31/YR4	0.868976	0.450260	0.340506	0.442961	0.384923
1/1/YR5	3/31/YR5	0.853590	0.360500	0.267798	0.350475	0.299162
4/1/YR5	6/30/YR5	0.838548	0.269063	0.196352	0.262856	0.220418
7/1/YR5	9/30/YR5	0.823539	0.182253	0.130621	0.177185	0.145918
10/1/YR5	12/31/YR5	0.808728	0.091569	0.064447	0.088592	0.071647
			Total	5.546353	Total	6.317104

c. Value of the Swap

Summary	Fixed-rate payer	Fixed-rate receiver
PV of payments received	$6.317104	$5.546353
PV of payments made	5.546353	6.317104
Value of swap	$0.770751	−$0.770751

Let's review here the valuation of an interest rate swap using the traditional approach using semiannual payments and semiannual forward rates from a Eurodollar futures contract. While the inputs in this illustration are not exactly the same as those in this chapter and the previous two chapters, the results are similar. What is important is that the results that we derive in this section will be the same as those derived in using the lattice approach demonstrated in Chapter 6.

First, let's look at the swap fixed rate. In Chapter 3 we showed that the formula for the swap fixed rate is

$$SFR = \frac{PV \text{ of floating payments}}{\sum\limits_{t=1}^{N} \text{notional principal} \times \dfrac{\text{Days}_t}{360} \times \text{FDF}_t}$$

Since we are using semiannual payments and ignoring the day count, then

$$\frac{\text{Days}_t}{360} = 0.5$$

Substituting into the formula for the swap fixed rate and factoring out the notional principal since it is the same for each period in our illustration, we get

$$SFR = \frac{PV \text{ of floating payments}}{0.5 \times \text{notional principal} \times \sum\limits_{t=1}^{N} \text{FDF}_t}$$

Now let's apply the above formula to our swap. All of the information needed is shown in Exhibit 5. Panel a of the exhibit shows the semiannual periods, the assumed forward rates, the end of period payments for our hypothetical 5-year swap with a notional principal of $100, and the forward discount factors. Panel b shows the present value of the floating payments given the end of period floating payment and forward discount factor for each period in panel a. The present value of the floating payments is $29.31153444 per $100 notional principal. The sum of the discount factors is 8.313822725 (see the last row and last column of panel a).

Exhibit 5: Swap Calculations Based on Semiannual Payments and Rounded Day Count

a. Semiannual Forward Rates, Floating Payments, and Discount Factors

(1) Period Starts	(2) Period Ends	(3) Forward Rate	(4) Floating Payment at End of Period	(5) Forward Discount Factors
1/1 YR1	6/30 YR1	6.96%	3.482499754	0.966346969
7/1 YR1	12/31 YR1	6.97%	3.483749998	0.933815183
1/1 YR2	6/30 YR2	7.00%	3.500000067	0.902236891
7/1 YR2	12/31 YR2	6.99%	3.492500025	0.871789638
1/1 YR3	6/30 YR3	7.03%	3.513750789	0.842196936
7/1 YR3	12/31 YR3	7.03%	3.515000816	0.813598927
1/1 YR4	6/30 YR4	7.09%	3.543754086	0.785753747
7/1 YR4	12/31 YR4	7.11%	3.556255474	0.758769949
1/1 YR5	6/30 YR5	7.19%	3.596265167	0.732429830
7/1 YR5	12/31 YR5	7.23%	3.613768418	0.706884656
				8.313822725

b. Present Value of Floating Payments

(1) Beginning Period	(2) End of Period	(3) Floating Payment at End of Period	(4) Present Value of the Floating Payment at End of Period
1/1 YR1	6/30 YR1	3.482499754	3.365303083
7/1 YR1	12/31 YR1	3.483749998	3.253178641
1/1 YR2	6/30 YR2	3.500000067	3.157829179
7/1 YR2	12/31 YR2	3.492500025	3.044725331
1/1 YR3	6/30 YR3	3.513750789	2.959270149
7/1 YR3	12/31 YR3	3.515000816	2.859800893
1/1 YR4	6/30 YR4	3.543754086	2.784518051
7/1 YR4	12/31 YR4	3.556255474	2.698379784
1/1 YR5	6/30 YR5	3.596265167	2.634011885
7/1 YR5	12/31 YR5	3.613768418	2.554517444
			29.31153444

Therefore, we know that

PV of floating payments = $29.31153444
notional principal   = $100

$$\sum_{t=1}^{N} FDF_t = 8.13822725$$

and then

$$SFR = \frac{\$29.31153444}{0.5 \times \$100 \times 8.13822725} = 0.070513 = 7.0513\%$$

Now let's show that the value of this swap is zero if the swap fixed rate is 7.0513%. We know that the present value of the floating payments is $29.31153444. The fixed payment for each period given a swap fixed rate of 7.0513% is found as follows:

$$\$100 \times 0.07513 \times 0.5 = \$3.52565$$

Since the sum of the discount factors is 8.13822725, then the present value of the fixed payments is $3.52565 × 8.313822725, which is equal to $29.3116 per $100 notional principal. The fixed and floating payments are equal (the difference being due to rounding). Consequently, the value of the swap is zero. When we value this same swap using the lattice approach in Chapter 6, we should find that the value of the swap is zero.

Now let's see how to value this swap if two years later rates increase as shown in panel a of Exhibit 6. The last column in the exhibit shows the floating payments based on the assumed forward rates in Columns (3) and (4). Panel b shows the period forward rates and the forward discount factors. Finally, Exhibit 8 shows the present value of the floating and fixed payments. and the value of the swap is shown at the bottom of the exhibit. The value of the swap is $0.15238 for the fixed-rate payer and −$0.15238 for the fixed-rate receiver.

Exhibit 7 shows the calculations for valuing the amortizing swap. Panel a of Exhibit 7 shows the floating payments using the forward rates in Exhibit 4. Panel b of Exhibit 7 shows the fixed payments assuming a swap fixed rate of 7.0111%. The rest of the exhibit shows the valuation of the fixed and floating payments.

Exhibit 6: Valuing a Swap Two Years Later After Rates Rise (Semiannual Payments and Rounded Day Count)

a. Semiannual Forward Rates and Floating Payments

(1) Beginning Period	(2) End of Period	(3) Current 6-Month LIBOR	(4) Forward Rate	(5) End of Period	(6) Floating Payments at End of Period
1/1/YR1	6/30/YR1	7.0275%		1	3.513751
7/1/YR1	12/31/YR1		7.0300%	2	3.515001
1/1/YR2	6/30/YR2		7.0875%	3	3.543754
7/1/YR2	12/31/YR2		7.1125%	4	3.556255
1/1/YR3	6/30/YR3		7.1925%	5	3.596265
7/1/YR3	12/31/YR3		7.2275%	6	3.613768

b. Period Forward Rates and Forward Discount Factors

(1) Beginning Period	(2) End of Period	(3) End of Period	(4) Forward Rate	(5) Period Forward Rate	(6) Forward Discount Factor
1/1/YR2	6/30/YR2	1	7.0275%	3.5138%	0.966055
7/1/YR2	12/31/YR2	2	7.0300%	3.5150%	0.933251
1/1/YR3	6/30/YR3	3	7.0875%	3.5438%	0.901311
7/1/YR3	12/31/YR3	4	7.1125%	3.5563%	0.870359
1/1/YR4	6/30/YR4	5	7.1925%	3.5963%	0.840145
7/1/YR4	12/31/YR4	6	7.2275%	3.6138%	0.810843

c. Valuing the Swap Two Years Later if Interest Rates Increase

(1) Beginning Period	(2) End of Period	(3) Forward Discount Factor	(4) Floating Cash Flow at End of Period	(5) PV of Floating Payment	(6) Fixed Payment at End of Period	(7) PV of Fixed Payment
1/1/YR2	6/30/YR2	0.966055	3.513751	3.394477	3.525635	3.405958
7/1/YR2	12/31/YR2	0.933251	3.515001	3.280380	3.525635	3.290304
1/1/YR3	6/30/YR3	0.901311	3.543754	3.194025	3.525635	3.177694
7/1/YR3	12/31/YR3	0.870359	3.556255	3.095219	3.525635	3.068568
1/1/YR4	6/30/YR4	0.840145	3.596265	3.021385	3.525635	2.962045
7/1/YR4	12/31/YR4	0.810843	3.613768	2.930199	3.525635	2.858737
			Total	18.91569		18.76331

d. Value of the Swap

Summary	Fixed-rate payer	Floating-rate receiver
PV of payments received	$18.91569	$18.76331
PV of payments made	18.76331	18.91569
Value of swap	$0.15238	−$0.15238

Exhibit 7: Valuing an Amortizing Swap with a Swap Fixed Rate of 7.0111 % (Semiannual Payments and Rounded Day Count)

a. Calculating the Floating Payments

Period Starts	Period Ends	Current 6-Month LIBOR	Forward Rate	End of Period	Varying Notional Principal	Floating Payment
1/1/YR1	6/30/YR1	6.9650%		1	100	3.482500
7/1/YR1	12/31/YR1		6.9675%	2	90	3.135375
1/1/YR2	6/30/YR2		7.0000%	3	80	2.800000
7/1/YR2	12/31/YR2		6.9850%	4	70	2.444750
1/1/YR3	6/30/YR3		7.0275%	5	60	2.108250
7/1/YR3	12/31/YR3		7.0300%	6	50	1.757500
1/1/YR4	6/30/YR4		7.0875%	7	40	1.417502
7/1/YR4	12/31/YR4		7.1125%	8	30	1.066877
1/1/YR5	6/30/YR5		7.1925%	9	20	0.719253
7/1/YR5	12/31/YR5		7.2275%	10	10	0.361377

b. Calculating the Fixed Payments using a Swap Fixed Rate of 7.0111 %

Period Starts	Period Ends	End of Period	Varying Notional Principal	Fixed Payments
1/1/YR1	6/30/YR1	1	100	3.505550
7/1/YR1	12/31/YR1	2	90	3.154995
1/1/YR2	6/30/YR2	3	80	2.804440
7/1/YR2	12/31/YR2	4	70	2.453885
1/1/YR3	6/30/YR3	5	60	2.103330
7/1/YR3	12/31/YR3	6	50	1.752775
1/1/YR4	6/30/YR4	7	40	1.402220
7/1/YR4	12/31/YR4	8	30	1.051665
1/1/YR5	6/30/YR5	9	20	0.701110
7/1/YR5	12/31/YR5	10	10	0.350555

(c) Calculation of Period Forward Rate and Forward Discount Rate

Period Starts	Period Ends	End of Period	Forward rate	Period Forward Rate	Forward Discount Factor
1/1/YR1	6/30/YR1	1	6.9650%	3.482%	0.966347
7/1/YR1	12/31/YR1	2	6.9675%	3.484%	0.933815
1/1/YR2	6/30/YR2	3	7.0000%	3.500%	0.902237
7/1/YR2	12/31/YR2	4	6.9850%	3.493%	0.871790
1/1/YR3	6/30/YR3	5	7.0275%	3.514%	0.842197
7/1/YR3	12/31/YR3	6	7.0300%	3.515%	0.813599
1/1/YR4	6/30/YR4	7	7.0875%	3.544%	0.785754
7/1/YR4	12/31/YR4	8	7.1125%	3.556%	0.758770
1/1/YR5	6/30/YR5	9	7.1925%	3.596%	0.732430
7/1/YR5	12/31/YR5	10	7.2275%	3.614%	0.706885

Exhibit 7 (Continued)
(d) Present Value of Floating and Fixed Payments

Beginning Period	End of Period	End of Period	Forward Discount Factor	Floating Payment	PV of Floating Payment	Fixed Payments	PV of Fixed Payments
1/1/YR1	6/30/YR1	1	0.966347	3.482500	3.365303	3.505550	3.3875776
7/1/YR1	12/31/YR1	2	0.933815	3.135375	2.927861	3.154995	2.9461822
1/1/YR2	6/30/YR2	3	0.902237	2.800000	2.526263	2.804440	2.5302692
7/1/YR2	12/31/YR2	4	0.871790	2.444750	2.131308	2.453885	2.1392715
1/1/YR3	6/30/YR3	5	0.842197	2.108250	1.775562	2.103330	1.7714181
7/1/YR3	12/31/YR3	6	0.813599	1.757500	1.429900	1.752775	1.4260559
1/1/YR4	6/30/YR4	7	0.785754	1.417502	1.113807	1.402220	1.1017996
7/1/YR4	12/31/YR4	8	0.758770	1.066877	0.809514	1.051665	0.7979718
1/1/YR5	6/30/YR5	9	0.732430	0.719253	0.526802	0.701110	0.5135139
7/1/YR5	12/31/YR5	10	0.706885	0.361377	0.255452	0.350555	0.2478020
					16.861770		16.86186

Panel c of Exhibit 7 shows the period forward rate and forward discount rate for each period. In panel d of Exhibit 7 it can be seen that the present value of the floating payments is equal to the present value of the fixed payments, the slight difference being due to rounding. Thus, the value of the swap is zero. The swap fixed rate could have been shown to be 7.0111%, the rate used in our illustration, using the formula for the swap fixed rate. We leave as an exercise for the reader to show that the denominator of the formula for the swap fixed rate is $240.5024. The numerator is the present value of the floating payments, $16.86177 (see panel d of Exhibit 7). Therefore,

$$SFR = \frac{\$16.86177}{\$240.5024} = 0.070111 = 7.0111\%$$

Finally, Exhibit 8 shows the value of our amortizing swap two years later using the assumed forward rates in Exhibit 6. Therefore, the swap's value as can be seen in panel d of Exhibit 8 is $0.060194 and −$0.060194 for the fixed-rate payer and fixed-rate receiver, respectively.

Exhibit 8: Valuing an Amortizing Swap Two Years Later After Rates Rise (Semiannual Payments and Rounded Day Count)

(a) New Floating Payments

Beginning Period	End of Period	Current 6-Month LIBOR	Forward Rate	End of Period	Varying Notional Principal	Floating Payment
1/1/YR2	6/30/YR2	7.0275%		1	60	2.108250
7/1/YR2	12/31/YR2		7.0300%	2	50	1.757500
1/1/YR3	6/30/YR3		7.0875%	3	40	1.417502
7/1/YR3	12/31/YR3		7.1125%	4	30	1.066877
1/1/YR4	6/30/YR4		7.1925%	5	20	0.719253
7/1/YR4	12/31/YR4		7.2275%	6	10	0.361377

(b) Period Forward Rates and Forward Discount Factor

Beginning Period	End of Period	End of Period	Forward Rate	Period Forward Rate	Forward Discount Factor
1/1/YR2	6/30/YR2	1	7.0275%	3.5138%	0.966055
7/1/YR2	12/31/YR2	2	7.0300%	3.5150%	0.933251
1/1/YR3	6/30/YR3	3	7.0875%	3.5438%	0.901311
7/1/YR3	12/31/YR3	4	7.1125%	3.5563%	0.870359
1/1/YR4	6/30/YR4	5	7.1925%	3.5963%	0.840145
7/1/YR4	12/31/YR4	6	7.2275%	3.6138%	0.810843

(c) Present Value of Floating and Fixed Payments

Beginning Period	End of Period	Forward Discount Factor	Floating Rate Payment	PV of Floating Payment	Fixed Payment	PV of Fixed Payment
1/1/YR2	6/30/YR2	0.966055	2.1082505	2.036686	2.103330	2.031933
7/1/YR2	12/31/YR2	0.933251	1.7575004	1.640190	1.752775	1.635780
1/1/YR3	6/30/YR3	0.901311	1.4175016	1.277610	1.402220	1.263837
7/1/YR3	12/31/YR3	0.870359	1.0668766	0.928566	1.051665	0.915326
1/1/YR4	6/30/YR4	0.840145	0.7192530	0.604277	0.701110	0.589034
7/1/YR4	12/31/YR4	0.810843	0.3613768	0.293020	0.350555	0.284245
				6.780349		6.720155

(d) Value of Swap

Summary	Fixed-rate payer	Fixed-rate receiver
PV of payments received	$6.780349	$6.720155
PV of payments made	6.720155	6.780349
Value of swap	$0.060194	−$0.060194

QUESTIONS

1. Assume we need to value the 5-year swap from Question 2 of the previous chapter three years after it has been initiated. The reference rate for the swap is 3-month LIBOR and the notional principal varies as shown in the following table:

Quarter Starts	Quarter Ends	Number of Days	Forward Rate	Varying NP ($million)
1/1/YR4	3/31/YR4	89	6.6550%	110
4/1/YR4	6/30/YR4	90	6.6700%	220
7/1/YR4	9/30/YR4	91	6.7500%	120
10/1/YR4	12/31/YR4	91	6.8250%	240
1/1/YR5	3/31/YR5	90	6.9600%	130
4/1/YR5	6/30/YR5	90	6.9750%	260
7/1/YR5	9/30/YR5	91	7.0600%	140
10/1/YR5	12/31/YR5	91	7.1450%	280

The floating and fixed payments are based on the "actual/360" day count convention. Use the table above to answer the following question and Questions 2-5.

What is the forward discount factor at the end of each quarter?

2. What is the present value of the floating payments three years after inception of the swap?

3. What is the present value of the fixed payments using a swap fixed rate of 6.5928%?

4. What is the value of the swap for the fixed-rate payer?

5. What is the value of the swap for the floating-rate payer?

SOLUTIONS TO QUESTIONS

1. The forward discount factors are shown in the last column.

Quarter Starts	Quarter Ends	Number of Days	Forward Rate	Varying NP	Fwd Discount Factor
1/1/YR4	3/31/YR4	89	6.6550%	110	0.9838137
4/1/YR4	6/30/YR4	90	6.6700%	220	0.9676776
7/1/YR4	9/30/YR4	91	6.7500%	120	0.9514436
10/1/YR4	12/31/YR4	91	6.8250%	240	0.9353076
1/1/YR5	3/31/YR5	90	6.9600%	130	0.9193116
4/1/YR5	6/30/YR5	90	6.9750%	260	0.9035559
7/1/YR5	9/30/YR5	91	7.0600%	140	0.8877136
10/1/YR5	12/31/YR5	91	7.1450%	280	0.8719651

2. The present value of the floating payments is $23,954,626.58 as shown below:

Quarter Starts	Quarter Ends	Number of Days	Varying NP	Floating Payment	Fwd Discount Factor	PV of Floating Payment
1/1/YR4	3/31/YR4	89	110	$1,809,790.28	0.9838137	$1,780,496.41
4/1/YR4	6/30/YR4	90	220	$3,668,500.00	0.9676776	$3,549,925.44
7/1/YR4	9/30/YR4	91	120	$2,047,500.00	0.9514436	$1,948,080.85
10/1/YR4	12/31/YR4	91	240	$4,140,500.00	0.9353076	$3,872,641.25
1/1/YR5	3/31/YR5	90	130	$2,262,000.00	0.9193116	$2,079,482.86
4/1/YR5	6/30/YR5	90	260	$4,533,750.00	0.9035559	$4,096,496.36
7/1/YR5	9/30/YR5	91	140	$2,498,455.56	0.8877136	$2,217,913.02
10/1/YR5	12/31/YR5	91	280	$5,057,072.22	0.8719651	$4,409,590.39
					Total	$23,954,626.58

3. The present value of the fixed payments based on a swap fixed rate of 6.5928% is $22,898,001.96 as shown below:

Quarter Starts	Quarter Ends	Number of Days	Varying NP	Fixed Payments	Fwd Discount Factors	PV of Fixed Payments
1/1/YR4	3/31/YR4	89	110	$1,792,873.37	0.9838137	$1,763,853.33
4/1/YR4	6/30/YR4	90	220	$3,626,036.02	0.9676776	$3,508,834.00
7/1/YR4	9/30/YR4	91	120	$1,999,813.81	0.9514436	$1,902,710.12
10/1/YR4	12/31/YR4	91	240	$3,999,627.61	0.9353076	$3,740,882.23
1/1/YR5	3/31/YR5	90	130	$2,142,657.65	0.9193116	$1,969,770.05
4/1/YR5	6/30/YR5	90	260	$4,285,315.30	0.9035559	$3,872,021.73
7/1/YR5	9/30/YR5	91	140	$2,333,116.11	0.8877136	$2,071,138.94
10/1/YR5	12/31/YR5	91	280	$4,666,232.22	0.8719651	$4,068,791.56
					Total	$22,898,001.96

4. The value of the roller coaster swap three years later from the perspective of the fixed-rate payer is:

> = PV of the floating payments − PV of the fixed payments
> = \$23,954,626.58 − \$22,898,001.96
> = \$1,056,624.62

5. The value of the roller coaster swap three years later from the perspective of the floating-rate payer is simply the opposite of that found in the previous question:

> = PV of the fixed payments − PV of the floating payments
> = \$22,898,001.96 − \$23,954,626.58
> = −\$1,056,624.62

Chapter 5

Lattice Approach to Valuation

In the previous chapter we described the traditional approach for valuing swaps. In this chapter we provide a more versatile model that can be used to value a wider range of swap products — from the plain vanilla swap to complex swap structures. The valuation model uses the lattice approach that is commonly used to value options on bonds and to value bonds with embedded options. In this chapter we will discuss the lattice approach to valuation. In the next two chapters we will apply this approach to the valuation of plain vanilla swaps. In Chapters 7 and 8, we will use the lattice approach to value more compex swap structures.

OVERVIEW OF THE LATTICE MODEL

The lattice model is commonly used in valuing derivative instruments. In the case of interest rate options and options embedded in bond structures, the lattice model is commonly used. As we will see, the values produced by a lattice model are arbitrage-free values.

In general, as explained in the previous chapter, in valuing the cash flows of a swap (i.e., the difference between the payments received and payments paid for each period) an arbitrage value for these cash flows is obtained by discounting at the forward rates implied from the Eurodollar CD futures contracts, or equivalently, the spot rates implied from the Eurodollar CD futures contracts.

The first complication in building a model to value swaps that we will discuss in later chapters (i.e., when we go beyond the plain vanilla swap) is that the future cash flows will depend on what happens to interest rates in the future. This means that future interest rate movements must be considered. This is incorporated into a valuation model by considering how interest rates can change based on some assumed interest rate volatility. Given the assumed interest rate volatility, an interest rate lattice representing possible future interest rates consistent with the volatility assumption can be constructed. It is from the interest rate lattice that two important elements in the valuation process are obtained. First, the interest rates in the lattice are used to generate the cash flows for the swap given the swap terms. Second, the interest rates in the lattice are used to compute the present value of the cash flows.

For a given interest rate volatility, there are several *interest rate models* that have been used in practice to construct an interest rate lattice. An interest rate model is a probabilistic description of how interest rates can change over the life of the swap. An interest rate model does this by making an assumption about the relationship between the level of short-term interest rates and the interest rate volatility as measured by the standard deviation. A discussion of the various interest rate models that have been suggested in the finance literature and that are used by practitioners in developing valuation models is beyond the scope of this chapter. What is important to understand is that the interest rate models commonly used are based on how short-term interest rates can evolve (i.e., change) over time. Consequently, these interest rate models are referred to as *one-factor models*, where "factor" means only one interest rate is being modeled over time. More complex interest rate models would consider how more than one interest rate changes over time. For example, an interest rate model can specify how the short-term interest rate and the long-term interest rate can change over time. Such a model is called a *two-factor model*.

Given an interest rate model and an interest rate volatility assumption, it can be assumed that interest rates can realize one of two possible rates in the next period. A valuation model that makes this assumption in creating an interest rate lattice is called a *binomial model*. There are valuation models that assume that interest rates can take on three possible rates in the next period and these models are called *trinomial models*. (We will illustrate this model in Appendix C.) There are even more complex models that assume in creating an interest rate lattice that more than three possible rates in the next period can be realized. Regardless of the assumption about how many possible rates can be realized in the next period, the interest rate lattice generated must produce a value for the Euro-dollar CD futures contract equal to its observed market price — that is, it must produce an arbitrage-free value. Moreover, the intuition and the methodology for using the interest rate lattice (i.e., the backward induction methodology described later) are the same.

Once an interest rate lattice is generated that (1) is consistent with both the interest rate volatility assumption and the interest rate model, and (2) generates the observed market price for each Euro-dollar CD futures contract, the next step is to use the interest rate lattice to generate the cash flows for the swap.

At this stage of our discussion, all of this sounds terribly complicated. While the building of a model to value swaps is more complex than building a model to value a plain vanilla swap described in the previous chapter, the basic principles are the same. In the case of valuing a plain vanilla swap, the model built is simply a set of forward or spot rates that are used to value the swap's cash flows. The spot or forward rates will produce an arbitrage-free value. To value more complicated swap structures such as swaptions and forward swaps, the interest rate lattice is used in conjunction with the swap terms to generate the future swap cash flows. Again, the interest rate lattice will produce an arbitrage-free value.

In this chapter, we will use the binomial model to demonstrate all of the issues and assumptions associated with valuing a swap. We demonstrate how to create an interest rate lattice (more specifically, a binomial interest rate lattice) given a volatility assumption and how the interest rate lattice can be used to value a swap's cash flows.

Once again, it must be emphasized that while the binomial model is used in this chapter to demonstrate how to value swaps, other models that allow for more than one interest rate in the next period all follow the same principles — they begin with the Euro-dollar CD futures contract, they produce an interest rate lattice that generates an arbitrage-free value obtained using a backward induction methodology, and they depend on assumptions regarding the future volatility of interest rates.

Exhibit 1: Binomial Interest Rate Lattice

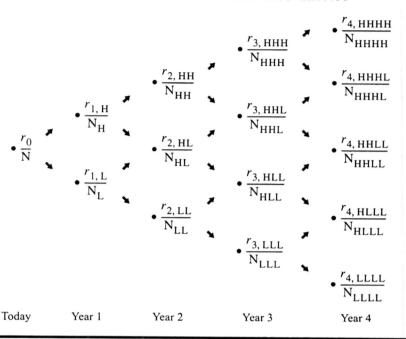

	Today	Year 1	Year 2	Year 3	Year 4

THE BINOMIAL INTEREST RATE LATTICE

In valuing more complex swaps, we will see that consideration must be given to interest rate volatility. This can be done by introducing an interest rate lattice. This lattice is nothing more than a graphical depiction of the one-period or short-term interest rates over time based on some assumption about interest rate volatility. How this lattice is constructed is illustrated below. This overview is presented to give the reader an appreciation only about the characteristics of the binomial interest rate lattice.

Exhibit 1 provides an example of a binomial interest rate lattice. In this lattice, each node (i.e., dot) represents a time period that is equal to one period from the node to the left. We will make the length of the period in our illustration six months. As noted earlier, a semiannual period is used rather than quarterly just to simplify the presentation and is sufficient to illustrate the valuation process. The methodology is the same when the cash flows are quarterly.

Each node is labeled with an N, representing, of course, node. There is a subscript at all the nodes except for the very first node. L represents the lower of the two 6-month rates and H represents the higher of the two 6-month rates. For example, node N_{HH} means that to get to that node the following path for 6-month rates occurred: the 6-month rate realized is the higher of the two rates in the prior 6-month period and then the higher of the two rates in the second 6-month period.

N_{HL} means that the higher of the two 6-month rates is realized in the first 6 months and the lower of the two 6-month rates is realized in the second 6-month period. However, we would get to the same node as N_{HL} if instead the lower of the two 6-month rates is realized in the first 6-month period and the higher of the two 6-month rates is realized in the second 6-month. That is, if we let the subscripts denote the path of interest rates, N_{HL} would be equal to N_{LH}. We didn't use both N_{HL} and N_{LH} in Exhibit 1 to avoid cluttering up the lattice with notation. It would get particularly messy as we move out further along the lattice. For example, at the node identified as N_{HHL} in Exhibit 1, three paths for the 1-year rate can get to that node: HHL, HLH, and LHH. Only N_{HHL} was arbitrarily selected for Exhibit 1.

Look at the point denoted by just N in Exhibit 1. This is the root of the lattice and is nothing more than the current 6-month spot rate, or equivalently the current 6-month rate, which we denote by r_0. What we have assumed in creating this lattice is that the 6-month rate can take on two possible values in the next 6-month period and the two rates have the same probability of occurring. One rate will be higher than the other.

The construction of the binomial interest rate lattice is explained in Appendix B. Exhibit 1 shows the notation for a 4-period binomial interest rate lattice.

The interest rates shown in the binomial interest rate lattice are forward rates. Basically, they are the 1-period rates starting in period t. There is not one forward rate for each 6-month period but a set of forward rates.

Thus, in valuing a plain vanilla swap we know that it is valued using forward rates and in previous chapters we have illustrated this by using 1-period forward rates. For each period, there is a unique forward rate. When we value swap structures using the lattice approach — no matter how complex they may be — we will see that we continue to use forward rates, although there is not just one forward rate for a given period, but a set of forward rates.

DETERMINING THE VALUE AT A NODE

To find the value of the future cash flows at a node, we first calculate the swap's value at the high and low nodes to the right of the node we are interested in. For example, in Exhibit 1, suppose we want to determine the swap's value at node N_H. The swap's value at node N_{HH} and N_{HL} must be determined. Hold aside for now how we get these two values because, as we will see, the process involves starting from the last period in the lattice and working backwards to get the final solution we seek. Because the procedure for solving for the final solution in any interest rate lattice involves moving backwards, the methodology is known as *backward induction.*

Effectively what we are saying is that if we are at some node, then the value at that node will depend on the future cash flows. In turn, the future cash flows depend on the value of the swap one period from that point at the node. The swap's value depends on whether the rate is the higher or lower rate reported at the two nodes to the right of the node that is the focus of our attention. So, the cash flow at a node will depend on (1) the swap's cash flow if the 6-month rate is the higher rate or (2) the swap's cash flow if the 6-month rate is the lower rate.

Let's return to the value at node N_H. The cash flow will be either the swap's value at N_{HH} or the swap's value at N_{HL}. In general, to get the swap's value at a node we follow the fundamental rule for valuation: the value is the present value of the expected cash flows. The appropriate discount rate to use is the 6-month rate at the node where we are computing the value. Now there are two present values in this case: the present value if the 6-month rate is the higher rate and one if it is the lower rate. Since it is assumed that the probability of both outcomes is equal (i.e., there is a 50% probability for each), an average of the two present values is computed.

Exhibit 2: Calculating a Swap's Value at a Node

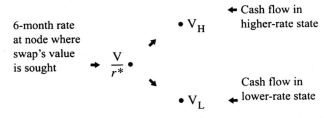

This is illustrated in Exhibit 2 for any node assuming that the 6-month rate is r^* at the node where the valuation is sought and letting:

V_H = the swap's value for the higher 6-month rate
V_L = the swap's value for the lower 6-month rate
$CF(r^*)$ = the arrears cash flow at $t + 1$ as a result of the interest rate r^* at t

The present value of these two swap values using the 6-month rate at the node, r^*, depends on the following components:

$V_H/(1 + r^*)$ = present value for the higher 6-month rate

$V_L/(1 + r^*)$ = present value for the lower 6-month rate

$CF(r^*)/(1 + r^*)$ = present value of the arrears cash flow at period $t + 1$ as a result of the interest rate r^* at t

Then, the value of the swap at the node is found as follows:

$$[(0.5 \times V_H) + (0.5 \times V_L) + CF(r^*)]/(1 + r^*)$$

CONSTRUCTING THE BINOMIAL INTEREST RATE LATTICE

As explained in Appendix B, the construction of any interest rate lattice is complicated, although the principle is simple to understand. This applies to the binomial interest rate lattice or a lattice based on more than two future rates in the next period. The fundamental principle is that when a lattice is used to value a bond, the resulting value should be arbitrage free.

Exhibit 3: Semiannual No Arbitrage Interest Rate Lattice from Eurodollar Futures Prices

	0.50	1.00	1.50	2.00	2.50	3.00	3.50	4.00	4.50
									13.4584%
								12.4902%	
							11.5207%		11.6836%
						10.7102%		10.8431%	
					9.9125%		10.0013%		10.1428%
				9.2477%		9.2977%		9.4131%	
			8.5798%		8.6053%		8.6824%		8.8052%
		8.0272%		8.0282%		8.0716%		8.1717%	
	7.4606%		7.4484%		7.4705%		7.5374%		7.6440%
6.9650%		6.9686%		6.9694%		7.0071%		7.0941%	
	6.4767%		6.4661%		6.4853%		6.5434%		6.6359%
		6.0496%		6.0503%		6.0831%		6.1585%	
			5.6134%		5.6300%		5.6805%		5.7608%
				5.2524%		5.2808%		5.3464%	
					4.8876%		4.9314%		5.0011%
						4.5844%		4.6413%	
							4.2810%		4.3416%
								4.0292%	
									3.7690%

Time in Years   0.50   1.00   1.50   2.00   2.50   3.00   3.50   4.00   4.50

Following the procedure outlined in Appendix B, the interest rate lattice is grown using the same procedure as described earlier. Exhibit 3 shows the binomial interest rate lattice for valuing any swap using the forward rates in Exhibit 5 of Chapter 4 and assuming annual interest rate volatility is 10%.

OBTAINING THE CASH FLOW AT EACH NODE OF THE LATTICE

From the interest rate lattice, the cash flow at each node is computed. Let's use the semiannual-pay swap earlier in this chapter to illustrate how to get each cash flow. The swap terms are:

swap term: 5 years
cash flows for fixed and floating: semiannual
notional principal: $100
swap fixed rate (SFR) = 7.0513%

From the perspective of the fixed-rate payer, the cash flow at a node is found using the following formula:

$$(F_{i,j-1} - \text{SFR}) \times NP_j \times 0.5$$

where

$F_{i,j-1}$ = the rate corresponding to the floating rate at node (i, $j-1$) that dictates the arrears cash flow at j. $j - 1$ means that the cash flow at j is determined by the forward rate at $j - 1$. (For example, $F_{3,7}$ is the forward rate that corresponds to period 7 (3.5 in years) and fourth from the top node ($i = 0, 1, 2, 3$) or 7.5374%.)

NP_j = the notional principal at j. The notional principal can change to whatever value is necessary (they are all constant for this plain vanilla swap).

In the above expression 0.5 is the daycount (semiannual in this case, 0.25 for quarterly, and so on) approximation.

For the fixed-rate receiver, the cash flow is:

$$(\text{SFR} - F_{i,j-1}) \times NP_j \times 0.5$$

Exhibit 4 shows the cash flows for the fixed-rate payer in our swap using the rates in Exhibit 3. For example, let's see how we get the cash flow in year 5 for the node where rates increase each period. We know from Exhibit 3:

$$F_{i,j-1} = F_{0,9} = F_{0,4.5 \text{ years}} = 13.4584\%$$

Then

$$(13.4584\% - 7.0513\%) \times 100 \times 0.5 = 3.2036$$

This is the value shown in Exhibit 4.

Let's try one more cash flow, the one assuming rates decline every period until year 5. Then

$$F_{i,j-1} = F_{9,9} = F_{9,4.5 \text{ years}} = 3.7690\%$$

Exhibit 4: Swap Cash Flow Lattice

	CF .5	CF 1	CF 1.5	CF 2	CF 2.5	CF 3.0	CF 3.5	CF 4	CF 4.5	CF 5
Notional==>	100.00	100.00	100.00	100.00	100.00	100.00	100.00	100.00	100.00	100.00
										3.2036
									2.7195	
								2.2347		2.3161
							1.8294		1.8959	
						1.4306		1.4750		1.5457
					1.0982		1.1232		1.1809	
				0.7643		0.7770		0.8156		0.8769
			0.4880		0.4884		0.5102		0.5602	
		0.2047		0.1985		0.2096		0.2431		0.2964
	-0.0431		-0.0413		-0.0409		-0.0221		0.0214	
		-0.2873		-0.2926		-0.2830		-0.2539		-0.2077
			-0.5008		-0.5005		-0.4841		-0.4464	
				-0.7190		-0.7106		-0.6854		-0.6452
					-0.8994		-0.8852		-0.8525	
						-1.0819		-1.0600		-1.0251
							-1.2334		-1.2050	
								-1.3851		-1.3549
									-1.5110	
										-1.6411
Time in Years	0.50	1.00	1.50	2.00	2.50	3.00	3.50	4.00	4.50	

The cash flow for the fixed-rate receiver is

$$(3.7690\% - 7.0513\%) \times 100 \times 0.5 = -\$1.6411$$

QUESTIONS

1. Using the semiannual interest rate lattice below, compute the pay fixed swap cash flows for a plain vanilla swap with a notional principal of $100 and a swap fixed rate of 7.0777%.

Time in Years	0.50	1.00	1.50	2.00	2.50	3.00	3.50	4.00	4.50
									29.1961%
								24.7073%	
							20.7991%		22.0033%
						17.6303%		18.6204%	
					14.8831%		15.6750%		16.5825%
				12.6554%		13.2869%		14.0330%	
			10.7026%		11.2165%		11.8133%		12.4972%
		9.1234%		9.5376%		10.0135%		10.5758%	
	7.7233%		8.0659%		8.4532%		8.9029%		9.4184%
6.5650%		6.8757%		7.1879%		7.5466%		7.9703%	
	5.8206%		6.0788%		6.3706%		6.7096%		7.0981%
		5.1818%		5.4171%		5.6874%		6.0068%	
			4.5812%		4.8011%		5.0566%		5.3494%
				4.0825%		4.2862%		4.5269%	
					3.6183%		3.8109%		4.0315%
						3.2303%		3.4117%	
							2.8720%		3.0383%
								2.5712%	
									2.2898%

2. Use the same interest rate lattice as in Question 1 to compute the pay fixed swap cash flows for a pay fixed swap where the notional principal varies as shown in the following table and the swap fixed rate is 7.5%.

Period (Yrs)	Notional
0.50	$100
1.00	120
1.50	100
2.00	120
2.50	100
3.00	120
3.50	100
4.00	120
4.50	100
5.00	120

SOLUTIONS TO QUESTIONS

1. The cash flows are as follows:

	CF .5	CF 1	CF 1.5	CF 2	CF 2.5	CF 3.0	CF 3.5	CF 4	CF 4.5	CF 5
Notional==>	100.00	100.00	100.00	100.00	100.00	100.00	100.00	100.00	100.00	100.00

CF Lattice

CF .5	CF 1	CF 1.5	CF 2	CF 2.5	CF 3.0	CF 3.5	CF 4	CF 4.5	CF 5
									11.0592
								8.8148	
							6.8607		7.4628
						5.2763		5.7714	
					3.9027		4.2987		4.7524
				2.7889		3.1046		3.4777	
			1.8125		2.0694		2.3678		2.7098
		1.0229		1.2300		1.4679		1.7491	
	0.3228		0.4941		0.6877		0.9126		1.1704
-0.2563		-0.1010		0.0551		0.2344		0.4463	
	-0.6285		-0.4994		-0.3535		-0.1840		0.0102
		-0.9479		-0.8303		-0.6951		-0.5355	
			-1.2482		-1.1383		-1.0105		-0.8641
				-1.4976		-1.3957		-1.2754	
					-1.7297		-1.6334		-1.5231
						-1.9237		-1.8330	
							-2.1028		-2.0197
								-2.2532	
									-2.3939

2. The cash flows are as follows:

	CF .5	CF 1	CF 1.5	CF 2	CF 2.5	CF 3.0	CF 3.5	CF 4	CF 4.5	CF 5
Notional==>	100.00	120.00	100.00	120.00	100.00	120.00	100.00	120.00	100.00	120.00

CF Lattice

CF .5	CF 1	CF 1.5	CF 2	CF 2.5	CF 3.0	CF 3.5	CF 4	CF 4.5	CF 5
									13.0177
								8.6037	
							7.9795		8.7020
						5.0651		5.5602	
					4.4299		4.9050		5.4495
				2.5777		2.8934		3.2665	
			1.9216		2.2299		2.5880		2.9983
		0.8117		1.0188		1.2567		1.5379	
	0.1340		0.3396		0.5719		0.8418		1.1510
-0.4675		-0.3121		-0.1561		0.0233		0.2352	
	-1.0077		-0.8527		-0.6776		-0.4742		-0.2412
		-1.1591		-1.0415		-0.9063		-0.7466	
			-1.7513		-1.6193		-1.4660		-1.2904
				-1.7087		-1.6069		-1.4865	
					-2.3290		-2.2135		-2.0811
						-2.1349		-2.0442	
							-2.7768		-2.6770
								-2.4644	
									-3.1261

Chapter 6

Swap Valuation Using the Lattice Approach

In the previous chapter we explained what an interest rate lattice is, how the rates are determined on the lattice, and how to compute the cash flows on a lattice. In this chapter we will see how to value a plain vanilla swap using the lattice approach. Remember that this approach is more computational intensive than the traditional approach described in Chapter 4. However, as will be seen, it can handle more complex swap structures. Since we will be using the same 5-year swap using semiannual payments and rounded day count and the same term structure that was illustrated at the end of Chapter 4, the results will (and should) be the same. We will also see how changes in the term structure and the interest rate volatility assumption affect the value of a swap.

VALUING THE SWAP USING THE BINOMIAL INTEREST RATE LATTICE

The binomial interest rate lattice that will be used is the one given in Exhibit 3 in the previous chapter will be used. The cash flow at each node is given in Exhibit 4 of the previous chapter. Using these two exhibits, we can now value this swap.

Cumulative Swap Valuation Lattice

The valuation is shown in Exhibit 1. We will refer to this lattice as the *cumulative swap valuation lattice*. Here is how the values in this lattice are obtained. Using the cash flow lattice given by Exhibit 4 of the previous chapter, each node shows the present value of all the nodes that take place after it. For example, take the middle node at year 3.0 in Exhibit 1 ($i = 3, j = 6$) where the value of 0.0576 is shown. This represents the cumulative present value of all the cash flows that feed into that node plus the cash flow that corresponds to that node at the 3-year point. To see how this is done, let's perform the following backward induction exercise to see how we arrive at 0.0576.

The values at year 4.5 are simply the discounted value of the cash flows at year 5.0:

$$0.8769/(1+8.8052\%/2) = 0.8400$$
$$0.2964/(1+7.6440\%/2) = 0.2854$$
$$-0.2077/(1+6.6359\%/2) = -0.2010$$
$$-0.6452/(1+5.7608\%/2) = -0.6272$$

The values at year 4.0 are going to be the discounted values of the values at year 4.5 plus the discounted value of arrears cash flows that take place at year 4.5. In other words these are the cumulative swap values at year 4.0:

$$(0.5 \times 0.8400 + 0.5 \times 0.2854 + 0.5602)/(1 + 8.1717\%/2)$$
$$= 1.0789$$

$$(0.5 \times 0.2854 + 0.5 \times -0.2010 + 0.0214)/(1 + 7.0941\%/2)$$
$$= 0.0614$$

Exhibit 1: Cumulative Swap Valuation Lattice

Time in Years	0.5	1	1.5	2	2.5	3	3.5	4	4.5
									3.0016
								5.0020	
							6.1485		2.1883
						6.6241		3.5340	
					6.5137		4.1502		1.4711
				5.9373		4.1876		2.2314	
			4.9360		3.7136		2.3679		0.8400
		3.5961		2.8297		2.0050		1.0789	
	1.9335		1.5689		1.1962		0.7837		0.2854
0.0000		0.0057		0.0278		0.0576		0.0614	
	-1.8472		-1.4743		-1.0569		-0.6203		-0.2010
		-3.2452		-2.4866		-1.6740		-0.8348	
			-4.2108		-3.0658		-1.8613		-0.6272
				-4.7334		-3.2089		-1.6227	
					-4.8508		-2.9556		-1.0001
						-4.5659		-2.3144	
							-3.9187		-1.3261
								-2.9206	
									-1.6108

$$(0.5 \times (-0.2010) + 0.5 \times (-0.6272) + (-0.4464))/(1 + 6.1585\%/2)$$
$$= -0.8348$$

The values at year 3.5 are going to be the discounted values of the values at year 4.0 plus the discounted value of arrears cash flows that take place at year 4.0. In other words these are the cumulative swap values at year 3.5:

$$(0.5 \times 1.0789 + 0.5 \times 0.0614 + 0.2431)/(1 + 7.5374\%/2)$$
$$= 0.7837$$

$$(0.5 \times 0.0614 + 0.5 \times (-0.8348) + (-0.2539))/(1 + 6.5434\%/2)$$
$$= -0.6203$$

Finally, to arrive at the middle node at year 3.0, we perform the analogous computation:

$$(0.5 \times 0.7837 + 0.5 \times (-0.6203) + (-0.0221))/(1 + 7.0071\%/2)$$
$$= 0.0576$$

One important feature of the above process should be noted. The discount rate is the floating rate that is used to compute the arrears cash flow. For example the 7.0071% is the rate that computes the -0.0221 (= $(7.0071\% - 7.0513\%) \times 100 \times 0.5$). This will always be the case — this approach allows us not to have to show 10 different lattices to value the swap (and in a later chapter to value a swaption). The alternative would be to present a separate lattice for each cash flow and discount it back using backward induction and then add them all together at the point where valuation is desired. Using this approach combines all the lattices into one and is easy to follow.[1] We will also see in later chapters that this approach enables tremendous versatility in the valuation of forward start swaps and swaptions.

Back to the valuation approach. Following this procedure throughout the lattice results in a swap value for the given SFR at time zero. It is simply a task of iterating on SFR until the swap

---

[1] It is certainly no more difficult than any other backward induction approach for other contingent claims.

value equals zero. This approach also allows extraordinary leverage for off market swaps (i.e., swaps where the SFR does not result in a zero swap value and other exotic structures — especially swaptions). The SFR that produces a zero swap value is 7.0513% — this is the value of the plain vanilla swap and agrees with what we found in Chapter 4 when we valued this swap using the traditional approach. Note that this is the same as the analytic equivalent explained in the previous chapter of summing the discount factors and dividing that into the total present value of the floating payments to arrive at the SFR. However, this approach allows far more versatility and is arguably more intuitive. It also offers an efficient and systematic framework for performing extensive analytics.

While in our illustration we valued a swap at inception that has a value of zero, the procedure for valuing a swap after rates change (i.e., valuing an off market swap) is the same. First, given the new Eurodollar CD futures prices, new forward rates are determined. Given the forward rates, a new interest rate lattice is generated. Then the swap (given its remaining term) is valued using the new interest rate lattice.

Valuing a Swap After Inception

In Chapter 4 we showed how using the traditional approach a plain vanilla swap can be valued two years after the swap's inception if interest rates rise. The new forward rates assumed were shown in Columns (3) and (6) of panel a of Exhibit 6 in Chapter 4 based on semiannual payments and rounded day count. To use the lattice approach to value a swap after rates change, the new rates are used to construct a new lattice. In panel a of Exhibit 2 these rates are reproduced. Panel b of Exhibit 2 shows the binomial interest rate lattice based on these rates. Based on this binomial interest rate lattice, panel c shows the cash flows for the pay fixed swap. In panel d the pay fixed swap value at each node is computed. The value of the swap two years later is shown at the root of the lattice in panel d. For a pay fixed swap it is $0.1524 per $100 of notional principal. This is the same value as computed using the traditional approach. (See panel d of Exhibit 6 in Chapter 4.)

Exhibit 2: Valuing a Swap After Rates Rise Using the Binomial Interest Rates Rise (Semiannual Pay and Rounded Day Count)

Panel a. New Interest Rates Two Years Later

(1) Beginning Period	(2) End of Period	(3) Current 6-Month LIBOR	(4) Forward Rate	(5) End of Period
1/1/YR1	6/30/YR1	7.0275%		1
7/1/YR1	12/31/YR1		7.0300%	2
1/1/YR2	6/30/YR2		7.0875%	3
7/1/YR2	12/31/YR2		7.1125%	4
1/1/YR3	6/30/YR3		7.1925%	5
7/1/YR3	12/31/YR3		7.2275%	6

Panel b. Interest Rate Lattice Two Years Later

```
                                              10.19%
                                      9.47%
                              8.74%           8.85%
                      8.13%           8.22%
              7.53%           7.58%           7.68%
      7.03%           7.06%           7.13%
              6.53%           6.58%           6.67%
                      6.13%           6.19%
                              5.72%           5.79%
                                      5.38%
                                              5.03%

Time in Years    0.5      1      1.5      2      2.5
```

Panel c. Pay Fixed Swap Cash Flows Two Years Later

```
                                                      1.5702
                                              1.2069
                                      0.8427          0.8981
                              0.5382          0.5828
                      0.2381          0.2666          0.3147
      -0.0119                 0.0023          0.0410
                      -0.2582         -0.2335         -0.1917
                              -0.4630         -0.4293
                                      -0.6677         -0.6314
                                              -0.8377
                                                      -1.0131

Time in Years    0.5      1      1.5      2      2.5      3
```

Exhibit 2 (Continued)
Panel d. Pay Fixed Swap Values Two Years Later

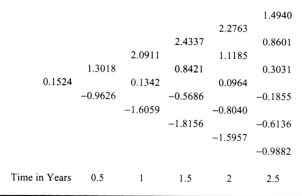

Time in Years	0.5	1	1.5	2	2.5

Valuing a Swap When There is a Varying Notional Principal

In Chapter 4 we explained how to compute the value of a swap where the notional principal changes over time in a predetermined way. In fact, we looked at a 5-year amortizing swap (i.e., a swap where the notional principal declines over time). In this section we will show how to value using the lattice approach the 5-year amortizing swap with semiannual payments. We will also value a 5-year accreting swap. The varying notional principal for each swap is given below:

Year	Amortizing Swap	Accreting Swap
0.5	$100	$100
1.0	90	110
1.5	80	120
2.0	70	130
2.5	60	140
3.0	50	150
3.5	40	160
4.0	30	170
4.5	20	180
5.0	10	190

Exhibit 3 shows the swap cash flow lattice for the amortizing swap with a swap fixed rate of 7.0513%. The corresponding cumulative swap valuation lattice for this amortizing swap is shown as Exhibit 4. Notice that with a swap fixed rate (SFR) of 7.0513% the value of this swap is −0.$00967 per $100 of notional for a pay fixed swap. What SFR would produce a zero value for this swap? We can iterate on the SFR to find that an SFR of 7.0111% would. The corresponding swap cash flow lattices and cumulative swap valuation lattice are shown in Exhibits 5 and 6.

Exhibit 7 shows the swap cash flow lattice for the accreting swap with a swap rate of 7.0676%. The corresponding cumulative swap valuation lattice for this accreting swap is shown as Exhibit 8. Notice that with a swap fixed rate of 7.0676% the value of this swap is zero.

Exhibit 3: Swap Cash Flow Lattice for an Amortizing Swap with an SFR = 7.0513%

	CF 0.5	CF 1	CF 1.5	CF 2	CF 2.5	CF 3.0	CF 3.5	CF 4	CF 4.5	CF 5
Notional==>	100.00	90.00	80.00	70.00	60.00	50.00	40.00	30.00	20.00	10.00
										0.3204
									0.5439	
								0.6704		0.2316
							0.7318		0.3792	
						0.7153		0.4425		0.1546
					0.6589		0.4493		0.2362	
				0.5350		0.3885		0.2447		0.0877
			0.3904		0.2931		0.2041		0.1120	
		0.1842		0.1390		0.1048		0.0729		0.0296
	−0.0431		−0.0331		−0.0246		−0.0088		0.0043	
		−0.2585		−0.2048		−0.1415		−0.0762		−0.0208
			−0.4007		−0.3003		−0.1936		−0.0893	
				−0.5033		−0.3553		−0.2056		−0.0645
					−0.5397		−0.3541		−0.1705	
						−0.5409		−0.3180		−0.1025
							−0.4934		−0.2410	
								−0.4155		−0.1355
									−0.3022	
										−0.1641
Time in Years	0.5	1	1.5	2	2.5	3	3.5	4	4.5	

Exhibit 4: Cumulative Swap Valuation Lattice an Amortizing Swap with an SFR = 7.0513%

```
                                                                        0.3002
                                                                0.7562
                                                        1.2435          0.2188
                                                1.6812          0.5332
                                        1.9847          0.8353          0.1471
                                2.1116          1.0544          0.3359
                        1.9963          1.1160          0.4730          0.0840
                1.6207          0.9822          0.4966          0.1617
        0.9283          0.5945          0.3411          0.1521          0.0285
-0.0967         -0.0633         -0.0269          0.0016          0.0082
        -1.0422         -0.6595         -0.3476         -0.1312         -0.0201
                -1.5714         -0.9251         -0.4364         -0.1268
                        -1.7771         -0.9580         -0.3808         -0.0627
                                -1.7222         -0.8230         -0.2453
                                        -1.4976         -0.6004         -0.1000
                                                -1.1635         -0.3492
                                                        -0.7932         -0.1326
                                                                -0.4402
                                                                        -0.1611

Time in Years   0.5     1.0     1.5     2.0     2.5     3.0     3.5     4.0     4.5
```

Exhibit 5: Swap Cash Flow Lattice for an Amortizing Swap with an SFR = 7.0111%

	CF.5	CF 1	CF 1.5	CF 2	CF 2.5	CF 3.0	CF 3.5	CF 4	CF 4.5	CF 5
Notional==>	100.00	90.00	80.00	70.00	60.00	50.00	40.00	30.00	20.00	10.00

```
                                                                        0.3224
                                                                0.5479
                                                        0.6764          0.2336
                                                0.7398          0.3832
                                        0.7254          0.4485          0.1566
                                0.6710          0.4573          0.2402
                        0.5491          0.3986          0.2507          0.0897
                0.4065          0.3051          0.2121          0.1161
        0.2023          0.1531          0.1148          0.0790          0.0316
-0.0230         -0.0170         -0.0125         -0.0008          0.0083
        -0.2405         -0.1907         -0.1314         -0.0702         -0.0188
                -0.3846         -0.2882         -0.1856         -0.0853
                        -0.4892         -0.3453         -0.1996         -0.0625
                                -0.5276         -0.3460         -0.1665
                                        -0.5309         -0.3120         -0.1005
                                                -0.4853         -0.2370
                                                        -0.4095         -0.1335
                                                                -0.2982
                                                                        -0.1621

Time in Years   0.5     1.0     1.5     2.0     2.5     3.0     3.5     4.0     4.5
```

Exhibit 6: Cumulative Swap Valuation Lattice an Amortizing Swap with an SFR = 7.0111 %

								0.3020
							0.7617	
						1.2545		0.2207
					1.6993		0.5389	
				2.0117		0.8464		0.1490
			2.1491		1.0728		0.3416	
		2.0460		1.1433		0.4842		0.0859
	1.6844		1.0203		0.5152		0.1674	
1.0076		0.6450		0.3688		0.1635		0.0305
0.0000		0.0014		0.0117		0.0204		0.0140	
	−0.9615		−0.6083		−0.3196		−0.1197		−0.0182
		−1.5058		−0.8861		−0.4174		−0.1210	
			−1.7252		−0.9298		−0.3693		−0.0608
				−1.6828		−0.8039		−0.2395	
					−1.4691		−0.5888		−0.0980
						−1.1443		−0.3434	
							−0.7816		−0.1306
							−0.4343	
								−0.1591

Time in Years	0.5	1.0	1.5	2.0	2.5	3.0	3.5	4.0	4.5

Exhibit 7: Swap Cash Flow Lattice for an Accreting Swap with an SFR = 7.0676%

	CF.5	CF 1	CF 1.5	CF 2	CF 2.5	CF 3.0	CF 3.5	CF 4	CF 4.5	CF 5
Notional==>	100.00	110.00	120.00	130.00	140.00	150.00	160.00	170.00	180.00	190.00

CF Lattice

									6.0712
								4.8803	
							3.7851		4.3851
						2.9140		3.3979	
					2.1337		2.4936		2.9214
				1.5260		1.7841		2.1109	
			0.9829		1.1532		1.3725		1.6507
		0.5758		0.6724		0.8032		0.9937	
	0.2161		0.2475		0.3021		0.3993		0.5475
−0.0513		−0.0594		−0.0687		−0.0484		0.0238	
	−0.3250		−0.3910		−0.4368		−0.4456		−0.4101
		−0.6108		−0.7121		−0.7877		−0.8182	
			−0.9453		−1.0782		−1.1791		−1.2415
				−1.2706		−1.4294		−1.5491	
					−1.6351		−1.8159		−1.9632
						−1.9866		−2.1837	
							−2.3686		−2.5898
							−2.7346	
								−3.1337

Time in Years	0.5	1.0	1.5	2.0	2.5	3.0	3.5	4.0	4.5

Exhibit 8: Cumulative Swap Valuation Lattice an Accreting Swap with an SFR = 7.0676%

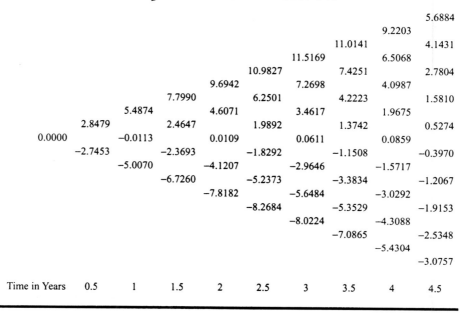

	5.6884
	9.2203
	11.0141	4.1431

Time in Years	0.5	1	1.5	2	2.5	3	3.5	4	4.5

Lattice values:

```
                                                                5.6884
                                                       9.2203
                                              11.0141          4.1431
                                     11.5169          6.5068
                            10.9827           7.4251          2.7804
                   9.6942           7.2698           4.0987
          7.7990           6.2501           4.2223          1.5810
 5.4874           4.6071           3.4617           1.9675
2.8479           2.4647           1.9892           1.3742          0.5274
0.0000  -0.0113           0.0109           0.0611           0.0859
       -2.7453          -2.3693          -1.8292          -1.1508          -0.3970
               -5.0070          -4.1207          -2.9646          -1.5717
                       -6.7260          -5.2373          -3.3834          -1.2067
                               -7.8182          -5.6484          -3.0292
                                       -8.2684          -5.3529          -1.9153
                                               -8.0224          -4.3088
                                                       -7.0865          -2.5348
                                                               -5.4304
                                                                        -3.0757
```

THE EFFECT OF CHANGES IN THE TERM STRUCTURE ON A SWAP'S VALUE

The swap illustration presented in this chapter is based on market inputs. It is critical to understand how changes in market variables will change the value of a swap. For example, we know that the value of a swap changes if rates change. In this section we will look at how changes in the shape of the term structure of interest rates affects the value of a swap and the swap fixed rate. This information is useful in understanding how swaps can be used in portfolio and risk management.

Exhibit 9 shows the original term structure of interest rates, labeled "Original TS." Using this term structure we computed a SFR of 7.0513%. (This is the SFR that produces a zero net present value for the plain vanilla swap for this term structure.) There are two other term structures shown in the exhibit. One is a steeper term structure than the original term structure and the other an inverted term structure (i.e., rates decline as maturity increases).

Exhibit 9: Term Structures Used for Swap Comparative Statics

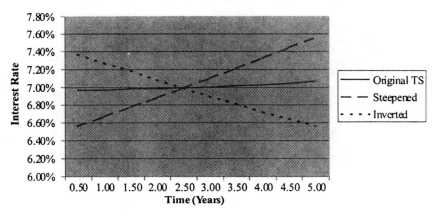

Exhibit 10: Swap Value as Original Term Structure Shifts
SFR = 7.0513%

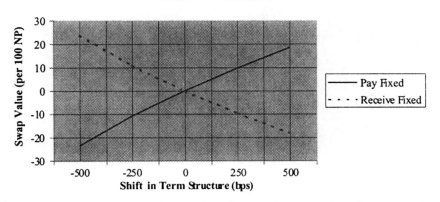

Exhibit 10 illustrates what happens to a swap's value as the original term structure is shifted in a parallel manner and holding the SFR at 7.0513%. The swap value is shown for both the fixed-rate payer and the fixed-rate receiver. Notice that the sum of the value of the two counterparty positions is equal to zero. As illustrated in Chapter 1, the fixed-rate payer gains if interest rates rise and loses if interest rate decline; the reverse is true for the floating-rate receiver. Therefore, one can use a swap to speculate or hedge against interest rate moves.

Exhibit 11: SFR as Original Term Structure Shifts

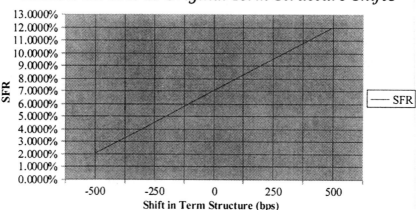

Exhibit 12: Swap Value as Steepened Term Structure Shifts
SFR = 7.0513%

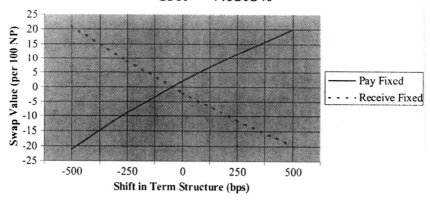

Exhibit 11 shows how the SFR changes as the original term structure is shifted in a parallel manner.

Exhibit 12 illustrates how the swap's value changes when the term structure steepens and shifts from its original position. Notice that with a steepening and no shift the value of the fixed-rate payer's position increases. This is because the steepened term structure implies an increase in the forward rates, suggesting an increase in the value of cash inflows to the pay fixed counterparty. This results in an increase in the swap's value. The opposite is true for the fixed receiver. Exhibit 13 shows the SFR that makes the swap value have a zero net present value using the steepened term structure. Note that the SFR to make the steepened only term structure swap zero is 7.4898%.

Exhibit 14 demonstrates what happens to the swap value for both counterparties as the term structure inverts and shifts from its original position. Notice that with an inversion and no shift the fixed-rate payer's position decreases in value. This is because the implied forward rates decrease, suggesting a decrease in cash inflows for the fixed payer. This results in a decline in the swap's value. The opposite is true for the fixed-rate receiver. Exhibit 15 indicates the SFR that makes the swap value have a zero net present value using the inverted only term structure swap zero is 6.6051%.

Exhibit 13: SFR as Steepened Term Structure Shifts

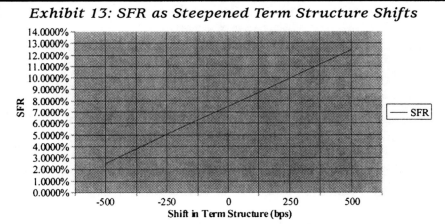

Exhibit 14: Swap Value as Inverted Term Structure Shifts
SFR = 7.0513%

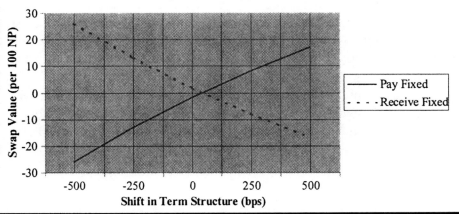

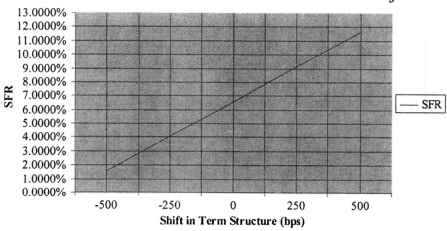

Exhibit 15: SFR as Inverted Term Structure Shifts

PLAIN VANILLA SWAP AND INTEREST RATE VOLATILITY

We conclude this chapter with the relationship between the value of a plain vanilla swap and the interest rate volatility assumed. As we stated at the outset of this chapter, the lattice approach is an alternative to the traditional approach. It is more computationally difficult, but it is more flexible in allowing us to handle more complex swap structures.

We also stated that the results should be the same for a plain vanilla swap whether we used the lattice approach or the traditional approach. Consequently, the volatility assumption made in constructing the interest rate lattice should not be expected to affect the value of a swap. That is, indeed, the case. Exhibit 16 shows for the three term structures the value of our swap and how that value does not change when the assumed interest rate volatility changes.

The beauty of the lattice approach is that where there are complex swap structures whose value depends on expected interest rate volatility, we can handle them. We will see this in later chapters.

Exhibit 16: Pay Fixed Swap Values as Volatility Changes

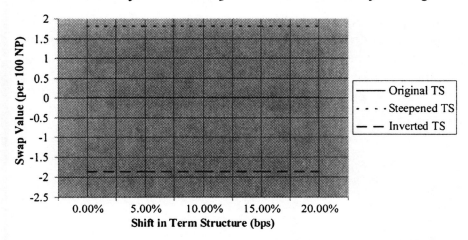

QUESTIONS

1. a. Using the semiannual interest rate lattice below (which is the same as the lattice used for Questions 1 and 2 in the previous chapter) compute the pay fixed swap values for a plain vanilla swap with a notional principal of $100 and a swap fixed rate of 7.0777%.

```
                                                                                  29.1961%
                                                                         24.7073%
                                                                20.7991%          22.0033%
                                                       17.6303%          18.6204%
                                              14.8831%          15.6750%          16.5825%
                                     12.6554%          13.2869%          14.0330%
                            10.7026%          11.2165%          11.8133%          12.4972%
                    9.1234%           9.5376%           10.0135%          10.5758%
            7.7233%           8.0659%           8.4532%           8.9029%           9.4184%
    6.5650%           6.8757%           7.1879%           7.5466%           7.9703%
            5.8206%           6.0788%           6.3706%           6.7096%           7.0981%
                    5.1818%           5.4171%           5.6874%           6.0068%
                            4.5812%           4.8011%           5.0566%           5.3494%
                                     4.0825%           4.2862%           4.5269%
                                              3.6183%           3.8109%           4.0315%
                                                       3.2303%           3.4117%
                                                                2.8720%           3.0383%
                                                                         2.5712%
                                                                                  2.2898%

Time in Years   0.50    1.00    1.50    2.00    2.50    3.00    3.50    4.00    4.50
```

b. Using a spreadsheet program compute the swap fixed rate that makes this swap have a zero value.

2. a. Use the same interest rate lattice as in Question 1 to compute the pay fixed swap value for a varying notional principal pay fixed swap where the notional principal varies as shown in the following table and the swap fixed rate is 7.5%.

Period (Yrs)	Notional
0.50	100
1.00	120
1.50	100
2.00	120
2.50	100
3.00	120
3.50	100
4.00	120
4.50	100
5.00	120

b. Using a spreadsheet program compute the swap fixed rate that makes this swap have a zero value.

SOLUTIONS TO QUESTIONS

1. a. The swap values are as follows:

0	0.5	1	1.5	2	2.5	3	3.5	4	4.5
									9.6504
								15.1322	
							17.7610		6.7231
						18.4323		10.3624	
					17.6469		11.8008		4.3886
				15.8017		11.6825		6.4917	
			13.1119		10.3786		6.9072		2.5504
		9.7927		8.2005		6.1000		3.4032	
	5.9494		5.3213		4.3447		2.9678		1.1177
1.7054		1.9199		1.8831		1.5812		0.9714	
	−1.9138		−1.1475		−0.5532		−0.1550		0.0098
		−4.6018		−3.2490		−2.0158		−0.9236	
			−6.3987		−4.4601		−2.6009		−0.8417
				−7.3451		−4.8420		−2.3887	
					−7.5347		−4.4992		−1.4930
						−7.0406		−3.5143	
							−5.9620		−1.9895
								−4.3752	
									−2.3669

Time in Years   0.5   1   1.5   2   2.5   3   3.5   4   4.5

b. The value lattice when the swap fixed rate is 7.4898%.

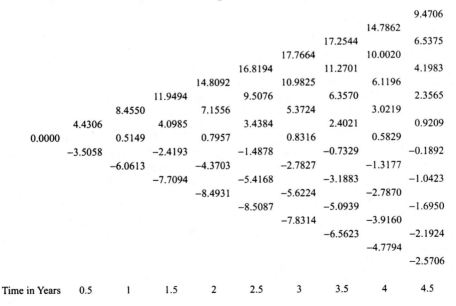

0	0.5	1	1.5	2	2.5	3	3.5	4	4.5
									9.4706
								14.7862	
							17.2544		6.5375
						17.7664		10.0020	
					16.8194		11.2701		4.1983
				14.8092		10.9825		6.1196	
			11.9494		9.5076		6.3570		2.3565
		8.4550		7.1556		5.3724		3.0219	
	4.4306		4.0985		3.4384		2.4021		0.9209
0.0000		0.5149		0.7957		0.8316		0.5829	
	−3.5058		−2.4193		−1.4878		−0.7329		−0.1892
		−6.0613		−4.3703		−2.7827		−1.3177	
			−7.7094		−5.4168		−3.1883		−1.0423
				−8.4931		−5.6224		−2.7870	
					−8.5087		−5.0939		−1.6950
						−7.8314		−3.9160	
							−6.5623		−2.1924
								−4.7794	
									−2.5706

Time in Years   0.5   1   1.5   2   2.5   3   3.5   4   4.5

2. a. The swap values are as follows:

	0.5	1	1.5	2	2.5	3	3.5	4	4.5
									11.3594
								16.2016	
							19.5358		7.8395
						19.4916		10.9744	
					18.8071		12.7536		5.0323
				16.2614		12.0619		6.7220	
			13.2739		10.6184		7.1859		2.8220
		9.2884		7.8638		5.9061		3.3228	
	4.8722		4.5268		3.8217		2.7042		1.0993
−0.0036		0.5645		0.8759		0.9166		0.6427	
	−3.9447		−2.7348		−1.6948		−0.8484		−0.2329
		−6.6682		−4.8062		−3.0590		−1.4480	
			−8.6289		−6.0950		−3.6310		−1.2568
				−9.3444		−6.1851		−3.0655	
					−9.5577		−5.7905		−2.0400
						−8.6182		−4.3091	
							−7.4546		−2.6370
								−5.2607	
									−3.0908

Time in Years

b. The swap values when the swap fixed rate is 7.4992%

Value Lattice

	0.5	1	1.5	2	2.5	3	3.5	4	4.5
									11.3598
								16.2024	
							19.5369		7.8399
						19.4931		10.9751	
					18.8089		12.7548		5.0327
				16.2635		12.0634		6.7228	
			13.2764		10.6203		7.1871		2.8225
		9.2912		7.8660		5.9076		3.3236	
	4.8755		4.5295		3.8237		2.7054		1.0997
0.0000		0.5675		0.8782		0.9182		0.6436	
	−3.9413		−2.7320		−1.6928		−0.8471		−0.2324
		−6.6651		−4.8039		−3.0574		−1.4471	
			−8.6261		−6.0930		−3.6297		−1.2563
				−9.3420		−6.1834		−3.0647	
					−9.5556		−5.7892		−2.0395
						−8.6166		−4.3083	
							−7.4533		−2.6365
								−5.2598	
									−3.0903

Time in Years

Chapter 7

Valuation of
Forward Start Swaps

T hus far we have looked at plain vanilla swaps — both swaps where the notional principal is constant over the life of the swap and swaps where the notional principal changes in a predetermined way. In this chapter and the next we will see how to value more complex swap structures. The valuation of these structures requires an approach that can handle changing rates in the future due to interest rate volatility. Of course, the approach that will be used is the lattice approach; that is the reason we discussed it in Chapters 5 and 6. In this chapter we will demonstrate how to value a forward start swap and in the next we look at how to value a swaption (i.e., an option on a swap).

FORWARD START SWAP

A *forward start swap* is a swap structure wherein the swap does not begin until some future date that is specified in the swap agreement. Thus, there is a beginning date for the swap at some time in the future and a maturity date. We use the notation "(y_s, y_e) forward start swap" to denote a forward start swap that starts y_s years from now and ends (matures) in y_e years after the start date. Notice that we use years in the notation, not periods.

    A forward start swap will also specify the swap fixed rate at which the counterparties agree to exchange payments commencing at the start date. We refer to this rate as the *forward swap fixed rate* for the forward start swap.

    In the next chapter we will look at swaptions. In a swaption, one of the counterparties (the buyer of the swaption) has the right, but not the obligation, to initiate a swap at or by some future date. In the case of a forward start swap, both counterparties must perform; that is, both counterparties parties are committing to make the designated payments in the future.

To illustrate the valuation of a forward start swap we will assume that the swap starts in two years and the swap then has a tenor of three years. Using our notation this is a (2,3) forward start swap. We will assume that the forward swap fixed rate is 7.1157%. In this illustration, we will use a 5-year swap based on a semiannual pay and a rounded day count.

USING THE CUMULATIVE SWAP VALUATION LATTICE

To value a forward start swap, it is necessary to first determine the possible values of the swap at the start date. Where can we obtain these values? In our discussion of the lattice approach in Chapter 5, we presented the *cumulative swap valuation lattice*. It is this lattice that can be used to obtain the possible swap values at the start date of the forward start swap. The values in the lattice are in terms of present value.

Exhibit 1 shows the cumulative swap valuation lattice for the 5-year swap for which the swap fixed rate is 7.1157%. For example, if the swap starts in year 2, then there are five possible values: 5.7720, 2.6611, −0.1438, −2.6608, and −4.9100. It might seem that the value of a forward start swap is the average value of the swap values for that period. In our illustration it would be $0.1437 for the pay fixed swap and −$0.1437 for the receive fixed swap if the swap starts in year 2.0. The problem with using a simple average is that the possible swap values for a given period may not have the same probability of occurrence. Instead of a simple averaging of the values at the period where the swap begins, the value at each node in Exhibit 1 should be weighted by the probability of realizing its value. We will see how this is done next.

Exhibit 1: Cumulative Swap Valuation Lattice for Forward Start Swaps at a Forward Swap Fixed Rate of 7.1157%

	0.5	1	1.5	2	2.5	3	3.5	4	4.5
									2.9714
								4.9432	
							6.0621		2.1579
						6.5109		3.4745	
					6.3742		4.0625		1.4405
				5.7720		4.0725		2.1713	
			4.7450		3.5715		2.2791		0.8091
		3.3795		2.6611		1.8883		1.0182	
	1.6913		1.3738		1.0519		0.6939		0.2544
−0.2678		−0.2157		−0.1438		−0.0607		0.0003	
	−2.0949		−1.6731		−1.2033		−0.7109		−0.2322
		−3.4709		−2.6608		−1.7936		−0.8963	
			−4.4127		−3.2140		−1.9526		−0.6585
				−4.9100		−3.3297		−1.6846	
					−5.0006		−3.0477		−1.0315
						−4.6877		−2.3766	
							−4.0114		−1.3576
								−2.9831	
									−1.6424

Time in Years   0.5   1   1.5   2   2.5   3   3.5   4   4.5

Exhibit 2: Lattice Showing the Number of Paths that Arrive at a Node

0	0.5	1	1.5	2	2.5	3	3.5	4	4.5
									1
								1	
							1		9
						1		8	
					1		7		36
				1		6		28	
			1		5		21		84
		1		4		15		56	
	1		3		10		35		126
0		2		6		20		70	
	1		3		10		35		126
		1		4		15		56	
			1		5		21		84
				1		6		28	
					1		7		36
						1		8	
							1		9
								1	
									1

Time in Years   0.5   1   1.5   2   2.5   3   3.5   4   4.5

OBTAINING THE WEIGHTS AT A NODE

When there are only two movements for the rate in the next period from a given node (i.e., in the binomial interest rate lattice), the number of paths that arrive at a given node can be calculated using the following relationship:

$$\frac{n!}{j!(n-j)!} \tag{1}$$

where n is the number of periods and j is the number of down states.

Exhibit 2 shows the number of paths that arrive at each node for a 5-year swap with semiannual payments. Let's illustrate equation (1) using the exhibit to explain the notation and then to demonstrate how to calculate the number of paths leading to each node in Exhibit 2. Look at year 2. Start at the top of year 2. At that node, there are no down states. Thus, j in equation (1) is 0. Since we are looking at year 2, the number of periods is 4. Thus, n is equal to 4. Substituting these values into equation (1) we have:[1]

$$\frac{4!}{0!(4-0)!} = \frac{4 \times 3 \times 2 \times 1}{1(4 \times 3 \times 2 \times 1)}$$

$$= \frac{24}{1(24)} = 1$$

This is a simple case since there is only 1 path that arrives at the top of the lattice. For the second node from the top at year 2, there is one down state so j is equal to 1. Since n is still 4 (as it is for all the nodes at year 2), then

$$\frac{4!}{1!(4-1)!} = \frac{4 \times 3 \times 2 \times 1}{1(3 \times 2 \times 1)}$$

$$= \frac{24}{1(6)} = 4$$

We'll do one more. Let's compute the number of paths to arrive at the node that is the third one down for year 2. In this case j is 2 and therefore,

$$\frac{4!}{2!(4-2)!} = \frac{4 \times 3 \times 2 \times 1}{(2 \times 1)(2 \times 1)}$$

$$= \frac{24}{2(2)} = 6$$

Given the lattice that shows the number of paths to arrive at a node, the probability of reaching a node can be computed. This is done by first adding up the total number of possible paths for a period and then for a given node dividing the number of paths that arrive at that node by the total number of possible paths for that period.

To illustrate this calculation, we will again use year 2. The total number of paths is 16 (= 1 + 4 + 6 + 4 + 1). For the top node at year 2, the probability is 1/16 or 6.25%. For the second node from the top of the lattice at year 2, the probability is 4/16 or 25.0%. Exhibit 3 shows in tabular form the number of paths that arrive at a node and the associated probability.

---

[1] 0! is equal to 1.

Exhibit 3: Calculating the Probability Weighted Value for Year 2

(1)	(2)	(3)	(4)
Cumulative swap value at node	No. of Paths that Arrive at Node	Probability of Realizing Node Value	Probability Weighted Value at Node
5.7720	1	6.25%	0.3608
2.6611	4	25.00%	0.6653
−0.1438	6	37.50%	−0.0539
−2.6608	4	25.00%	−0.6652
−4.9100	1	6.25%	−0.3069
Total	16	100.00%	0.0000

An alternative to the procedure just described for computing the probability of getting to a node is to use the formula given below. The formula is appropriate only when there is an up and down movement in the next period and the probability is 50% each. The formula is:

$$\frac{n!}{j!(n-j)!}(0.5)^n \tag{2}$$

For example, consider the top node at year 2. Since j is 0 and n is 4, we have

$$\frac{4!}{0!(4-0)!}(0.5)^4 = \frac{24}{1(24)}(0.0625)$$

$$= 0.0625 = 6.25\%$$

This value agrees with the probability shown in Exhibit 3.

For the second node from the top at year 2, j is 1 and n is 4. Therefore,

$$\frac{4!}{1!(4-1)!}(0.5)^4 = \frac{24}{1(6)}(0.0625)$$

$$= 0.25 = 25\%$$

Note the symmetry of probabilities in the lattice for a given period. This will always be the case in the binomial lattice. Consequently, only the probabilities for the top half of the binomial lattice need be computed.

VALUE OF FORWARD START SWAP

Given the cumulative swap valuation lattice and the probability associated for each value of that lattice, the value of a forward start swap can be computed. This is done at a starting period for the forward rate swap as follows. Calculate at each node for the starting period the product of the cumulative swap value at the node and the corresponding probability. Then, sum up these products. The summation is the value of the forward start swap.

The calculations are shown in Exhibit 3 for a (2,3) forward start swap. For year 2, Column (1) shows the five swap values from the cumulative swap valuation lattice (Exhibit 1). Column (3) shows the probability corresponding to each of the five swap values. The last column shows the product of the swap value in Column (1) and the corresponding probability in Column (3). The last row of the last column is the sum of these products and is the value of our (2,3) forward start swap. The value is zero for the forward start swap party that pays fixed and therefore zero for the party that receives fixed.

Exhibit 4 shows the probability weighted cumulative swap valuation lattice. The two rows at the bottom of the lattice show for each counterparty the value of a forward start swap for each period. Notice that for year 2.0, the value agrees with what was computed in Exhibit 3.

It is a straightforward extension to value varying notional principal forward start swaps. For the (2,3) forward rate swap, simply adjust the values in the cumulative swap valuation lattice in Exhibit 1 at each node for the varying notional principal and use the same number of paths that arrive at a node (and associated probability) to value the swap.

THE EFFECT OF CHANGES IN THE TERM STRUCTURE ON A FORWARD START SWAP'S VALUE

In Chapter 6 we demonstrated how changes in the term structure affect the value of a plain vanilla swap. In this section we will do the same for the forward start swap using the same term structures used in Chapter 6. Exhibit 9 of Chapter 6 shows the original term structure, a steeper term structure, and an inverse term structure.

Exhibit 4: Probability Weighted Cumulative Swap Values with an SFR of 7.1157% and Value of Forward Start Swaps

Lattice of probability-weighted cumulative swap values (triangular array as printed):

```
 0.005804
 0.037931   0.019309
 0.101283   0.108577   0.04736
 0.132745   0.237486   0.222171   0.101733
 0.062609   0.222725   0.373921   0.3818     0.199194
-0.057141   7.71E-05   0.189743   0.442561   0.55805    0.360748
-0.108034  -0.196072  -0.018958   0.328713   0.665276   0.593131
-0.072529  -0.320356  -0.194393  -0.376034  -0.05394    0.515174   0.844887
-0.023864  -0.184258  -0.420365  -0.665211  -0.627396  -0.107826   0.845652
-0.003208  -0.074269  -0.166669  -0.502185  -0.55159   -0.867734  -1.047472
-0.011653  -0.031339  -0.312157  -0.306873  -0.073245  -0.156268  -0.2678
```

Time in Years	0.5	1	1.5	2	2.5	3	3.5	4	4.5
FWD Start Pay Fixed Swaps==>	−0.2018	−0.1307	−0.0707	0.0000	0.0515	0.1014	0.1204	0.1219	0.0756
FWD Start Receive Fixed Swaps==>	0.2018	0.1307	0.0707	0.0000	−0.0515	−0.1014	−0.1204	−0.1219	−0.0756

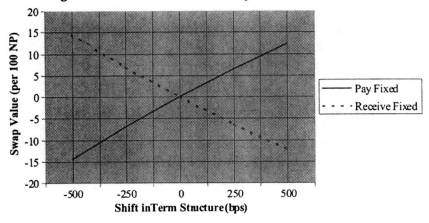

Exhibit 5: (2, 3) Forward Start Swap Value as Original Term Structure Shifts SFR = 7.1157%

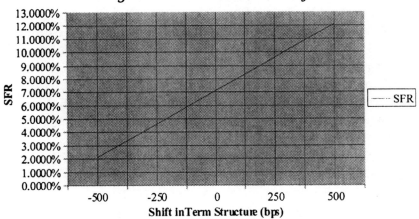

Exhibit 6: (2, 3) Forward Start Swap SFR as Original Term Structure Shifts

Exhibit 5 shows how the value of the (2,3) forward start swap changes for a parallel shift in the original term structure. Notice how small the range of values is. This is because the number of cash flows for the (2,3) forward start swap is much smaller than for the other swaps such as the plain vanilla and amortizing swap analyzed in previous chapters and so the discounted values of these reduced number of cash flows is smaller. Exhibit 6 shows the swap fixed rate for a parallel shift in the original term structure.

Exhibit 7 shows the value of various forward start swaps as the original term structure shifts. The swaps shown in the exhibit are the (1,4), (2,3), (3,2), and (4,1) forward start swaps. Also shown in the exhibit for comparative purposes is the value of the plain vanilla swap as the original term structure shifts. Panel a of Exhibit 7 shows this for the pay fixed party and panel b shows this for the received fixed party.

FORWARD START SWAPS AND INTEREST RATE VOLATILITY

Recall from Chapter 6 that in investigating the impact of a change in the interest rate volatility assumed for a plain vanilla swap (with constant or varying notional principal), the interest rate volatility assumed does not affect a swap's value or the swap fixed rate. This is not the case for a forward start swap. Exhibit 8 shows the effect of the assumed interest rate volatility on a forward start swap's value. Notice that the higher the interest rate volatility assumed, the higher the value of the forward rate swap.

The lower panel of Exhibit 8 also shows the effect of interest rate volatility on the swap fixed rate. If we were to compute the swap fixed rate for (1,4), (2,3), and (3,2) forward start swaps using the traditional approach we would get 7.0765%, 7.1085%, and 7.1528%, respectively. Notice that these are exactly what we get with a zero volatility. (This produces an interest lattice consisting of only the forward rates implied by the spot term structure).

So why is there a difference as volatility increases? This is due to the fact that our term structure model has an implied drift rate that is an increasing function of interest rate volatility. As volatility increases, so will the implied drift rate; the drift rate implies that the rates are rising on average so as volatility increases and the drift rate increases so does the implied forward rates. As the implied forward rates increase so will the swap fixed rate that produces a zero net present value. This is seen as we move down any column in Exhibit 8.

Also note that this effect increases as the start of the swap moves further out into the future. The longer the start of the swap is delayed, the greater the affect of the drift rate on the implied forward rates implied by the interest rate model. Hence this increases swap fixed rates as the delay increases (moving right to left in Exhibit 8).

Exhibit 7: Value of a Plain Vanilla Swap and Several Forward Start Swaps as the Original Term Structure Shifts

(a) Pay Fixed Swap

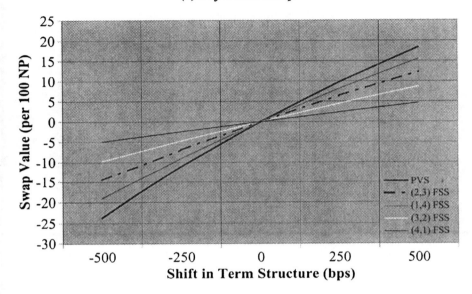

(b) Receive Fixed Swap

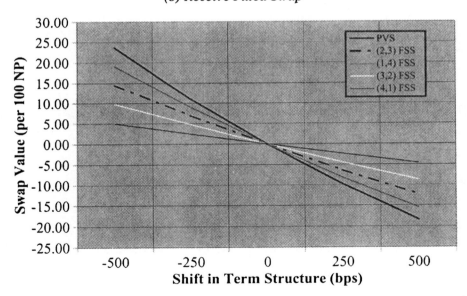

Exhibit 8: The Effect of Assumed Interest Rate Volatility on Forward Start Swap Value and SFR

Pay Fixed Forward Start Swap Values

Vol	(1, 4)	(2, 3)	(3, 2)
0.00%	−0.0041	−0.0191	−0.0333
5.00%	−0.0032	−0.0143	−0.0250
10.00%	0	0	0
15.00%	0.0049	0.0238	0.0418
20.00%	0.0118	0.0567	0.1003

Pay Fixed Forward Start Swap SFR's

Vol	(1, 4)	(2, 3)	(3, 2)
0.00%	7.0765%	7.1085%	7.1528%
5.00%	7.0768%	7.1103%	7.1574%
10.00%	7.0777%	7.1157%	7.1710%
15.00%	7.0791%	7.1246%	7.1938%
20.00%	7.0811%	7.1370%	7.2257%

A possible explanation for this is the convexity bias. The traditional approach ignores the affect that volatility has on the convexity bias. We would argue that the lattice approach can incorporate this phenomenon and may represent a more robust valuation methodology for these swaps and any delayed start swap structures.

QUESTIONS

1. a. Using the semiannual interest rate lattice below (which is the same as the lattice used for the Questions 1 and 2 in the previous two chapters) and Exhibit 2 in the chapter, compute the pay fixed swap values for a (3,2) plain vanilla forward start swap with a notional principal of $100 and a swap fixed rate of 7.0%.

```
                                                                           29.1961%
                                                                24.7073%
                                                     20.7991%              22.0033%
                                          17.6303%              18.6204%
                               14.8831%              15.6750%              16.5825%
                    12.6554%              13.2869%              14.0330%
         10.7026%              11.2165%              11.8133%              12.4972%
          9.1234%               9.5376%              10.0135%              10.5758%
7.7233%               8.0659%               8.4532%               8.9029%               9.4184%
6.5650%    6.8757%               7.1879%               7.5466%               7.9703%
          5.8206%               6.0788%               6.3706%               6.7096%               7.0981%
           5.1818%               5.4171%               5.6874%               6.0068%
            4.5812%               4.8011%               5.0566%               5.3494%
             4.0825%               4.2862%               4.5269%
              3.6183%               3.8109%               4.0315%
               3.2303%               3.4117%
                2.8720%               3.0383%
                 2.5712%
                  2.2898%

Time in Years   0.50      1.00      1.50      2.00      2.50      3.00      3.50      4.00      4.50
```

b. Using a spreadsheet program compute the swap fixed rate that makes this swap have a zero value.

2. a. Use the same interest rate lattice as in Question 1 to compute the pay fixed swap value for a (4,1) forward start swap pay fixed swap where the notional principal varies as shown in the following table and the swap fixed rate is 8.0%.

Period (Yrs)	Notional
0.50	100
1.00	120
1.50	100
2.00	120
2.50	100
3.00	120
3.50	100
4.00	120
4.50	100
5.00	120

b. Using a spreadsheet program compute the swap fixed rate that makes this swap have a zero value.

SOLUTIONS TO QUESTIONS

1. a. All of the forward start swap values using an SFR of 7.0% are as follows:

FWD Start Swap Value Lattice

```
                                                                        0.018915
                                                                        0.059365
                                                              0.139504
                                                   0.289967            0.32595
                                        0.556341             0.650829
                             0.999301             1.107606            0.717697
                  1.666386             1.64731              1.150235
       2.511239127         2.099375             1.461837            0.760167
3.117868259        2.081957             1.411113            0.84067
2.0270  1.092416227         0.78306              0.538281            0.28564
       -0.806831266        -0.340397            -0.117821           -0.012582
            -1.081661885        -0.759393            -0.438562            -0.185794
                 -0.768948            -0.668708           -0.408545
                      -0.445538            -0.440145           -0.253044
                           -0.22972             -0.239916
                                -0.107679           -0.107456
                                     -0.045694
                                          -0.016793
```

Time in Years	0.5	1	1.5	2	2.5	3	3.5	4
FWD Start Pay Fixed Swaps==>	2.3110	2.5220	2.6390	2.6768	2.5985	2.4113	2.0745	1.5857
FWD Start Receive Fixed Swaps==>	-2.3110	-2.5220	-2.6390	-2.6768	-2.5985	-2.4113	-2.0745	-1.5857

Note that the (3,2) pay fixed plain vanilla forward start swap has a value of $2.4113.

b. The forward start swap value lattice when the swap fixed rate is 8.3319%.

FWD Start Swap Value Lattice

```
                                                                        0.01778
                                                                        0.054997
                                                              0.126712
                                                   0.256334            0.289544
                                        0.472766             0.557026
                             0.798818             0.895504            0.586177
                  1.196723             1.207454            0.858488
       1.430347965         1.255103             0.910688            0.490622
0.663479579        0.599823             0.495714            0.340711
-3.4851  -1.178177341        -0.534877            -0.218806           -0.057661
       -3.379487005        -1.881772            -1.061702            -0.52332
            -2.260911913        -1.66542             -1.019497            -0.46439
                 -1.298469            -1.151863           -0.72002
                      -0.677437            -0.676608           -0.393867
                           -0.328099            -0.345037
                                -0.147617           -0.148025
                                     -0.060853
                                          -0.021896
```

Time in Years	0.5	1	1.5	2	2.5	3	3.5	4
FWD Start Pay Fixed Swaps==>	-2.7160	-2.0087	-1.3837	-0.8238	-0.3657	0.0000	0.2337	0.3355
FWD Start Receive Fixed Swaps==>	2.7160	2.0087	1.3837	0.8238	0.3657	0.0000	-0.2337	-0.3355

Notice that the (3,2) forward start swap has a value of zero.

2. a. The forward start swap values with a SFR of 8.0% are as follows:

FWD Start Swap Value Lattice

0.5	1	1.5	2	2.5	3	3.5	4	
								0.021675
								0.061494
							0.14718	
						0.290725		0.327978
					0.552578		0.657552	
				0.933805		1.043491		0.681083
			1.46276		1.474175		1.054817	
		1.876760539		1.618133		1.157194		0.615836
	1.412335045		1.077572		0.809404		0.526715	
-2.2759		-0.653745063		-0.214804		-0.025632		0.03425
	-3.045433675		-1.670299		-0.92649		-0.449274	
		-2.1533616		-1.575188		-0.956517		-0.431624
			-1.300113		-1.155487		-0.728223	
				-0.679687		-0.677393		-0.393381
					-0.340042		-0.36139	
						-0.151139		-0.1514
							-0.064689	
								-0.022655

Time in Years	0.5	1	1.5	2	2.5	3	3.5	4
FWD Start Pay Fixed Swaps==>	-1.6331	-0.9303	-0.4301	0.0823	0.4141	0.6807	0.7827	0.7216
FWD Start Receive Fixed Swaps==>	1.6331	0.9303	0.4301	-0.0823	-0.4141	-0.6807	-0.7827	-0.7216

Note that the varying notional principal (4,1) forward start swap has a value of $0.7216.

b. The swap values when the swap fixed rate is 8.7002%

FWD Start Swap Value Lattice

0.5	1	1.5	2	2.5	3	3.5	4	
								0.020959
								0.058981
							0.139558	
						0.271355		0.307013
					0.503362		0.601659	
				0.818221		0.921216		0.605268
			1.187608		1.215171		0.880984	
		1.253110091		1.131031		0.839226		0.460339
	-0.021409917		0.209311		0.270402		0.228829	
-5.4581		-1.964537022		-0.975609		-0.46266		-0.163913
	-4.548211849		-2.57324		-1.482252		-0.753579	
		-2.834414229		-2.098433		-1.292007		-0.59251
			-1.610304		-1.439969		-0.913804	
				-0.813656		-0.813996		-0.474732
					-0.397967		-0.424022	
						-0.174216		-0.174842
							-0.073721	
								-0.025605

Time in Years	0.5	1	1.5	2	2.5	3	3.5	4
FWD Start Pay Fixed Swaps==>	-4.5696	-3.5458	-2.7866	-1.9384	-1.3313	-0.7111	-0.3141	0.0000
FWD Start Receive Fixed Swaps==>	4.5696	3.5458	2.7866	1.9384	1.3313	0.7111	0.3141	0.0000

Note that the varying notional principal (4,1) forward start swap has a value of zero at an SFR of 8.7002%.

Chapter 8

Valuing a Swaption

There are options on interest rate swaps. These derivative contracts are called *swaptions* and grant the option buyer the right to enter into an interest rate swap at a future date. The time until expiration of the swap, the term of the swap, and the swap fixed rate are specified. The swap fixed rate is the strike rate for the option. In this chapter we will explain how to value a swaption using the lattice approach. In the next chapter we discuss how the various inputs into the swaption valuation model affect the value of a swaption.

TYPES OF SWAPTIONS

There are two types of swaptions. A *pay fixed swaption* (also called a *payer's swaption*) entitles the option buyer to enter into an interest rate swap in which the buyer of the option pays a fixed rate and receives a floating rate. If the option buyer has the right to enter into the swap at the expiration date of the option, the option is referred to as a *European style swaption*. In contrast, if the option buyer has the right to enter into the swap at any time until the expiration date, the option is referred to as an *American style swaption*. Throughout this chapter when we refer to a swaption we will mean a European style swaption. For example, suppose that a pay fixed swaption has a strike rate equal to 7%, a term of three years, and expires in two years. This means that at the end of two years the buyer of this pay fixed swaption has the right to enter into a 3-year interest rate swap in which the buyer pays 7% (the swap fixed rate which is equal to the strike rate) and receives the reference rate.

In a *receive fixed swaption* (also called a *receiver's swaption*) the buyer of the swaption has the right to enter into an interest rate swap that requires paying a floating rate and receiving a fixed rate. For example, if the strike rate is 6.75%, the swap term is four years, and the option expires in one year, the buyer of this receiver fixed swaption has the right at the end of the next year to enter into an 4-year interest rate swap in which the buyer receives a swap fixed rate of 7% (i.e., the strike rate) and pays the reference rate.

We will let "(y_e, y_t) swaption" denote a swaption that expires in year y_e on a swap with a tenor of y_t years. So, a (2,3) swaption is one that expires in 2 years for a swap that has a tenor of 3 years.

THE ROLE OF THE CUMULATIVE SWAP VALUATION LATTICE

In our illustration we will use the 5-year interest rate lattice based on semiannual rates and rounded day count that we used in Chapter 5. The lattice is reproduced as Exhibit 1. Since we will be valuing a pay fixed swaption with a strike rate of 7% in our illustration later, Exhibit 2 shows the pay fixed swap cash flow lattice for a plain vanilla swap with a notional principal of $100 based on a swap fixed rate of 7%. The methodology described in Chapter 5 was used to construct Exhibit 2. Also using the methodology in that chapter, the cumulative swap valuation lattice can be constructed.

Exhibit 1: Semiannual No Arbitrage Interest Rate Lattice

Time in Years	0.50	1.00	1.50	2.00	2.50	3.00	3.50	4.00	4.50
									13.4584%
								12.4902%	
							11.5207%		11.6836%
						10.7102%		10.8431%	
					9.9125%		10.0013%		10.1428%
				9.2477%		9.2977%		9.4131%	
			8.5798%		8.6053%		8.6824%		8.8052%
		8.0272%		8.0282%		8.0716%		8.1717%	
	7.4606%		7.4484%		7.4705%		7.5374%		7.6440%
6.9650%		6.9686%		6.9694%		7.0071%		7.0941%	
	6.4767%		6.4661%		6.4853%		6.5434%		6.6359%
		6.0496%		6.0503%		6.0831%		6.1585%	
			5.6134%		5.6300%		5.6805%		5.7608%
				5.2524%		5.2808%		5.3464%	
					4.8876%		4.9314%		5.0011%
						4.5844%		4.6413%	
							4.2810%		4.3416%
								4.0292%	
									3.7690%

Exhibit 2: Pay Fixed Swap Cash Flow Lattice for Plain Vanilla Swap with a Strike Rate of 7%

	CF 0.5	CF 1	CF 1.5	CF 2	CF 2.5	CF 3.0	CF 3.5	CF 4	CF 4.5	CF 5
Notional==>	100.00	100.00	100.00	100.00	100.00	100.00	100.00	100.00	100.00	100.00
CF Lattice										3.2292
									2.7451	
								2.2603		2.3418
							1.8551		1.9215	
						1.4563		1.5007		1.5714
					1.1239		1.1489		1.2066	
				0.7899		0.8026		0.8412		0.9026
			0.5136		0.5141		0.5358		0.5859	
		0.2303		0.2242		0.2352		0.2687		0.3220
	-0.0175		-0.0157		-0.0153		0.0036		0.0470	
		-0.2616		-0.2669		-0.2574		-0.2283		-0.1820
			-0.4752		-0.4748		-0.4585		-0.4207	
				-0.6933		-0.6850		-0.6598		-0.6196
					-0.8738		-0.8596		-0.8268	
						-1.0562		-1.0343		-0.9995
							-1.2078		-1.1793	
								-1.3595		-1.3292
									-1.4854	
										-1.6155
Time in Years	0.50	1.00	1.50	2.00	2.50	3.00	3.50	4.00	4.50	5.00

Just to repeat how the values in Exhibit 2 are determined, let's look at year 1.5. We know from Chapter 5 that the cash flow at a node in the lattice is found as follows:

$$(F_{i,j-1} - \text{SFR}) \times NP_j \times 0.5$$

where $F_{i,j-1}$ is the floating rate at node $(i,j-1)$ that dictates the arrears cash flow at j, SFR is the swap fixed rate, and NP_j is the notional principal at j. For our semiannual pay swap and rounded day count, the formula for the cash flow for a $100 notional principal is:

$$(\text{LIBOR at node} - \text{SFR}) \times \$100 \times 0.5$$

For a swap fixed rate of 7%, the formula is then:

$$(\text{LIBOR at node} - 0.07) \times \$100 \times 0.5$$

Let's use the three LIBOR values shown at year 1.5 to illustrate the calculation. The three values are 8.0272%, 6.9686%, and 6.0496%. The corresponding cash flow at each node is:

$$(0.080272 - 0.07) \times \$100 \times 0.5 = \$0.5136$$
$$(0.069686 - 0.07) \times \$100 \times 0.5 = -\$0.0157$$
$$(0.060496 - 0.07) \times \$100 \times 0.5 = -\$0.4752$$

For the cash flow lattice shown in Exhibit 2, the corresponding cumulative swap valuation lattice is shown in Exhibit 3. From the root of Exhibit 3 it can be seen that the value of the 5-year pay fixed swap is 0.2132.[1] This lattice will be the basis for all pay fixed swaption valuations with a strike rate of 7%. We will see that all permutations of pay fixed swaptions are simply an exercise of the backward induction methodology.

EXPIRATION VALUES AND THE SWAPTION VALUATION LATTICE

We will use the cumulative swap valuation lattice as shown in Exhibit 3 to produce corresponding pay fixed swaption valuation lattices. We will value four different pay fixed swaptions — (1,4), (2,3), (3,2), and (4,1) pay fixed swaptions.

Exhibit 3: Pay Fixed Cumulative Swap Valuation Lattice for a Plain Vanilla Swap with a Strike Rate of 7%

Value Lattice

Time in Years	0.50	1.00	1.50	2.00	2.50	3.00	3.50	4.00	4.50
									3.0256
								5.0489	
							6.2173		2.2125
						6.7142		3.5814	
					6.6246		4.2200		1.4955
				6.0689		4.2792		2.2793	
			5.0880		3.8266		2.4386		0.8645
		3.7684		2.9639		2.0980		1.1271	
	2.1262		1.7241		1.3111		0.8551		0.3101
0.2132		0.1819		0.1643		0.1517		0.1101	
	−1.6500		−1.3162		−0.9404		−0.5482		−0.1762
		−3.0656		−2.3479		−1.5788		−0.7858	
			−4.0500		−2.9478		−1.7886		−0.6023
				−4.5929		−3.1128		−1.5734	
					−4.7315		−2.8824		−0.9751
						−4.4690		−2.2648	
							−3.8450		−1.3010
								−2.8708	
									−1.5856

[1] This is because the swap fixed rate that produces a zero swap value is 7.0513% (see Chapter 6) and the lattice shown in Exhibit 3 corresponds to the lower swap fixed rate resulting in lower negative cash flows for the fixed-rate payer — hence the positive swap value.

Exhibit 4: (4,1) Pay Fixed Swaption with a Strike Rate of 7%

	0.50	1.00	1.50	2.00	2.50	3.00	3.50	4.00
								5.048867
							4.080103	
						3.260828		3.581393
					2.56019		2.790793	
				1.953041		2.113332		2.27931
			1.441984		1.526504		1.632364	
		1.0307		1.054647		1.071036		1.127147
	0.715378		0.702152		0.667458		0.596158	
0.483679033		0.453428		0.401957		0.313741		0.110104
	0.285668		0.236302		0.164471		0.053308	
		0.13641		0.085926		0.025867		0
			0.044771		0.01258		0	
				0.006129		0		0
					0		0	
						0		0
							0	
								0
Time in Years 0.50	1.00	1.50	2.00	2.50	3.00	3.50	4.00	

Let's begin with the (4,1) pay fixed swaption. Exhibit 4 presents the results of the procedure for valuing the (4,1) pay fixed swaption. Here is how we get the values in this lattice. Look at year 4.0, the year when the option expires. The values for that year shown in Exhibit 4 are called the *expiration values*. The expiration value at the expiration date will be either:

- zero if the value at the corresponding node in Exhibit 3 is negative or
- the cumulative swap value at the corresponding node in Exhibit 3 if the value is positive

The reason the expiration value is zero if the swap value at the node in Exhibit 3 is negative is that the owner of a swaption does not have to exercise the option. That is, the swaption owner will allow the swaption to expire unexercised.

The expiration value at a node can be expressed as follows:

max(cumulative swap value, 0)

Look at Exhibit 4. The five expiration values starting from the top of year 4.0 are the same as in Exhibit 3 because the corresponding swap value is positive. (They do differ in terms of the number of decimal places.) For the lower four expiration values in year 4.0 in Exhibit 4, the value is zero because the corresponding swap value in Exhibit 3 is negative.

APPLYING THE BACKWARD INDUCTION METHODOLOGY TO OBTAIN A SWAPTION'S VALUE

Once the expiration values are computed at the swaption's expiration date, year 4.0 in our (4,1) swaption, it is simply an exercise of backward induction thereafter using the interest rate lattice to compute the discount factors. For example, the top value at year 3.5 in Exhibit 4 is computed as follows:

$$0.5(5.048867 + 3.581393)/(1 + 0.115207/2) = 4.080103$$

For the lower value at year 1.5, the value in Exhibit 4 is found as follows:

$$0.044771 = 0.5(0.085926 + 0.006129)/(1 + 0.056134/2)$$

Repeating this process throughout the lattice in Exhibit 4 results in a (4,1) pay fixed swaption value of $0.48368 per $100 of notional principal.

Before presenting a similar lattice for the other pay fixed swaptions, let's comment on this valuation framework. Notice that the swaption lattice relies completely on both the interest rate and the swap value lattices. Therefore, computing swaption values as the inputs to the model change is very easy. It becomes obvious then that we can further extend the swaption valuation to value swaptions with a varying notional principal. To do this we simply base the swaption lattice on the corresponding varying notional principal swap value lattice. It is this kind of flexibility that makes this systematic approach so attractive.

Exhibit 5: (3,2) Pay Fixed Swaption with a Strike Rate of 7%

```
                                                        6.714189
                                            5.237138
                                3.963815                4.279219
                    2.854828                3.057054
        1.963271                1.99078                 2.097959
1.299758            1.229311                1.084329
0.834288592         0.733214                0.559406            0.151704
        0.426928            0.288213                0.07347
                0.148292            0.035656                0
                        0.017341                0
                                        0                      0
                                                0
                                                               0

Time in Years    0.5      1      1.5      2      2.5      3
```

Exhibit 6: (2,3) Pay Fixed Swaption with a Strike Rate of 7%

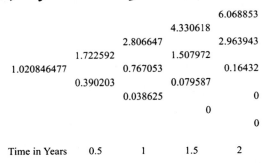

```
                                            6.068853
                                4.330618
                    2.806647                2.963943
        1.722592                1.507972
1.020846477         0.767053                0.16432
        0.390203                0.079587
                0.038625                0
                            0
                                        0

Time in Years    0.5      1      1.5      2
```

Exhibit 7: (1,4) Pay Fixed Swaption with a Strike Rate of 7%

```
                            3.768448
                1.904158
0.962612161                 0.18193
                0.088112
                            0

Time in Years    0.5      1
```

The swaption lattices shown in Exhibits 5, 6, and 7 correspond to the (3,2), (2,3), and the (1,4) pay fixed swaptions, respectively. The lattices are computed in the same manner as the lattice for the (4,1) pay fixed swaption except that the expiration values take place at different times within the swap value lattice.

Exhibit 8: Receive Fixed Swap Cash Flow Lattice for a Swap Fixed Rate of 6.75%

	CF 0.5	CF 1	CF 1.5	CF 2	CF 2.5	CF 3.0	CF 3.5	CF 4	CF 4.5	CF 5
Notional==>	100.00	100.00	100.00	100.00	100.00	100.00	100.00	100.00	100.00	100.00
CF Lattice										−3.3542
									−2.8701	
								−2.3853		−2.4668
							−1.9801		−2.0465	
						−1.5813		−1.6257		−1.6964
					−1.2489		−1.2739		−1.3316	
				−0.9149		−0.9276		−0.9662		−1.0276
			−0.6386		−0.6391		−0.6608		−0.7109	
		−0.3553		−0.3492		−0.3602		−0.3937		−0.4470
	−0.1075		−0.1093		−0.1097		−0.1286		−0.1720	
		0.1366		0.1419		0.1324		0.1033		0.0570
			0.3502		0.3498		0.3335		0.2957	
				0.5683		0.5600		0.5348		0.4946
					0.7488		0.7346		0.7018	
						0.9312		0.9093		0.8745
							1.0828		1.0543	
								1.2345		1.2042
									1.3604	
										1.4905

We will repeat the approach above for a receive fixed swaption. We will use a swap fixed rate (i.e., strike rate) of 6.75% instead of 7% which was used for the pay fixed swaption. Exhibit 8 is the cash flow lattice for a receive fixed swap with a swap fixed rate of 6.75%. In general the cash flow at a lattice is found as follows:

$$(\text{SFR} - F_{i,j-1}) \times NP_j \times 0.5$$

Substituting the strike rate for the swap fixed rate,

$$(\text{strike rate} - F_{i,j-1}) \times NP_j \times 0.5$$

Therefore, given LIBOR at a node, the cash flow is determined as follows:

$$(\text{strike rate} - \text{LIBOR at node}) \times \$100 \times 0.5$$

For a swap fixed rate of 6.75%, the formula is then:

$$(0.0675 - \text{LIBOR at node}) \times \$100 \times 0.5$$

Exhibit 9: Receive Fixed Swap Values for a Plain Vanilla Swap with a Strike Rate of 6.75%

Value Lattice

0.5	1	1.5	2	2.5	3	3.5	4	4.5
								-3.1427
							-5.2772	
						-6.5527		-2.3306
					-7.1534		-3.8124	
				-7.1657		-4.5602		-1.6145
			-6.7103		-4.7258		-2.5127	
		-5.8291		-4.3777		-2.7830		-0.9843
	-4.6087		-3.6182		-2.5510		-1.3626	
-3.0658		-2.4810		-1.8711		-1.2033		-0.4305
-1.2524	-1.0409		-0.8301		-0.6105		-0.3474	
0.6888		0.5452		0.3725		0.1966		0.0552
	2.1898		1.6719		1.1149		0.5469	
		3.2665		2.3728		1.4340		0.4808
			3.9077		2.6444		1.3331	
				4.1503		2.5253		0.8531
					3.9966		2.0233	
						3.4856		1.1786
							2.6282	
								1.4629
Time in Years 0.5	1	1.5	2	2.5	3	3.5	4	4.5

Again, we will use the three LIBOR values shown at year 1.5 to illustrate the calculation. The three values are 8.0272%, 6.9686%, and 6.0496%. The corresponding value for the cash flow at each node at year 1.5 is:

$$(0.0675 - 0.080272) \times \$100 \times 0.5 = -\$0.6386$$
$$(0.0675 - 0.069686) \times \$100 \times 0.5 = -\$0.1093$$
$$(0.0675 - 0.060496) \times \$100 \times 0.5 = \$0.3502$$

Exhibit 9 shows the corresponding receive fixed swap values for a plain vanilla swap with a strike rate of 6.75%. Notice that the value of the swap is negative. This is due to the fact that the swap is worth zero when the swap fixed rate is 7.0513%; since we have decreased the swap fixed rate, the receive fixed counterparty has lost value relative to the higher swap fixed rate, therefore, the swap becomes negative.

We now follow the same process as in a pay fixed swaption to value a receive fixed swaption. Exhibits 10, 11, 12, and 13 show the valuation lattices for the (1,4), (2,3), (3,2), and (4,1) receive fixed swaptions.

Exhibit 10: (4,1) Receive Fixed Swaption with a Strike Rate of 6.75%

	0.5	1	1.5	2	2.5	3	3.5	4
								0
							0	
						0		0
					0		0	
				0		0		0
			0.014208		0		0	
		0.05855		0.029636		0		0
	0.141993		0.107592		0.06165		0	
0.26506334		0.23603		0.193563		0.127906		0
	0.406595		0.380916		0.338965		0.264775	
		0.603494		0.5929		0.572008		0.546874
			0.862581		0.882706		0.914036	
				1.180683		1.243102		1.333119
					1.540674		1.637813	
						1.913548		2.023274
							2.277007	
								2.628219

Time in Years

Exhibit 11: (3,2) Receive Fixed Swaption with a Strike Rate of 6.75%

	0.5	1	1.5	2	2.5	3
						0
					0	
				0		0
			0		0	
		0.060451		0		0
	0.217494		0.125755		0	
0.47399846		0.390762		0.260876		0
	0.763517		0.683001		0.539935	
		1.185723		1.149288		1.114885
			1.760178		1.828178	
				2.469873		2.644397
					3.241297	
						3.996617

Time in Years

Exhibit 12: (2,3) Receive Fixed Swaption with a Strike Rate of 6.75%

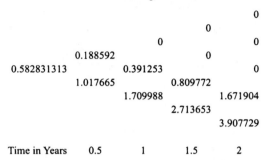

```
                                                    0
                                          0
                               0                    0
                  0.188592                0
   0.582831313                 0.391253             0
                  1.017665                0.809772
                               1.709988             1.671904
                                          2.713653
                                                    3.907729


Time in Years      0.5          1          1.5       2
```

Exhibit 13: (1,4) Receive Fixed Swaption with a Strike Rate of 6.75%

```
                               0
                  0
   0.51242675                  0
                  1.060544
                               2.189777


Time in Years      0.5          1
```

QUESTIONS

1. a. Using the semiannual interest rate lattice below (which is the same as the lattice used for the Questions 1 and 2 in the previous three chapters), compute the (1,4), (2,3), and (4,1) pay fixed swaption values with a notional principal of $100 and a swaption strike rate of 7.75%.

```
                                                                29.1961%
                                                    24.7073%
                                        20.7991%                22.0033%
                            17.6303%                18.6204%
                14.8831%                15.6750%                16.5825%
     12.6554%               13.2869%                14.0330%
10.7026%                11.2165%                11.8133%                12.4972%
 9.1234%                9.5376%                10.0135%                10.5758%
7.7233%       8.0659%             8.4532%                8.9029%                9.4184%
6.5650%       6.8757%    7.1879%            7.5466%                7.9703%
5.8206%       6.0788%             6.3706%                6.7096%                7.0981%
         5.1818%        5.4171%            5.6874%                6.0068%
                   4.5812%            4.8011%                5.0566%                5.3494%
                         4.0825%            4.2862%                4.5269%
                               3.6183%                3.8109%                4.0315%
                                     3.2303%                3.4117%
                                           2.8720%                3.0383%
                                                 2.5712%
                                                       2.2898%

Time in Years  0.50   1.00   1.50   2.00   2.50   3.00   3.50   4.00   4.50
```

b. Repeat the computations for the corresponding receive fixed swaption with a strike rate of 7.25%.

2. Use the same interest rate lattice as in Question 1 to compute the (1,4), (2,3), and (4,1) pay fixed swaption values where the notional principal varies as shown in the following table and the swaption strike rate is 8.0%.

Period (Yrs)	Notional
0.50	$100
1.00	120
1.50	100
2.00	120
2.50	100
3.00	120
3.50	100
4.00	120
4.50	100
5.00	120

SOLUTIONS TO QUESTIONS

1. a. The appropriate swap value lattice using a swaption strike rate of 7.75% is:

Time in Years:

	0.5	1	1.5	2	2.5	3	3.5	4	4.5
									9.3571
								14.5677	
							16.9345		6.4203
						17.3458		9.7744	
					16.2970		10.9350		4.0781
				14.1826		10.5405		5.8847	
			11.2154		8.9576		6.0096		2.2340
		7.6104		6.4959		4.9130		2.7812	
	3.4716		3.3263		2.8661		2.0449		0.7967
-1.0768		-0.3723		0.1092		0.3583		0.3377	
	-4.5110		-3.2222		-2.0778		-1.0978		-0.3148
		-6.9828		-5.0783		-3.2669		-1.5665	
			-8.5370		-6.0209		-3.5592		-1.1690
				-9.2179		-6.1152		-3.0385	
					-9.1237		-5.4694		-1.8225
						-8.3307		-4.1696	
							-6.9414		-2.3206
								-5.0346	
									-2.6992

The (4,1) pay fixed swaption lattice is:

Time in Years:

	0.5	1	1.5	2	2.5	3	3.5	4
								14.56772
							11.02455	
						8.40189		9.774399
					6.386823		7.260504	
				4.780297		5.322312		5.884694
			3.500258		3.778735		4.091288	
		2.501261		2.59484		2.659		2.781198
	1.745883		1.730464		1.658429		1.49297	
1.192116241		1.125345		1.005666		0.798047		0.33766
	0.716612		0.597602		0.425188		0.16335	
		0.349589		0.225865		0.079417		0
			0.119691		0.038777		0	
				0.019001		0		0
					0		0	
						0		0
							0	
								0

The (3,2) pay fixed swaption lattice is:

	0.5	1	1.5	2	2.5	3
						17.34585
					12.97745	
				9.543086		10.5405
			6.759112		7.316434	
		4.611722		4.698541		4.913012
	3.048327		2.885077		2.528775	
1.962360865		1.720363		1.304321		0.358299
	1.005224		0.673937		0.173619	
		0.348594		0.08452		0
			0.041314		0	
				0		0
					0	
						0

Time in Years 0.5 1 1.5 2 2.5 3

The (2,3) pay fixed swaption lattice is:

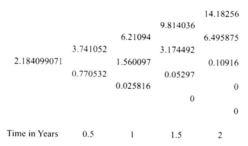

	0.5	1	1.5	2
				14.18256
			9.814036	
		6.21094		6.495875
	3.741052		3.174492	
2.184099071		1.560097		0.10916
	0.770532		0.05297	
		0.025816		0
			0	
				0

Time in Years 0.5 1 1.5 2

The (1,4) pay fixed swaption lattice is:

	0.5	1
		7.610374
	3.663708	
1.773634354		0
	0	
		0

1. b. The receive fixed swap value lattice with a swaption strike rate of 7.25% is:

0.5	1	1.5	2	2.5	3	3.5	4	4.5
								−9.5753
							−14.9875	
						−17.5492		−6.6455
					−18.1539		−10.2117	
				−17.3009		−11.5789		−4.3090
			−15.3867		−11.3898		−6.3361	
		−12.6258		−10.0144		−6.6772		−2.4693
	−9.2334		−7.7636		−5.7958		−3.2438	
−5.3144		−4.8100		−3.9657		−2.7313		−1.0354
−0.9924		−1.3325		−1.4285		−1.2678		−0.8090
2.5794		1.6792		0.9440		0.3966		0.0734
	5.2120		3.7178		2.3364		1.0884	
		6.9467		4.8601		2.8465		0.9256
			7.8250		5.1683		2.5552	
				7.9419		4.7478		1.5775
					7.3712		3.6823	
						6.2130		2.0743
							4.5442	
								2.4520

Time in Years   0.5   1   1.5   2   2.5   3   3.5   4   4.5

The (4,1) receiver swaption lattice is:

0.5	1	1.5	2	2.5	3	3.5	4
							0
						0	
					0		0
				0		0	
			0		0		0
		0.027566		0		0	
	0.11386		0.058082		0		0
0.276918		0.210541		0.121703		0	
0.518361644		0.461364		0.379983		0.253694	
0.793836		0.743909		0.665575		0.526532	
	1.172513		1.153056		1.119859		1.088393
		1.661874		1.702998		1.776876	
			2.246826		2.3679		2.555209
				2.882382		3.060418	
					3.501158		3.682255
						4.054995	
							4.544194

Time in Years   0.5   1   1.5   2   2.5   3   3.5   4

The (3,2) receiver swaption lattice is:

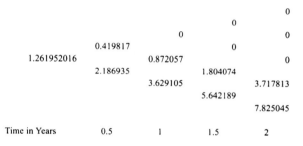

```
                                                              0
                                                      0
                                              0               0
                                      0               0
                      0.125585                0               0
          0.44695                 0.262628              0
0.966032242           0.802834              0.54644               0
          1.548535               1.39824              1.132157
                      2.384369              2.335037              2.336439
                                 3.494051              3.664407
                                           4.813134              5.168309
                                                      6.158357
                                                              7.371235

Time in Years    0.5        1        1.5       2       2.5       3
```

The (2,3) receiver swaption lattice is:

```
                                                      0
                                              0
                      0.419817                0               0
1.261952016                       0.872057              0
          2.186935               1.804074              0
                      3.629105              3.717813
                                 5.642189
                                           7.825045

Time in Years         0.5        1        1.5       2
```

The (1,4) receiver swaption lattice is:

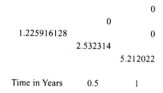

```
                              0
                      0
1.225916128                   0
          2.532314
                      5.212022

Time in Years        0.5        1
```

2. The appropriate swap value lattice using a strike rate of 8% is:

	0.5	1	1.5	2	2.5	3	3.5	4	4.5
									11.0976
								15.7423	
							18.8391		7.5692
						18.6064		10.4953	
					17.6825		12.0238		4.7553
				14.9409		11.1306		6.2270	
			11.7021		9.4347		6.4294		2.5397
		7.5070		6.4725		4.9374		2.8153	
	2.8247		2.8735		2.5901		1.9263		0.8128
−2.2759		−1.3075		−0.5728		−0.0820		0.1253	
	−6.0909		−4.4541		−2.9648		−1.6431		−0.5226
		−8.6134		−6.3008		−4.0811		−1.9731	
			−10.4009		−7.3951		−4.4387		−1.5489
				−10.8750		−7.2255		−3.5966	
					−10.8813		−6.6083		−2.3341
						−9.6729		−4.8448	
							−8.2802		−2.9325
								−5.7998	
									−3.3874

Time in Years: 0.5, 1, 1.5, 2, 2.5, 3, 3.5, 4, 4.5

The (4,1) pay fixed swaption lattice is:

	0.5	1	1.5	2	2.5	3	3.5	4
								15.74234
							11.88304	
						9.022884		10.4953
					6.822153		7.753493	
				5.064805		5.636768		6.227043
			3.66865		3.948429		4.268993	
		2.587899		2.665137		2.702964		2.815251
	1.780547		1.743251		1.636035		1.407595	
1.197326278		1.110713		0.961974		0.707403		0.125257
	0.69271		0.554544		0.357058		0.060596	
		0.315026		0.180824		0.02946		0
			0.091833		0.014385		0	
				0.007048		0		0
					0		0	
						0		0
							0	
								0

Time in Years: 0.5, 1, 1.5, 2, 2.5, 3, 3.5, 4

The (3,2) pay fixed swaption lattice is:

	0.5	1	1.5	2	2.5	3
						18.60642
					13.83868	
				10.08487		11.13057
			7.045843		7.607327	
		4.726138		4.760911		4.937361
	3.064625		2.837616		2.368571	
1.932902369		1.639803		1.1432		0
	0.928074		0.554739		0	
		0.270365		0		0
			0		0	
				0		0
					0	
						0

Time in Years   0.5   1   1.5   2   2.5   3

The (2,3) pay fixed swaption lattice is:

	0.5	1	1.5	2
				14.94088
			10.16286	
		6.347292		6.472534
	3.779548		3.110809	
2.183399911		1.503709		0
	0.730592		0	
		0		0
			0	
				0

Time in Years   0.5   1   1.5   2

The (1,4) pay fixed swaption lattice is:

		7.507042
	3.613963	
1.749552302		0
	0	
		0

Chapter 9

Factors that Affect the Value of a Swaption

In this chapter we look at how changes in both the market inputs to the swaption valuation and terms of the swaption affect the value of a swaption. This chapter is in the same spirit of the sections in Chapters 6 and 8 where we demonstrated the factors that affect the value of a plain vanilla swap and a forward start swap, respectively. In particular, in this chapter we will see how volatility of interest rates plays a crucial role in swaption valuation. Unlike plain vanilla swaps, the role of volatility is crucial. This suggests that swaptions are far more appropriate an instrument when the user is making a volatility play on interest rates. As we will see, not all the factors investigated have a predictable effect on swaption values.

EXPIRATION OF THE SWAPTION

Increasing the expiration of a swaption can either increase or decrease the swaption's value. This is because as the expiration increases the tenor of the underlying swap decreases, and so the resulting effect on a swaption's value will depend on the current level of interest rates, the volatility, and the strike price. Holding the tenor of the underlying swap constant and increasing the expiration also has an unpredictable outcome on the swaption's value because the interaction of the other variables will dictate the effect.

The two graphs in Exhibit 1 illustrate how for a given volatility at a strike rate of 7%, lengthening the expiration dates of a pay fixed swaption (top graph) and receive fixed swaption (bottom graph) are not monotonic relationships. Notice that the (2,3) swaptions are more valuable than the (4,1) swaptions. The relationship between swaption value and swaption expiration depends largely on the shape and the level of the term structure as well as the strike rate. For example, the pay fixed swaption with a strike rate of 6.7% will be mono-tonic; the strike rate of 7.5% of the receive fixed swaption will also exhibit a monotonic relationship. The following table which shows the value of a pay fixed swaption with a strike rate of 6.75% and a received fixed swaption with a strike rate of 7.25% illustrates this

Swaption	Pay fixed swaption with strike = 6.75%	Receive fixed swaption with strike = 7.25%
(4,1)	0.5959	0.4269
(3,2)	1.0750	0.8167
(2,3)	1.4146	1.1193
(1,4)	1.5594	1.2384

Exhibit 1: Effect of Time to Expiration on Swaption Values Assuming a Strike Rate of 7%

a. Pay Fixed Swaption Values

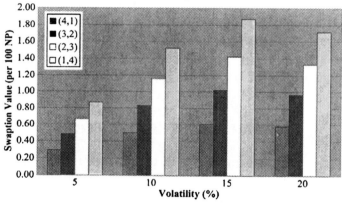

b. Receive Fixed Swaption Values

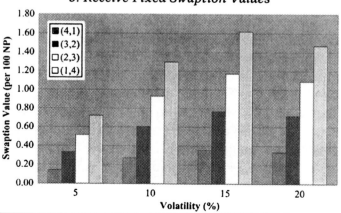

STRIKE RATE

Exhibits 2, 3, 4, and 5 illustrate the effects of changing the strike rate for a given volatility on the value of (4,1), (3,2), (2,3), and (1,4) swaptions. (The strike rate for the pay fixed swaption is 6.75% and for the receive fixed swaption is 7.5%.) The top graph of each exhibit shows the results for a pay fixed swaption and the bottom graph of each exhibit for a receive fixed swaption.

Notice how the top and bottom graphs in these exhibits are mirror images of each other, suggesting that as the strike rate increases from low to high, the two swaptions behave in opposite manner. Specifically, for every volatility, increasing the strike rate will decrease the value of the pay fixed swaption and increase the value of the receive fixed swaption.

This should be intuitive. Since the strike rate represents the fixed rate of the underlying swap, it will have a completely opposite effect depending on which leg of the swap the counterparty is contracting. For the pay fixed swaption, the owner of the swaption has the right to enter into the underlying swap as the fixed-rate payer; so as the strike rate increases, the owner of the pay fixed swaption is essentially given the right to enter into a swap to pay a higher interest rate. Clearly this will have less value to the swaption owner than a lower fixed rate. Conversely, the owner of a receive fixed swaption is entering into an agreement that gives the owner the right to enter into a swap arrangement as the fixed-rate receiver; so as the contracted fixed rate increases, the swaption owner has the right to enter into a swap to receive a higher fixed rate. This will have more value to the swaption owner than a lower fixed rate.

The relationship may be easier to see in Exhibit 6. This exhibit illustrates, using a simple line graph, the effect of different strike rates on a (2,3) pay fixed swaption (PFS) and a (2,3) receive fixed swaption (RFS). The graph in Exhibit 6 is just a cross-sectional slice of Exhibits 2, 3, 4, and 5 at a volatility of 10% and clearly shows that increasing the strike rate negatively impacts the pay fixed swaption and positively impacts the receive fixed swaption.

Exhibit 2: The Effect of Strike Rates and Volatility on (4,1) Swaption Values

a. Pay Fixed Swaption Values

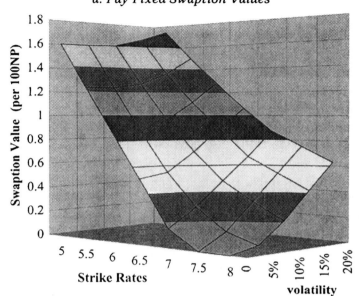

b. Receive Fixed Swaption Values

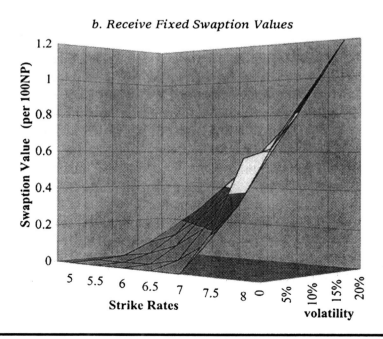

Exhibit 3: The Effect of Strike Rates and Volatility on (3,2) Swaption Values

a. Pay Fixed Swaption Values

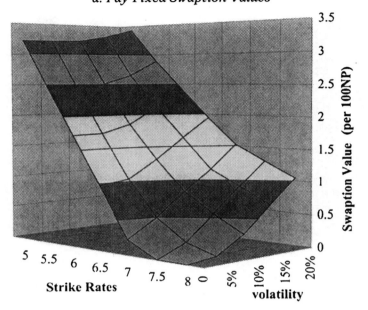

b. Receive Fixed Swaption Values

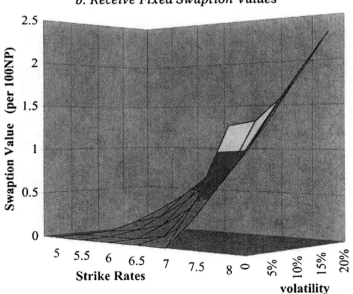

Exhibit 4: The Effect of Strike Rates and Volatility on (2,3) Swaption Values

a. Pay Fixed Swaption Values

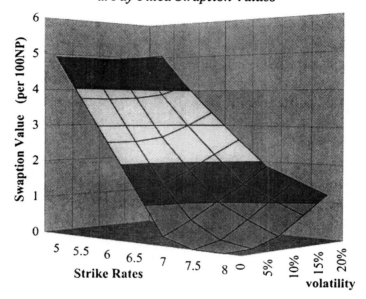

b. Receive Fixed Swaption Values

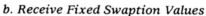
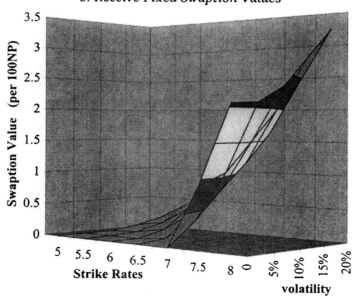

Exhibit 5: The Effect of Strike Rates and Volatility on (1,4) Swaption Values

a. Pay Fixed Swaption Values

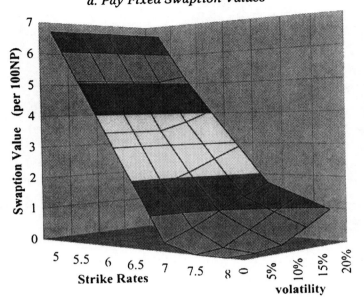

b. Receive Fixed Swaption Values

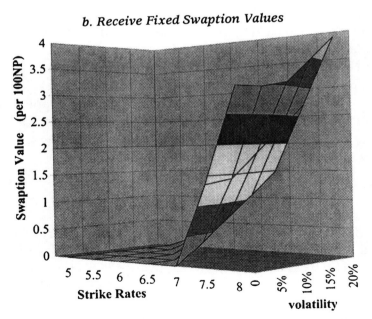

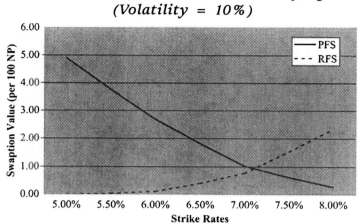

Exhibit 6: (2,3) Swaption Values with Varying Strikes (Volatility = 10%)

ASSUMED INTEREST RATE VOLATILITY

The other noticeable effect in Exhibits 2, 3, 4, and 5 is the relationship between the swaption value and the magnitude of interest rate volatility. Regardless of the type of swaption, increasing volatility will increase a swaption's value. In other words, as with all options, volatility increases the value a swaption. The exhibits show that regardless of the level of the strike rate, volatility will increase a swaption's value.

Exhibit 7 shows, using simple line graphs, the effects of volatility on a (2,3) pay fixed swaption (PFS) and a (2,3) receiver fixed swaption (RFS) with a strike rate of 6.75%. The graphs in this exhibit are just cross-sectional slices of Exhibits 2, 3, 4, and 5 at a strike rate of 6.75%. The graphs clearly demonstrate that increasing volatility increases the value of both types of swaptions.

CHANGES IN THE TERM STRUCTURE

Exhibits 8 and 9 show the effects of a shifting term structure on each swaption variation — (4,1), (3,2), (2,3), and (1,4) for a pay fixed swaption and a receive fixed swaption, respectively. Not surprisingly, the effects of shifting term structure are the opposite of changing the strike rate. And for the same reasons, we see that the behaviors of the pay fixed swaption and receive fixed swaption mirror one another.

Since the buyer of the pay fixed swaption has the right to enter into the underlying swap as a fixed rate payer (floating rate receiver), as interest rates increase the value of that right will increase. Conversely, the buyer of the receive fixed swaption has the right to enter into the underlying swap as a fixed rate receiver (floating rate payer), so as interest rates decrease the value of that right will increase. Exhibits 8 and 9 clearly demonstrate this relationship.

Exhibit 7: (2,3) Swaption Values with Varying Volatilities (Strike Rate = 6.75%)

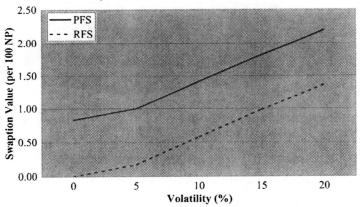

Exhibit 8: Pay Fixed Swaption Values as Term Structure Shifts (Strike Rate = 6.75%, Volatility = 10%)

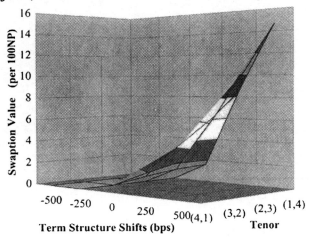

Exhibit 9: Receive Fixed Swaption Values as Term Structure Shifts (Strike Rate = 7.5%, Volatility = 10%)

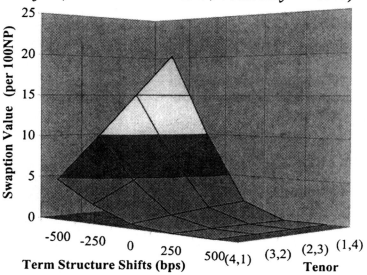

Exhibit 10: Term Structures Analyzed

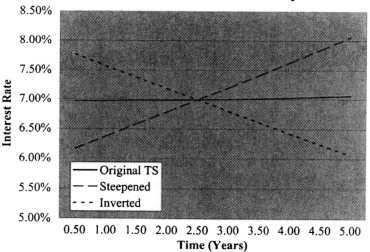

Now let's analyze the effects of the shape of the term structure on the value of a swaption. Exhibit 10 shows the three different term structures used in this analysis. Note that these term structures are steeper (i.e., have a larger slope) than the term structure shapes used in Chapter 6. We intentionally did this in order to highlight the effects on swaption values. The original term structure is the term structure used for all the analysis so far.

The results reported in Exhibits 11 and 12 are interesting. Notice how the shape of the term structure significantly impacts the value of a swaption. In particular, notice how a steeper term structure has a positive effect on the pay fixed swaption and a negative effect on the receive fixed swaption. The opposite is true for the inverted term structure. Inverting the term structure negatively impacts the value of a pay fixed swaption while positively impacts the value of a receive fixed swaption.

The intuition behind this is the same as for the shifting term structures. Steepening the term structure implies that forward rates are increasing more than was implied by the original term structure; the result of this is that the net cash inflows on the underlying swap are increased so that the pay fixed swaption increases in value. The receiver swaption loses value if the term structure steepens since as the implied forward rates increase, the net cash outflows of the underlying swap are increased so the receive fixed swaption decreases in value.

Exhibit 11: Pay Fixed Swaption Values as Term Structure Changes Shape (Strike Rate = 6.75%, Volatility = 10%)

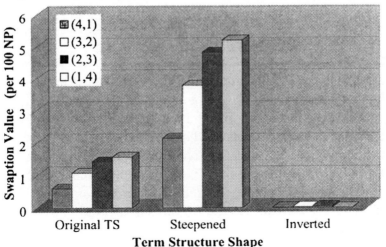

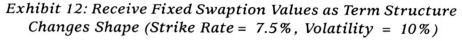

Exhibit 12: Receive Fixed Swaption Values as Term Structure Changes Shape (Strike Rate = 7.5%, Volatility = 10%)

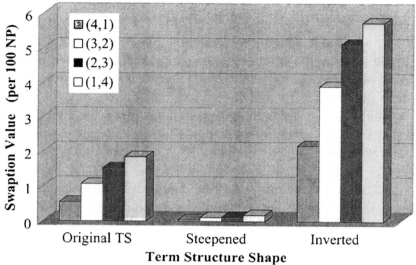

Exhibit 13: Summary of Findings of the Effect of Factors on a Swaption's Value

Effect	Payer Swaption	Receiver Swaption
Increase Volatility	+	+
Increase Strike Rate	–	+
Increase Interest Rates	+	–
Inverting TS	–	+
Steepening TS	+	–
Increase Expiration	?	?

Similarly, when we inverted the term structure the implied forward rates decrease and so the net cash outflows on the underlying pay fixed swap increase, and the net cash inflows on the underlying receive fixed swap increase. This change in the net cash flows of the underlying swap has a negative impact on the pay fixed swap and a positive impact the receive fixed swap. The bar charts shown in Exhibits 11 and 12 clearly illustrate this phenomenon.

Exhibit 13 summarizes the findings presented in this chapter.

QUESTIONS

1. Based on the following graph, answer the questions below.

Swaption Values with Varying Volatilities

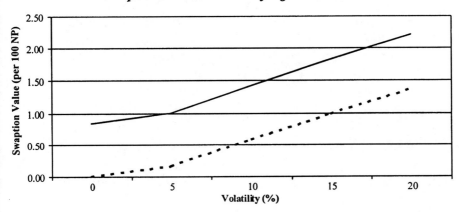

a. Which graph represents the receive fixed swaption and which graph represents the pay fixed swaption?
b. Do the graphs have the correct shape?
c. What is the effect that volatility has on the swaption value?

2. Based on the following graph, answer the questions below.

Swaption Values with Varying Strikes

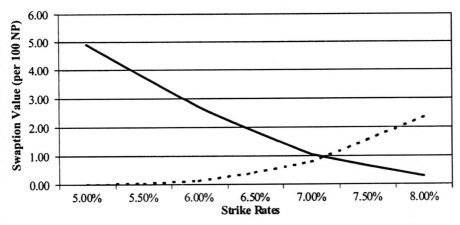

a. Which graph represents the receive fixed swaption?
b. Which graph represents the pay fixed swaption?
c. Do the graphs have the correct shape?
d. What is the affect of the strike rate on the swaption's value?

3. The table below presents some swaption values with varying expirations. The values are all per $100 of notional principal.

Tenor	Swaption 1	Swaption 2
(4,1)	0.9495	0.6187
(3,2)	1.7034	1.1025
(2,3)	2.1971	1.3654
(1,4)	2.2819	1.2349

Using the table above answer the following questions:

a. Which swaption is the receive fixed swaption and which swaption is the pay fixed swaption?
b. Are the swaption values plausible?
c. What is the effect of time to option expiration on the value of a swaption?

SOLUTIONS TO QUESTIONS

1.a. Without more information we are unable to determine which swaption is the pay fixed or the receive fixed swaption. Which swaption has a higher value will depend on the level of interest rates and the shape of the term structure. Since this information is not given we are unable to make the determination.

b. The graphs have the correct shape — as volatility of the short rate increases so will the value of the swaptions.

c. Volatility will have a positive effect on swaptions because they are contingent claims that have a limited liability. In other words, the most the owner of a swaption can ever lose is the amount paid for the option so as volatility increases the potential profit increases and the amount of potential loss stays the same. This results in an increase in a swaption's value.

2. a. The dotted graph is the receive fixed swaption. It increases in value as the strike rate increases since for a given level and shape of the term structure, the value of the underlying receive fixed swap increases as the receive fixed rate increases. Consequently, the value of the swaption on that swap will also increase.

b. The solid line represents the pay fixed swaption. It increases in value as the strike rate decreases since for a given level and shape of the term structure, the value of the underlying pay fixed swap increases as the pay fixed rate decreases. Consequently, the value of the swaption on that swap will also increase.

c. Both graphs have the correct shape.

d. See the explanation to parts a and b.

3. a. Without further information we are unable to determine which swaption is the pay fixed or the receive fixed swaption. Which swaption has a higher value will depend on the level of interest rates

and the shape of the term structure. Since this information is not given we are unable to make the determination. Additionally, whether the effect of time to expiration is monotonic is a function of the other variables that affect a swaption's value.

b. The values are plausible and simply reflect the property that the effect of time to expiration on a swaption's value depends on the other variables and is not monotonic.

c. See parts a and b.

Chapter 10

Valuing Non-LIBOR Based Swaps and Basis Swaps

In previous chapters, our focus has been on swap structures where the reference rate is LIBOR and swaps where one leg of the swap is fixed and the other floating. In this chapter, we extend the valuation framework to swaps where both legs of the swap are floating and swaps where the floating payment is not LIBOR.

VALUING BASIS SWAPS USING THE TRADITIONAL APPROACH

Below we will show how to value a basis swap and a swap in which the fixed rate is based on a Constant Maturity Treasury rate using the traditional approach to swap valuation.

Basis Swap

A swap in which the payments of both counterparties are based on different reference rates is called a *basis swap*. The application of the traditional approach described in Chapter 4 to valuing basis swaps will be demonstrated using a swap in which the payments of one of the counterparties are based on the 90-day Treasury bill (T-bill) rate and that party receives floating payments based on 3-month LIBOR. The spread between LIBOR and the T-bill rate is called the Treasury-eurodollar CD spread, or simply the *TED spread*.

To illustrate the process we will evaluate a 1-year swap that pays LIBOR and receives the T-bill rate plus a spread. We will call this a *pay LIBOR TED swap*. To begin, we replicate in Exhibit 1 the information for the quarterly swap introduced in Chapter 2. The information in Exhibit 2 is the same as in Exhibit 1 except that it pertains to the T-bill futures contract. Note that in the last column of Exhibit 2 we have payment information for the forward rates obtained from prices of the T-bill futures contract.

Exhibit 1: LIBOR and Forward Rates from Eurodollar CD Futures

(1)	(2)	(3)	(4)	(5)	(6)	(7)	(8)	(9)
Quarter Starts	Quarter Ends	Number of Days	Actual/ 360	Current 3-Month LIBOR	Eurodollar CD Price	Forward Rate	End of Quarter	Payment per 100 NP
1/1/YR1	3/31/YR1	90	0.2500	6.99%			1	1.746250
4/1/YR1	6/30/YR1	90	0.2500		93.055	6.945%	2	1.736250
7/1/YR1	9/30/YR1	91	0.2528		93.035	6.965%	3	1.760597
10/1/YR1	12/31/YR1	91	0.2528		93.030	6.970%	4	1.761861

Exhibit 2: T-Bill and Forward Rates from T-Bill Futures

(1)	(2)	(3)	(4)	(5)	(6)	(7)	(8)	(9)
Quarter Starts	Quarter Ends	Number of Days	Actual/ 360	Current 3-Month T- Bill Rate	T-Bill Futures Price	Forward Rate	End of Quarter	Payment per 100 NP
1/1/YR1	3/31/YR1	90	0.2500	5.97%			1	1.4925
4/1/YR1	6/30/YR1	90	0.2500		93.950	6.05%	2	1.5125
7/1/YR1	9/30/YR1	91	0.2528		93.870	6.13%	3	1.5495
10/1/YR1	12/31/YR1	91	0.2528		93.830	6.17%	4	1.5596

Exhibit 3: Forward Discount Factors for LIBOR

(1)	(2)	(3)	(4)	(5)	(6)	(7)	(8)
Quarter Starts	Quarter Ends	Number of Days	Actual/ 360	End of Quarter	LIBOR Forward Rate	Period Forward Rate	Forward Discount Factor
1/1/YR1	3/31/YR1	90	0.2500	1	6.99%	0.0175	0.98284
4/1/YR1	6/30/YR1	90	0.2500	2	6.94%	0.0174	0.96606
7/1/YR1	9/30/YR1	91	0.2528	3	6.97%	0.0176	0.94935
10/1/YR1	12/31/YR1	91	0.2528	4	6.97%	0.0176	0.93291

Exhibits 3 and 4 are the same as presented in earlier chapters for a 1-year swap and have the same interpretation. The two floating payments for each period are found as follows:

T-bill payment for period j

$$= (TB_{j-1} + Spread) \times \frac{\text{days in quarter}}{360} \times NP_j$$

LIBOR payment for period $j = L_{j-1} \times \frac{\text{days in quarter}}{360} \times NP_j$

Exhibit 4: Present Values of LIBOR Leg of Pay LIBOR TED Swap

(1) Quarter Starts	(2) Quarter Ends	(3) End of Quarter	(4) Forward Discount Factor	(5) Payment per 100 NP	(6) PV of Floating Payment
1/1/YR1	3/31/YR1	1	0.98284	1.746250	1.716279
4/1/YR1	6/30/YR1	2	0.96606	1.736250	1.677328
7/1/YR1	9/30/YR1	3	0.94935	1.760597	1.671422
10/1/YR1	12/31/YR1	4	0.93291	1.761861	1.643663
				Total	6.708694

Exhibit 5: Present Values of T-Bill Leg of Pay LIBOR TED Swap with a Spread of Zero

(1) Quarter Starts	(2) Quarter Ends	(3) End of Quarter	(4) Forward Discount Factor	(5) Payment per 100 NP	(6) PV of Floating Payment	(7) Spread
1/1/YR1	3/31/YR1	1	0.98284	1.4925	1.466885	0
4/1/YR1	6/30/YR1	2	0.96606	1.5125	1.461173	
7/1/YR1	9/30/YR1	3	0.94935	1.5495	1.471047	
10/1/YR1	12/31/YR1	4	0.93291	1.5596	1.455011	
				Total	5.854114	

The net payment (i.e., cash flow) for the pay LIBOR TED swap can then be expressed as:

$$CF_j = (TB_{j-1} + Spread - L_{j-1}) \times \frac{\text{days in quarter}}{360} \times NP_j$$

where

TB_{j-1} = T-bill rate at $j-1$

L_{j-1} = LIBOR at $j-1$

NP_j = notional principal at j ($100 in our illustration)

"*Spread*" is the adjustment to the T-bill rate in order to equate the present value of the two payment streams. This is the term we iterate on in place of the swap fixed rate in a plain vanilla swap.

The total value in Exhibit 4 represents the present value of the LIBOR leg of the swap. Exhibit 5 is the same as Exhibit 4 except that we have replaced the payments with the T-bill payment plus the spread (TB_{j-1} + *Spread*) where *Spread* has been set to zero as seen in the last column. Note that the total present value of the T-bill payments is $5.854114 using LIBOR for discounting. The objective now is to compute the value for *Spread* that equates the two payment streams; in other words, what value for *Spread* produces a swap with a value of zero? We simply iterate on the *Spread*. Exhibit 6 illustrates the results. It can be seen that a spread of 88.74 basis points is the correct adjustment. We use LIBOR as the discount rate since it is the most representative of the risk of swap counterparties.

This illustrates that the appropriate T-bill spread is 0.8874% on an annualized basis. So the pay LIBOR counterparty would receive the T-bill rate plus 0.8874% and pay LIBOR.[1]

Constant Maturity Treasury Swap

A popular swap is one in which the floating leg is tied to a longer-term rate such as the 2-year Treasury note (T-note) rate. The reference rate in a swap tied to a fixed maturity Treasury is the Constant Maturity Treasury rate published by the Federal Reserve. For this reason, the swap is referred to as a *Constant Maturity Treasury swap* and denoted by *CMT swap* or *CMS*. In this swap the fixed-rate payer would pay the swap fixed rate each period in exchange for the 2-year T-note rate as specified by the 2-year Constant Maturity Treasury rate.

Exhibit 6: Present Values of T-Bill Leg of Pay LIBOR TED Swap with a Spread of 88.74 Basis Points

(1) Quarter Starts	(2) Quarter Ends	(3) End of Quarter	(4) Forward Discount Factor	(5) Payment per 100 NP	(6) PV of Floating Payment	(7) Spread
1/1/YR1	3/31/YR1	1	0.98284	1.7143	1.684926	0.8874%
4/1/YR1	6/30/YR1	2	0.96606	1.7343	1.675493	
7/1/YR1	9/30/YR1	3	0.94935	1.7738	1.683999	
10/1/YR1	12/31/YR1	4	0.93291	1.7840	1.664276	
				Total	6.708694	

[1] Using rounded day count at (0.25) and non-rounded interest rates the *Spread* is 0.8879% on an annual basis.

Exhibit 7: The Floating Leg Payments for the CMT Swap

(1)	(2)	(3)	(4)	(5)	(6)
Time	2-Year Treasury Forward Rate	End of Period	Payment per 100 NP	LIBOR Forward Discount Factor	PV of Payments
0	6.30%	1	1.575000	0.982837	1.547969
0.25	6.50%	2	1.625000	0.966064	1.569854
0.50	6.70%	3	1.693611	0.949350	1.607829
0.75	6.80%	4	1.718889	0.932913	1.603574
				Total	6.329226

To find the appropriate swap fixed rate, we proceed in the same way as we did for a plain vanilla swap. That is, we begin with the implied 2-year forward rates from the U.S. Treasury term structure. (Appendix A shows how forward rates are derived from the term structure.) For example, suppose we want to value a quarterly-pay CMT swap with a tenor of one year. We will assume that the 2-year forward rates for each quarter are those shown in Column (2) of Exhibit 7. From these rates, the quarterly payments per $100 notional principal are shown in Column (4). We will use 3-month LIBOR to discount payments in this swap. As discussed above, we use LIBOR because it is the appropriate rate for most swap market participants. The forward discount factors using 3-month LIBOR are shown in Column (5) of Exhibit 7 and were taken from Column (4) of Exhibits 4, 5, and 6.

To compute the swap fixed rate for this CMT swap we use the forward rates in Exhibit 7 to produce the payments on the floating leg. These payments are shown in Exhibit 7 which also presents the present value of these payments as well as their total present value.

The goal now is to simply find the swap fixed rate using the same discount rates that produce the same present value of the floating leg payments. The swap fixed rate turns out to be 6.5723%. The counterparty in this swap would pay 6.5723% every quarter in exchange for the 2-year T-note rate.

The CMT swap and the LIBOR TED swap show that valuing swaps with alternative floating rates is not difficult. All that needs to be done is to obtain the implied forward rates for that reference rate and build the payments and present value tables. Once the tables are created, it is a simple task of computing the appropriate *Spread* (for the basis swap) or swap fixed rate (for the CMT swap) that produces a value for the swap of zero. The analyst needs to ensure that the proper discount rate is used when transitioning from the payment table to the present value table. Mostly, LIBOR is the appropriate rate in the swap market, but it will depend on the parties involved.

VALUATION USING THE LATTICE APPROACH

To value a plain vanilla swap structure, the traditional approach can be used. However, when more complex swap structures such as forward start swaps or swaptions are valued, the lattice approach is necessary. In the next section, we will see how to value a swaption for a basis swap. Here we will show how the lattice approach is used to value a basis swap.

To illustrate the lattice approach, we will value the swap that pays LIBOR in return for the 90-day T-bill rate plus a spread that we valued using the traditional approach earlier. We begin by building two interest rate lattices — one for each floating rate. Exhibit 8 shows these two lattices. The T-bill lattice is created in the same manner as the LIBOR lattice except the forward rates and volatility correspond to the T-bill rates. We use the T-bill futures prices to get the forward rates and assume a volatility of 7.5%. It cannot be overemphasized that the lattice structures can be constructed to accommodate any periodicity of rate — varying periods are also easily accommodated. We make the valuation procedure uniform in this illustration so as to not complicate the process. It is the mechanics and intuition that are important. Neither one of these changes with nonuniform periodicity of the lattice.

Now that we have the two interest rate lattices, we need to produce the cash flows associated with a pay LIBOR swap. Each cash flow (CF) at period j is computed as follows ignoring the exact day count (i.e., each period is 0.25 of one year):

$$CF_j = (TB_{j-1} + Spread - L_j) \times 0.25 \times NP_j$$

where the notation is the same as used earlier in this chapter. Again, the term *Spread* is the adjustment to the T-bill rate in order to equate the present value of the two payment streams. This is the term we iterate on in place of the swap fixed rate. The *Spread* for our swap is 88.79 basis points.

To illustrate the equation for obtaining the cash flow, look at $j = 4$. Hence, we are looking at the cash flow at period 3 in the interest rate lattices in Exhibit 8. Look at the top node for period 3. In this illustration,

$TB_{4-1} = 6.89\% = 0.0689$ (from bottom lattice of Exhibit 8)

$L_{4-1} = 8.07\% = 0.0807$ (from top lattice of Exhibit 8)

$NP_4 = \$100$

$Spread = 0.008879$

Exhibit 8: 1-Year Interest Rate Lattices for LIBOR TED Swap
a. LIBOR Interest Rate Lattice

				8.07%
			7.68%	
		7.29%		7.30%
	6.99%		6.95%	
		6.60%		6.61%
			6.29%	
				5.98%

LIBOR

Period	1	2	3
Time in Years	0.25	0.5	0.75

10% volatility assumed.

b. T-Bill Interest Rate Lattice

				6.89%
			6.60%	
		6.28%		6.39%
	5.97%		6.12%	
		5.82%		5.93%
			5.68%	
				5.50%

Period	1	2	3
Time in Years	0.25	0.50	0.75

7.5% volatility assumed.

Exhibit 9: Cash Flows for a Pay LIBOR Receive T-Bill Swap with a Spread of 88.79 Basis Points

Pay LIBOR CF

				-0.073
			-0.048	
		-0.032		-0.005
	-0.032		0.015	
		0.027		0.053
			0.070	
				0.103
Period	1	2	3	4
Time in years	0.25	0.5	0.75	1

then

$$(0.0689 + 0.008879 - 0.0807) \times 0.25 \times \$100 = -\$0.073$$

This value is shown at period 4 in Exhibit 9. To determine the cash flows for the bottom node at period 2, we use

$TB_{2-1} = 5.82\% = 0.0582$ (from bottom lattice of Exhibit 8)

$L_{2-1} = 6.60\% = 0.0660$ (from top lattice of Exhibit 8)

$NP_2 = \$100$

$Spread = 0.008879$

then

$$(0.0582 + 0.008879 - 0.066) \times 0.25 \times \$100 = \$0.027$$

Now in order to produce the value lattice we follow the same procedure described in Chapter 6 as we did with all the other swaps valued using the lattice approach. We use LIBOR as the discount rate since, as noted earlier, it is the most representative of the risk of swap counterparties. The value lattice is shown in Exhibit 10. The value of this swap is zero. This value is expected since we explained earlier that the appropriate T-bill spread is 0.8879% to produce a value of zero for the swap. (Note that the difference relative to the traditional approach is due to rounded day count.[2])

---

[2] See footnote 1.

Exhibit 10: Pay LIBOR Receive T-Bill Swap Value Lattice with a Spread of 88.79 Basis Points

```
                                          -0.071
                                -0.085
                      -0.054              -0.005
            0.000               0.038
                      0.118               0.052
                                0.145
                                          0.102
Period                1        2        3
Time in years    0    0.25     0.5      0.75
```

VALUING AN OPTION ON A BASIS SWAP

In Chapter 8 we demonstrated how to value a swaption on a plain vanilla swap. The procedure is the same for a basis swap and a CMT swap. To illustrate the procedure, we will find the value of a swap that pays LIBOR in exchange for the 90 day T-bill rate. To do so, we build two interest rate lattices — one for each floating rate. The two interest rate lattices that we will use in our illustration are shown in Exhibit 11.

In our illustration, we will assume that the *Spread* is 0.5%. Using the same formula as given earlier for computing the cash flow for a period, Exhibit 12 shows the cash flow lattice based on receiving the T-bill rate plus 50 basis points and paying LIBOR. The value of this swap is −$0.522 per $100 notional principal, as shown in Exhibit 13.[3]

Options on basis swaps have strike rates that represent the spread over the higher credit quality interest rate. In our LIBOR TED spread swap, it is the spread over the T-bill rate. For example, the swaption will be priced relative to the spread.[4]

---

[3] If we wanted to find the spread that would make this swap have a value of zero, we would iterate on the *Spread*. The interested reader can show that this value is 0.87%.

[4] We have simplified the valuation framework slightly in that we have implicitly assumed that the two floating rates are independent when creating the lattices. We could produce lattices with an assumed correlation between the two rates, but the mechanics of the valuation framework would not change. For short dated basis swaptions this simplification will not have a significant effect on the valuation results. The correlation between rates was also ignored in the traditional approach discussed earlier.

Exhibit 11: 1.5-Year Interest Rate Lattices for Pay LIBOR TED Spread Swaption

a. LIBOR Interest Rate Lattice

					8.906%
				8.541%	
			8.070%		8.059%
		7.679%		7.728%	
	7.292%		7.302%		7.292%
6.985%		6.949%		6.993%	
	6.598%		6.607%		6.598%
		6.287%		6.328%	
			5.978%		5.970%
				5.725%	
					5.402%

Period	1	2	3	4	5
Time in Years	0.25	0.50	0.75	1.00	1.25

10% volatility assumed

b. T-Bill Interest Rate Lattice

					7.407%
				7.162%	
			6.891%		6.872%
		6.599%		6.644%	
	6.277%		6.393%		6.375%
5.970%		6.122%		6.164%	
	5.823%		5.931%		5.914%
		5.679%		5.719%	
			5.503%		5.487%
				5.305%	
					5.091%

Period	1	2	3	4	5
Time in Years	0.25	0.50	0.75	1.00	1.25

7.5% volatility assumed

Exhibit 12: Cash Flow Lattice for a Pay LIBOR Receive T-Bill Swap with a Spread of 0.5%

Period 1	2	3	4	5	6
0.25	0.50	0.75	1.00	1.25	1.50
					-0.250
				-0.220	
			-0.170		-0.172
		-0.145		-0.146	
	-0.129		-0.102		-0.104
-0.129		-0.082		-0.082	
	-0.069		-0.044		-0.046
		-0.027		-0.027	
			0.006		0.004
				0.020	
					0.047

Exhibit 13: Value Lattice for a Pay LIBOR Receive T-Bill Swap with a Spread of 0.5%

Period	1	2	3	4	5
0	0.25	0.5	0.75	1	1.25
					-0.244
				-0.417	
			-0.506		-0.168
		-0.543		-0.276	
	-0.542		-0.311		-0.102
-0.522		-0.303		-0.153	
	-0.263		-0.142		-0.045
		-0.094		-0.047	
			0.005		0.004
				0.045	
					0.047

We will illustrate the valuation procedure using the lattice approach to value a (0.5,1) pay LIBOR TED swaption with a strike rate of 1%. This is an option to enter into a swap six months (0.5 means two quarters) from now that pays LIBOR and receives the T-bill rate plus 100 basis points. Once we have the value lattice the approach is the same. The swaption lattice is created in the same way as illustrated in Chapter 8.

Exhibit 14: (0.5,1) Pay LIBOR TED Swaption

```
                                           0.000
                                   0.086
                           0.179           0.176
                                   0.277
                                           0.387
         Period                      1       2
         Time in years     0      0.250   0.500
```

The swaption lattice is shown in Exhibit 14. The value of this option is $0.179 per $100 notional principal. Note that the value of this swaption will depend on the characteristics of both LIBOR and the T-bill. The effect of changes in each interest rate can be analyzed as explained in Chapter 9.

To show where some of the swaption values in Exhibit 14 come from, we illustrate the value lattice with a spread of 1%. The swap value lattice is shown in Exhibit 15. The terminal values for the swaption are simply the maximum of zero or the swap value — that is, max(swap value, 0). The other values are found by backward induction and discounting using LIBOR. For example, the value in Exhibit 14 for period 1 at the top node is obtained from

$$(0.5 \times 0 + 0.5 \times 0.176)/(1 + 0.07292/4) = 0.086$$

Our focus above was on a swaption on a LIBOR TED swap. Swaptions on Constant Maturity Treasury swaps are found in the same manner as for swaptions on plain vanilla swaps. The only trick is to produce the appropriate interest rate lattice. The lattice will represent the appropriate floating leg (in our previous CMT swap example this would be the 2-year T-note). The arbitrage conditions that are to be evaluated when creating the lattices must be setup correctly before creating the lattice. Once the lattice is created, the procedure is the same.

Exhibit 15: Swap Value Lattice for a Pay LIBOR TED Swap with a Spread of 1%

						−0.122
					−0.175	
				−0.146		−0.046
			−0.067		−0.033	
		0.050		0.050		0.020
	0.184		0.176		0.090	
		0.332		0.221		0.078
			0.387		0.197	
				0.369		0.127
					0.289	
						0.170
Period		1	2	3	4	5
Time in years	0	0.25	0.5	0.75	1	1.25

QUESTIONS

1. The following two tables present the 1-year information for both LIBOR and the U.S. Treasury bill.

LIBOR

Quarter Starts	Quarter Ends	Number of Days	Current 3-Month LIBOR	Eurodollar CD Price
1/1/YR1	3/31/YR1	90	7.00%	
4/1/YR1	6/30/YR1	90		92.90
7/1/YR1	9/30/YR1	91		92.85
10/1/YR1	12/31/YR1	91		92.80

T-Bill Rate

Quarter Starts	Quarter Ends	Number of Days	Current 3-Month LIBOR	T-Bill Futures
1/1/YR1	3/31/YR1	90	6.00%	
4/1/YR1	6/30/YR1	90		93.69994
7/1/YR1	9/30/YR1	91		93.63996
10/1/YR1	12/31/YR1	91		93.45991

Using the "Actual/360" day count convention and the traditional approach compute the appropriate spread over the Treasury bill rate for a 1-year TED swap with a notional principal of $100.

2. Using the following two interest rate lattices for LIBOR and the Treasury bill rate and rounding the day count to 0.25 years, repeat the computation from Question 1 for a 1-year pay LIBOR TED swap with a notional principal of $100.

```
              LIBOR                    8.34%
                               7.88%
                     7.46%             7.54%
           7.00%               7.13%
                     6.75%             6.83%
                               6.45%
                                       6.18%

   Time in Years   0.25      0.5     0.75
```

```
T-Bill Rate                          7.30%
                          6.85%
               6.54%                 6.78%
      6.00%                6.35%
               6.06%                 6.29%
                          5.89%
                                     5.83%

Time in Years    0.25     0.5    0.75
```

3. Using the 2-year Treasury forward rates in the following exhibit and the LIBOR information from Question 1, compute the swap rate for a 1-year CMT swap with a notional principal where the floating payment is made quarterly and is based on the 2-year Constant Maturity Treasury rate.

Quarter Starts	Quarter Ends	2-Year CMT Forward Rate	Number of Days in Period
1/1/YR1	3/31/YR1	7.00%	90
4/1/YR1	6/30/YR1	7.10%	90
7/1/YR1	9/30/YR1	7.20%	91
10/1/YR1	12/31/YR1	7.25%	91

4. Using the following interest rate lattices, compute the value of a 6-month pay LIBOR TED swaption on a 1-year swap with a strike rate of 1.5% and a notional principal of $100.

```
LIBOR                                          9.42%
                                     8.91%
                          8.51%                8.52%
               7.99%                 8.06%
      7.56%                7.70%               7.71%
7.00%          7.23%                 7.29%
      6.84%                6.97%               6.98%
               6.54%                 6.60%
                          6.30%                6.31%
                                     5.97%
                                               5.71%

Time in Years    0.25     0.5     0.75     1     1.25
```

T-Bill rate

	0.25	0.5	0.75	1	1.25
					8.00%
				7.59%	
			7.30%		7.42%
		6.85%		7.04%	
	6.54%		6.78%		6.88%
6.00%		6.35%		6.53%	
	6.06%		6.29%		6.39%
		5.89%		6.06%	
			5.83%		5.92%
				5.62%	
					5.50%

Time in Years   0.25   0.5   0.75   1   1.25

SOLUTIONS TO QUESTIONS

1. The payments per \$100 notional principal are computed in the same manner as in earlier chapters and are shown in the following two tables.

LIBOR

Quarter Starts	Quarter Ends	Number of Days	Forward Rate	End of quarter	Payment per 100 NP
1/1/YR1	3/31/YR1	90	7.00%	1	1.750000000
4/1/YR1	6/30/YR1	90	7.100%	2	1.775000000
7/1/YR1	9/30/YR1	91	7.150%	3	1.807361111
10/1/YR1	12/31/YR1	91	7.200%	4	1.820000000

T-Bill Rate

Quarter Starts	Quarter Ends	Number of Days	Forward Rate	End of quarter	Payment per 100 NP
1/1/YR1	3/31/YR1	90	6.00%	1	1.703552090
4/1/YR1	6/30/YR1	90	6.30%	2	1.778565945
7/1/YR1	9/30/YR1	91	6.36%	3	1.813489596
10/1/YR1	12/31/YR1	91	6.54%	4	1.859004345

The LIBOR based forward discount factors are found in the same manner as in earlier chapters and are shown in the following table.

LIBOR

Quarter Starts	Quarter Ends	End of Quarter	LIBOR Forward Rate	Period Forward Rate	Forward Discount Factor
1/1/YR1	3/31/YR1	1	7.00%	1.7500%	0.982800983
4/1/YR1	6/30/YR1	2	7.10%	1.7750%	0.965660509
7/1/YR1	9/30/YR1	3	7.15%	1.8074%	0.948517375
10/1/YR1	12/31/YR1	4	7.20%	1.8200%	0.931562929

The next two tables show that the appropriate spread is 0.814%. (Note that it does not matter if it is a pay LIBOR or receive LIBOR TED swap because the computations do not change.)

LIBOR

Quarter Starts	Quarter Ends	End of Quarter	Forward Discount Factor	Payment per 100 NP	PV of Floating Payment
1/1/YR1	3/31/YR1	1	0.982800983	1.75	1.71990172
4/1/YR1	6/30/YR1	2	0.965660509	1.775	1.714047403
7/1/YR1	9/30/YR1	3	0.948517375	1.807361	1.714313416
10/1/YR1	12/31/YR1	4	0.931562929	1.82	1.695444531
				Total	6.843707

T-Bill Rate

Quarter Starts	Quarter Ends	End of Quarter	Forward Discount Factor	Payment per 100 NP	PV of Floating Payment	Spread
1/1/YR1	3/31/YR1	1	0.982800983	1.703567	1.674267352	0.814%
4/1/YR1	6/30/YR1	2	0.965660509	1.778581	1.717505323	
7/1/YR1	9/30/YR1	3	0.948517375	1.813505	1.720140719	
10/1/YR1	12/31/YR1	4	0.931562929	1.859019	1.731793606	
				Total	6.843707	

2. The appropriate cash flow lattice and corresponding swap value lattice are given below based a spread of 0.815%. This spread produces a zero swap value. Due to the rounded day count, the results are not exactly the same as computed for Question 1. Repeating Question 1 using the rounded day count produces the same result.

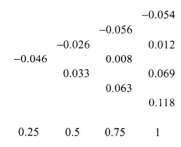

Spread over T-Bill Rate   0.815%

Pay LIBOR CF

```
                                              -0.054
                                  -0.056
                      -0.026                   0.012
          -0.046                    0.008
                       0.033                   0.069
                                   0.063
                                               0.118

          0.25        0.5        0.75          1
```

Pay LIBOR Values

```
                                   -0.053
                       -0.075
           -0.039                   0.012
 0.000                   0.047
            0.131                   0.068
                         0.153
                                    0.116

 0         0.25        0.5         0.75
```

3. The forward discount factors for the swap are:

Quarter Starts	Quarter Ends	Number of Days	Actual/ 360	End of Quarter	LIBOR Forward Rate	Period Forward Rate	Forward Discount Factor
1/1/YR1	3/31/YR1	90	0.25	1	7.00%	1.7500%	0.982801
4/1/YR1	6/30/YR1	90	0.25	2	7.10%	1.7750%	0.965661
7/1/YR1	9/30/YR1	91	0.252778	3	7.15%	1.8074%	0.948517
10/1/YR1	12/31/YR1	91	0.252778	4	7.20%	1.8200%	0.931563

The resulting floating payments and the total present value of the floating payments are:

End of Period	Cash Flow per $100	Forward Discount Factor	PV of Cash Flows
1	1.75	0.982801	1.719902
2	1.775	0.965661	1.714047
3	1.82	0.948517	1.726302
4	1.832639	0.931563	1.707218
		Total	6.867469

The swap rate is 7.1361% as shown below (using the formula from Chapter 3):

$$SFR = \frac{PV \text{ of floating payments}}{\sum_{t=1}^{5} \text{notional principal} \times \frac{\text{Days}_t}{360} \times \text{FDF}_t}$$

$$= \frac{6.867469}{96.2358} = 7.1361\%$$

4. The appropriate lattices are shown below. The value of this swaption is $0.644 per $100 notional principal:

Cash Flow Lattice
Pay LIBOR CF

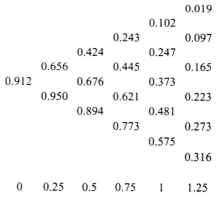

						0.020
					0.046	
				0.074		0.099
			0.088		0.121	
		0.119		0.144		0.168
	0.125		0.155		0.185	
		0.181		0.205		0.227
			0.212		0.241	
				0.257		0.278
					0.288	
						0.321

0.25	0.50	0.75	1.00	1.25	1.50

Swap Value Lattice

						0.019
					0.102	
				0.243		0.097
			0.424		0.247	
		0.656		0.445		0.165
	0.912		0.676		0.373	
		0.950		0.621		0.223
			0.894		0.481	
				0.773		0.273
					0.575	
						0.316

0	0.25	0.5	0.75	1	1.25

(.5,1) Swaption Lattice

		0.424
	0.540	
0.644		0.676
	0.772	
		0.894

0.000	0.250	0.500

Chapter 11

Controlling Interest Rate Risk with Swaps

I n previous chapters we demonstrated how the value of a swap changes when interest rates change. For this reason, swaps are used to control the interest rate risk of a financial entity or a portfolio. Swaps are a cost effective means of altering exposure to interest rate risk compared to rebalancing a portfolio using cash market instruments and futures contracts. In this chapter, we will explain how swaps are used to control interest rate risk.

ILLUSTRATION OF HOW A SWAP CAN BE USED TO CONTROL INTEREST RATE RISK

We begin this chapter with an application of swaps to alter the exposure of two financial entities. Specifically, we will demonstrate how an interest rate swap can be used to hedge interest rate risk by altering the cash flow characteristics of an entity so as to better match the cash flow characteristics of assets and liabilities.

Suppose a bank has a portfolio consisting of 4-year commercial loans with a fixed interest rate. The principal value of the portfolio is $100 million, and the interest rate on all the loans in the portfolio is 11%. The loans are interest-only loans; interest is paid semiannually, and the principal is paid at the end of four years. That is, assuming no default on the loans, the cash flow from the loan portfolio is $5.5 million every six months for the next four years and $100 million at the end of four years. To fund its loan portfolio, assume that the bank can borrow at 6-month LIBOR for the next four years.

The risk that the bank faces is that 6-month LIBOR will be 11% or greater. To understand why, remember that the bank is earning 11% annually on its commercial loan portfolio. If 6-month LIBOR is 11% when the borrowing rate for the bank's loan resets, there will be no spread income for that 6-month period. Worse, if 6-month LIBOR rises above 11%, there will be a loss for that 6-month period; that is, the cost of funds will exceed the interest rate earned on the loan portfolio. The bank's objective is to lock in a spread over the cost of its funds.

The other party in the interest rate swap illustration is a life insurance company that has committed itself to pay an 8% rate for the next four years on a guaranteed investment contract (GIC) it has issued. The amount of the GIC is $100 million. Suppose that the life insurance company has the opportunity to invest $100 million in what it considers an attractive 4-year floating-rate instrument in a private placement transaction. The interest rate on this instrument is 6-month LIBOR plus 120 basis points. The coupon rate is set every six months.

The risk that the life insurance company faces in this instance is that 6-month LIBOR will fall so that the company will not earn enough to realize a spread over the 8% rate that it has guaranteed to the GIC policyholders. If 6-month LIBOR falls to 6.8% or less at a coupon reset date, no spread income will be generated. To understand why, suppose that 6-month LIBOR at the date the floating-rate instrument resets its coupon is 6.8%. Then the coupon rate for the next six months will be 8% (6.8% plus 120 basis points). Because the life insurance company has agreed to pay 8% on the GIC policy, there will be no spread income. Should 6-month LIBOR fall below 6.8%, there will be a loss for that 6-month period.

We can summarize the asset/liability problems of the bank and the life insurance company as follows.

Bank:
1. has lent long term and borrowed short term
2. if 6-month LIBOR rises, spread income declines

Life insurance company:
1. has lent short term and borrowed long term
2. if 6-month LIBOR falls, spread income declines

Now let's suppose the market has available a 4-year interest rate swap with a notional amount of $100 million. Suppose the swap terms available to the bank are as follows:

1. every six months the bank will pay 9.50% (annual rate)
2. every six months the bank will receive LIBOR

Suppose the swap terms available to the insurance company are as follows:

1. every six months the life insurance company will pay LIBOR
2. every six months the life insurance company will receive 9.40%

Now let's look at the positions of the bank and the life insurance company after the swap. Exhibit 1 summarizes the position of each institution before and after the swap. Consider first the bank. For every 6-month period for the life of the swap, the interest rate spread will be as follows:

Annual interest rate received:		
From commercial loan portfolio	=	11.00%
From interest rate swap	=	6-month LIBOR
Total	=	11.00% + 6-month LIBOR

Annual interest rate paid:		
To borrow funds	=	6-month LIBOR
On interest rate swap	=	9.50%
Total	=	9.50% + 6-month LIBOR

Outcome:		
To be received	=	11.0% + 6-month LIBOR
To be paid	=	9.50% + 6-month LIBOR
Spread income	=	1.50% or 150 basis points

Thus, whatever happens to 6-month LIBOR, the bank locks in a spread of 150 basis points assuming no loan defaults or early payoff of a loan.

Now let's look at the effect of the interest rate swap on the life insurance company:

Annual interest rate received:		
From floating-rate instrument	=	1.20% + 6-month LIBOR
From interest rate swap	=	9.40%
Total	=	10.60% + 6-month LIBOR

Annual interest rate paid:		
To GIC policyholders	=	8.00%
On interest rate swap	=	6-month LIBOR
Total	=	8.00% + 6-month LIBOR

Outcome:		
To be received	=	10.60% + 6-month LIBOR
To be paid	=	8.00% + 6-month LIBOR
Spread income	=	2.60% + 6-month LIBOR

Regardless of what happens to 6-month LIBOR, the life insurance company locks in a spread of 260 basis points assuming the issuer of the floating-rate instrument does not default.

Exhibit 1: Position of Bank and Life Insurance Company Before and After Swap

Position before interest rate swap:

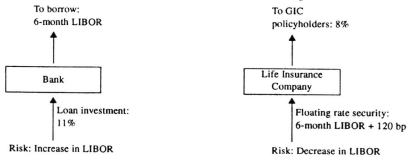

Position after interest rate swap:

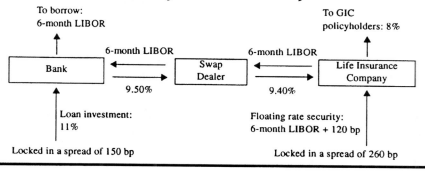

The interest rate swap has allowed each party to accomplish its asset/liability objective of locking in a spread.[1] It also permits the two financial institutions to alter the cash flow characteristics of its assets: from fixed to floating in the case of the bank, and from floating to fixed in the case of the life insurance company.

PRINCIPLES OF INTEREST RATE RISK CONTROL WITH SWAPS

The general principle in controlling interest rate risk with swaps is to combine the dollar exposure of the current portfolio and the dollar exposure of swap positions so that the total dollar exposure is equal to the target dollar exposure desired by the portfolio manager or risk manager. This means that the manager must be able to fairly accurately measure the dollar exposure of both the current portfolio and the swaps employed to alter the exposure.

There are two commonly used measures for approximating the change in the dollar value of a bond or bond portfolio to changes in interest rates: *price value of a basis point* (PVBP) and *duration*. PVBP, also called the *dollar value of an 01* (DV01), is the dollar price change resulting from a one-basis-point change in yield. Duration is the approximate percentage change in price of a security (or market value of a portfolio) for a 100-basis-point change in rates. Given the percentage price change, the dollar price change (or change in market value) for a given change in rates can be computed.

There are two measures of duration: modified and effective. *Modified duration* assumes that when rates change, the cash flows of the bond or financial instrument do not change. *Effective duration* is the appropriate measure that should be used for bonds and other financial instruments whose expected cash flows change when rates change (e.g., bond with embedded options and swaptions). In this chapter when we refer to duration, we mean effective duration. Moreover, since the manager is interested in dollar price exposure, it is the effective dollar duration that should be used. (For a one basis point change in rates, PVBP is equal to the effective dollar duration for a one-basis-point change in rates.)

---

[1] Whether the size of the spread is adequate is not an issue to us in this illustration.

To estimate the effective dollar duration for a bond, it is necessary to have a good valuation model. It is the valuation model that is used to determine what the new values for the bonds in the portfolio will be if rates change. The difference between the current values of the bonds in the portfolio and the new values estimated by the valuation model when rates are changed is the dollar price exposure. Consequently, the starting point in controlling interest rate risk is the development of a reliable valuation model. A reliable valuation model is also needed to value the swaps that the manager wants to use to control interest rate exposure.

Suppose that a manager seeks a target duration for the portfolio based on expectations of interest rates, client-specified exposure, or maximum exposure mandated by regulators. Given the target duration, a target dollar duration for a small basis point change in interest rates can be obtained. Since duration is the approximate percentage change in value for a 100 basis point change in rates, the target dollar duration can be found by dividing the target duration by 100 and then multiplying the dollar value of the portfolio by this value. If the target dollar duration for a 25 basis point change is sought, then this value is found by dividing the target dollar duration for a 100 basis point change by 4. For example, suppose that the manager of a $500 million portfolio wants a target duration of 4. This means that for a 100 basis point change in rates, the target dollar duration is found by first dividing 4 by 100 to get 4% and then multiplying $500 million by 4%. The resulting value of $20 million is the dollar duration for a 100 basis point change in rates. For a 25 basis point change (i.e., one fourth of the 100 basis point change), the target dollar duration is $5 million.

The manager must then determine the dollar duration of the current portfolio. The current dollar duration for a 25 basis point change in interest rates is found in the same way. Suppose that the current duration for the portfolio is 6. Then the current dollar duration for a 100 basis point change in rates is found by first dividing 6 by 100 to get 6% and then multiplying $500 million by 6% to get $30 million. For a 25 basis point change in rates, the current dollar duration is $7.5 million.

The target dollar duration is then compared to the current dollar duration. Assuming that swaps are used to control the interest rate risk, the difference between the two dollar durations is the dollar exposure that must be provided by the swap positions. If the target dollar duration exceeds the current dollar duration, the swap positions must be such that they increase the dollar exposure by the difference. Once swap positions are taken, the portfolio's dollar duration is equal to the sum of the current dollar duration without the swap positions and the dollar duration of the swap position. That is,

> portfolio's dollar duration
>   = current dollar duration without swap positions
>   + dollar duration of swap positions

The objective is to control the portfolio's interest rate risk by establishing swap positions such that the portfolio's dollar duration is equal to the target dollar duration. Thus,

> portfolio's dollar duration = target dollar duration

Or, equivalently,

> target dollar duration
>   = current dollar duration without swap positions
>   + dollar duration of swap positions   (1)

DOLLAR DURATION OF A SWAP

Effectively, a position in an interest rate swap is a leveraged position. This agrees with our "package of cash instruments" economic interpretation of an interest rate swap explained in Chapter 1. Specifically, it is a leveraged position involving either buying a fixed-rate bond and financing it on a floating-rate basis (i.e., fixed-rate receiver position) or buying a floating-rate bond and financing it on a fixed-rate basis (i.e., fixed-rate payer position). So, we would expect that the dollar duration of a swap is a multiple of the bond that effectively underlies the swap.

To see how to calculate the dollar duration, let's work with the economic interpretation of a swap as a package of cash flows from buying and selling cash market instruments. From the perspective of the fixed-rate receiver, the position can be viewed as follows:

long a fixed-rate bond + short a floating-rate bond

The fixed-rate bond is a bond with a coupon rate equal to the swap's fixed rate, a maturity equal to the term of the swap, and a par value equal to the swap's notional principal.

This means that the dollar duration of an interest rate swap from the perspective of a fixed-rate receiver is just the difference between the dollar durations of the two bond positions that comprise the swap. That is,

dollar duration of a swap for a fixed-rate receiver
= dollar duration of a fixed-rate bond
  − dollar duration of a floating-rate bond

Most of the interest rate sensitivity of a swap will result from the dollar duration of the fixed-rate bond since the dollar duration of the floating-rate bond will be small. The dollar duration of a floating-rate bond is smaller the closer the swap is to its reset date. If the dollar duration of the floating-rate bond is close to zero then:

dollar duration of a swap for a fixed-rate receiver
= dollar duration of a fixed-rate bond

Thus, adding an interest rate swap to a portfolio in which the manager pays a floating-rate and receives a fixed-rate increases the dollar duration of the portfolio by roughly the dollar duration of the underlying fixed-rate bond. This is because it effectively involves buying a fixed-rate bond on a leveraged basis.

We can use the package of cash market instruments economic interpretation to compute the dollar duration of a swap for the fixed-rate payer. The dollar duration is:

dollar duration of a swap for a fixed-rate payer
= dollar duration of a floating-rate bond
  − dollar duration of a fixed-rate bond

Again, assuming that the dollar duration of the floater is small, we have

dollar duration of a swap for a fixed-rate payer
  = −dollar duration of a fixed-rate bond

Consequently, a manager who adds a swap to a portfolio involving paying fixed and receiving floating decreases the dollar duration of the portfolio by an amount roughly equal to the dollar duration of the fixed-rate bond.

The dollar duration of a portfolio that includes a swap is:

dollar duration of assets − dollar duration of liabilities
  + dollar duration of a swap position

Let's look at our bank/life insurance illustration in terms of duration mismatch. The bank has a long duration for its assets (the fixed-rate loans) and a short duration for its liabilities (the short-term funds it borrows). Effectively, the position of the bank is as follows:

bank's dollar duration
  = dollar duration of assets − dollar duration of liabilities > 0

The bank entered into an interest rate swap in which it pays fixed and receives floating. As just explained, the dollar duration of that swap position is negative. Thus, adding the swap position moves the bank's dollar duration position closer to zero and, therefore, reduces interest rate risk.

For the life insurance company, the duration of the liabilities is long while the duration of the floating-rate assets is short. That is,

life insurance company's dollar duration
  = dollar duration of assets − dollar duration of liabilities < 0

The life insurance company entered into an interest rate swap in which it pays floating and receives fixed. This swap position has a positive duration. By adding it to a portfolio it moves the duration closer to zero, thereby reducing interest rate risk.

Exhibit 2: Current Term Structure and a 25 Basis Point Shift in the Term Structure

(1) Time in Years	(2) Current Spot	(3) Minus 25 bps	(4) Plus 25bps	(5) Current Forward	(6) Forward − 25bps	(7) Forward + 25bps
0.5	6.96%	6.71%	7.21%	6.96%	6.71%	7.21%
1.0	6.97%	6.72%	7.22%	6.97%	6.72%	7.22%
1.5	6.98%	6.73%	7.23%	7.00%	6.75%	7.25%
2.0	6.98%	6.73%	7.23%	6.99%	6.74%	7.24%
2.5	6.99%	6.74%	7.24%	7.03%	6.78%	7.28%
3.0	7.00%	6.75%	7.25%	7.03%	6.78%	7.28%
3.5	7.01%	6.76%	7.26%	7.09%	6.84%	7.34%
4.0	7.02%	6.77%	7.27%	7.11%	6.86%	7.36%
4.5	7.04%	6.79%	7.29%	7.19%	6.94%	7.44%
5.0	7.06%	6.81%	7.31%	7.23%	6.98%	7.48%

CALCULATING THE DOLLAR DURATION OF A SWAP

Now let's see how to compute the dollar duration of a swap. Suppose that we know what the dollar duration of a portfolio is without swap positions for a parallel shift in the term structure of interest rates. We will denote the number of basis points for the shift as Δy. The goal is then to compute the dollar duration of the swap positions for the same Δy shift in the term structure.

To illustrate how this is done, we will use the 5-year swap with a notional principal of $100 based on semiannual payments and rounded day count. The term structure of interest rates is the same as in Exhibit 5 of Chapter 4. Column (5) of Exhibit 2 reproduces the rates.[2]

We will compute the dollar duration of this swap for a 25 basis point change in yield. Columns (3) and (4) of Exhibit 2 show the rates for a 25 basis point decrease and increase, respectively. Exhibits 3 and 4 show the interest rate lattice for a 25 basis point downward and upward shift in the term structure, respectively.[3]

[2] Column (2) is found using the principles reviewed in Appendix A.
[3] Note that the interest rate lattice resulting from a shift in the term structure is found by reconstructing an arbitrage-free lattice using the new rates in the term structure. It is not constructed by taking the current interest rate lattice and changing the rate at each node by the number of basis points that the term structure is shifted.

Exhibit 3: The Interest Rate Lattice After a 25 Basis Point Downward Shift

Time in Years	0.50	1.00	1.50	2.00	2.50	3.00	3.50	4.00	4.50	
	6.7150%	7.1929%	7.7404%	8.2725%	8.9182%	9.5592%	10.3311%	11.1139%	12.0535%	12.9894%
		6.2443%	6.7196%	7.1815%	7.7421%	8.2985%	8.9687%	9.6482%	10.4640%	11.2764%
			5.8335%	6.2345%	6.7211%	7.2042%	7.7859%	8.3758%	9.0840%	9.7893%
				5.4123%	5.8347%	6.2541%	6.7591%	7.2713%	7.8860%	8.4984%
					5.0653%	5.4293%	5.8678%	6.3124%	6.8461%	7.3776%
						4.7133%	5.0939%	5.4799%	5.9432%	6.4047%
							4.4222%	4.7572%	5.1594%	5.5601%
								4.1299%	4.4790%	4.8268%
									3.8884%	4.1903%
										3.6377%

Exhibit 4: The Interest Rate Lattice After a 25 Basis Point Upward Shift

	0.50	1.00	1.50	2.00	2.50	3.00	3.50	4.00	4.50
									13.9276%
								12.9271%	
							11.9275%		12.0909%
						11.0893%		11.2223%	
					10.2659%		10.3546%		10.4964%
				9.5773%		9.6269%		9.7423%	
			8.8872%		8.9121%		8.9891%		9.1121%
		8.3141%		8.3142%		8.3573%		8.4576%	
	7.7283%		7.7152%		7.7368%		7.8036%		7.9105%
7.2150%		7.2176%		7.2178%		7.2552%		7.3422%	
	6.7092%		6.6978%		6.7165%		6.7745%		6.8673%
		6.2658%		6.2659%		6.2984%		6.3739%	
			5.8145%		5.8307%		5.8811%		5.9616%
				5.4396%		5.4678%		5.5334%	
					5.0618%		5.1055%		5.1754%
						4.7467%		4.80?%	
							4.4322%		4.4929%
								4.1702%	
									3.9004%

Time in Years   0.50   1.00   1.50   2.00   2.50   3.00   3.50   4.00   4.50

Exhibit 5: Current Value of Swap

(1) Beginning Period	(2) End of Period	(3) Rounded Day Count	(4) Forward Rate	(5) End of Period CF	(6) Forward Discount Factor	(7) Fixed Payments with SFR =7.0513%	(8) PV Floating	(9) PV Fixed
1/1/YR1	6/30/YR1	0.5	6.96%	3.4825	0.966347	3.525635	3.3653	3.4070
7/1/YR1	12/31/YR1	0.5	6.97%	3.4837	0.933815	3.525635	3.2532	3.2923
1/1/YR2	6/30/YR2	0.5	7.00%	3.5000	0.902237	3.525635	3.1578	3.1810
7/1/YR2	12/31/YR2	0.5	6.99%	3.4925	0.87179	3.525635	3.0447	3.0736
1/1/YR3	6/30/YR3	0.5	7.03%	3.5138	0.842197	3.525635	2.9593	2.9693
7/1/YR3	12/31/YR3	0.5	7.03%	3.5150	0.813599	3.525635	2.8598	2.8685
1/1/YR4	6/30/YR4	0.5	7.09%	3.5438	0.785754	3.525635	2.7845	2.7703
7/1/YR4	12/31/YR4	0.5	7.11%	3.5563	0.75877	3.525635	2.6984	2.6751
1/1/YR5	6/30/YR5	0.5	7.19%	3.5963	0.73243	3.525635	2.6340	2.5823
7/1/YR5	12/31/YR5	0.5	7.23%	3.6138	0.706885	3.525635	2.5545	2.4922
						Total	29.3115	29.3115
						Swap Value	0	

Exhibit 5 shows the current value of the swap assuming a swap fixed rate of 7.0513%. The value of the swap is zero. Exhibit 6 shows using the traditional approach the floating payments, the period forward rates, the forward discount factors, and the present value of the floating and fixed payments for each period for a 25 basis point downward shift in the term structure. The value of the swap for the fixed pay party is –$1.0446 per $100 notional principal. Exhibit 7 shows the swap value using the lattice approach. The value of the swap for the fixed-rate payer is –$1.0446 per $100 notional principal and $1.0446 per $100 notional principal for the floating-rate payer, the same as with the traditional approach.

Exhibit 8 does the same as Exhibit 6 for a 25 basis point upward shift in the term structure and Exhibit 9 for the lattice approach. In this case, the value of the swap for the fixed-rate payer is $1.0316 per $100 notional principal and –$1.0316 per $100 notional principal for the floating-rate payer.

The results for a 25 basis point shift in the term structure are summarized below:

	Pay fixed swap	Receive fixed swap
downward shift	–$1.0446	$1.0446
upward shift	$1.0316	–$1.0316

Exhibit 6: Valuation of a Pay Fixed Swap After a Downward Shift of 25 Basis Points Using the Traditional Approach (SFR = 7.0513%)

(1)	(2)	(3)	(4)	(5)	(6)	(7)	(8)	(9)
Beginning Period	End of Period	Rounded Day Count	Forward Rate	End of Period CF	Forward Discount Factor	Fixed Payments with SFR =7.0513%	PV Floating	PV Fixed
1/1/YR1	6/30/YR1	0.5	6.71%	3.3575	0.967516	3.525635	3.2484	3.4111
7/1/YR1	12/31/YR1	0.5	6.72%	3.3587	0.936075	3.525635	3.1440	3.3003
1/1/YR2	6/30/YR2	0.5	6.75%	3.3750	0.905514	3.525635	3.0561	3.1925
7/1/YR2	12/31/YR2	0.5	6.74%	3.3675	0.876014	3.525635	2.9500	3.0885
1/1/YR3	6/30/YR3	0.5	6.78%	3.3888	0.847301	3.525635	2.8713	2.9873
7/1/YR3	12/31/YR3	0.5	6.78%	3.3900	0.81952	3.525635	2.7782	2.8893
1/1/YR4	6/30/YR4	0.5	6.84%	3.4188	0.792429	3.525635	2.7091	2.7938
7/1/YR4	12/31/YR4	0.5	6.86%	3.4313	0.76614	3.525635	2.6288	2.7011
1/1/YR5	6/30/YR5	0.5	6.94%	3.4713	0.740438	3.525635	2.5703	2.6105
7/1/YR5	12/31/YR5	0.5	6.98%	3.4888	0.715476	3.525635	2.4961	2.5225
						Total	28.4524	29.4970
						Swap Value		−1.0446

Exhibit 7: Valuation of a Pay Fixed Swap After a Downward Shift of 25 Basis Points Using the Lattice Approach (SFR = 7.0513%)

```
                                                                                  2.7880
                                                                        4.6168
                                                              5.6231              1.9998
                                                    5.9829              3.1918
                                          5.7756              3.6810              1.3052
                                5.1175              3.6124              1.9284
                      4.0465              3.0489              1.9503              0.6940
            2.6471              2.0892              1.4911              0.8111
   0.9331              0.7633              0.6004              0.4132              0.1574
-1.0446              -0.8554             -0.6379             -0.4000             -0.1746
           -2.7562             -2.1999             -1.5889             -0.9480             -0.3133
                     -4.0222             -3.0823             -2.0800             -1.0424
                               -4.8613             -3.5390             -2.1505             -0.7254
                                         -5.2644             -3.5682             -1.8051
                                                   -5.2704             -3.2103             -1.0860
                                                             -4.8831             -2.4743             -1.4011
                                                                       -4.1426             -1.4011
                                                                                 -3.0607
                                                                                           -1.6763

Time in Years   0.5      1      1.5      2      2.5      3      3.5      4      4.5
```

Exhibit 8: Valuation of a Pay Fixed Swap After an Upward Shift of 25 Basis Points Using the Traditional Approach (SFR = 7.0513%)

(1)	(2)	(3)	(4)	(5)	(6)	(7)	(8)	(9)
Beginning Period	End of Period	Rounded Day Count	Forward Rate	End of Period CF	Forward Discount Factor	Fixed Payments with SFR = 7.0513%	PV Floating	PV Fixed
1/1/YR1	6/30/YR1	0.5	7.21%	3.6075	0.965181	3.525635	3.4819	3.4029
7/1/YR1	12/31/YR1	0.5	7.22%	3.6087	0.931563	3.525635	3.3618	3.2844
1/1/YR2	6/30/YR2	0.5	7.25%	3.6250	0.898975	3.525635	3.2588	3.1695
7/1/YR2	12/31/YR2	0.5	7.24%	3.6175	0.86759	3.525635	3.1385	3.0588
1/1/YR3	6/30/YR3	0.5	7.28%	3.6388	0.837129	3.525635	3.0461	2.9514
7/1/YR3	12/31/YR3	0.5	7.28%	3.6400	0.807728	3.525635	2.9401	2.8478
1/1/YR4	6/30/YR4	0.5	7.34%	3.6688	0.779143	3.525635	2.8585	2.7470
7/1/YR4	12/31/YR4	0.5	7.36%	3.6813	0.751479	3.525635	2.7664	2.6494
1/1/YR5	6/30/YR5	0.5	7.44%	3.7213	0.724518	3.525635	2.6961	2.5544
7/1/YR5	12/31/YR5	0.5	7.48%	3.7388	0.698406	3.525635	2.6112	2.4623
						Total	30.1594	29.1278
						Swap Value	1.0316	

Exhibit 9: Valuation of a Pay Fixed Swap After an Upward Shift of 25 Basis Points Using the Lattice Approach (SFR = 7.0513%)

									3.2143
								5.3851	
							6.6701		2.3761
						7.2598		3.8745	
					7.2447		4.6165		1.6367
				6.7485		4.7586		2.5332	
			5.8156		4.3727		2.7832		0.9855
		4.5340		3.5636		2.5157		1.3456	
	2.9216		2.3665		1.7878		1.1524		0.4133
1.0316		0.8580		0.6881		0.5126		0.2967	
	−0.9478		−0.7549		−0.5283		−0.2939		−0.0890
		−2.4752		−1.8950		−1.2699		−0.6277	
			−3.5650		−2.5951		−1.5730		−0.5291
				−4.2056		−2.8511		−1.4408	
					−4.4331		−2.7017		−0.9143
						−4.2499		−2.1547	
							−3.6954		−1.2511
								−2.7808	
									−1.5453
Time in Years 0.5	1	1.5	2	2.5	3	3.5	4	4.5	

The dollar duration per $100 notional principal per 25 basis point shift in the term structure is computed by subtracting from the above values the swap value before the shift in the term structure. Since the swap value before the shift is zero, the above values are also the dollar durations for a 25 basis point shift in the term structure.

Now let's look at how to use these values. Suppose that a manager has a portfolio with cash market instruments that has a market value of $500 million and a current duration of 6. Concerned with a rise in interest rates, the manager wants to reduce the current duration from 6 to 4. That is, the target duration is 4. The situation is then as follows for a rise in interest rates of, say, 25 basis points. The portfolio's value will decline by 6% for a 100 basis point increase in rates and therefore 1.5% for a 25 basis point change in rates. Translated into dollars, the change in the dollar value of the position will be about −$7.5 million for a 25 basis point increase in rates. For the target duration of 4, the decrease in dollar value will be 1% for a 25 basis point increase in rates or −$5 million. So, we have

> current dollar duration for a 25 basis point rate increase
> = −$7.5 million

> target dollar duration for a 25 basis point rate increase
> = −$5.0 million

The difference between these values is −$2.5 million and is the excess interest rate risk exposure that the manager wants the swap positions taken to protect against.

If the manager wants to use our hypothetical 5-year swap to control this interest rate risk, he or she must take a position in the swap such that (1) the swap position increases in value when interest rates increase and (2) the notional principal is such that the increase in value of the swap is approximately $2.5 million. The reason is that if a swap position is created that increases in value when rates increase by 25 basis points, the portfolio's position will be as follows for a 25 basis point increase in rates:

> portfolio dollar duration with swaps
> = current dollar duration without the swap position
> + dollar duration of the swap position

portfolio dollar duration with swaps
    = –$7.5 million + $2.5 million = –$5 million

Thus, the portfolio dollar duration with the right notional principal for the swap will give the target dollar duration of –$5 million for a 25 basis point increase in rates.

Now let's see what position we want to take in the swap. The swap must increase in value when rates increase. For the pay fixed swap we know that the swap value will increase when rates increase. (This can be verified using the values reported above.) Thus, this is the position that will be taken in the swap. Next, we must determine how much the notional principal should be to produce a $2.5 million increase in value for a 25 basis point increase in rates. From the table above we know that the swap value will increase by $1.0316 per $100 notional principal for a 25 basis point increase in rates. Dividing $1.0316 by $100 gives 1.0316%, which is the change in the value of the swap as a percentage of the notional principal. To determine the correct notional principal to adjust the portfolio duration so that it will be approximately equal to the target duration, we then divide the $2.5 million by 1.0316%. The resulting value is $242,352,565. So, a position in a 5-year pay fixed swap with a swap fixed rate of 7.0513% and a notional principal of $242,352,565 should be taken by the manager who seeks to alter the portfolio's current duration from 6 to a target duration of 4.[4]

A few points to note. First, the change in the value of the swap is not the same for an upward shift and downward shift in the term structure. For this reason, some managers prefer to take the average of the absolute change in the swap's value rather than the change in the swap value if rates move adversely — upward in our illustration. The average change in the absolute values for our swap for a 25 basis point shift is $1.0381 = ($1.0446 + $1.0316). Dividing $2.5 million by 1.0381% gives a notional principal of $240,826,787.

Second, in our illustration the target duration is less than the current duration for the portfolio. If the target duration sought by

---

[4] Some individuals may be concerned by how large the notional principal is relative to the size of the portfolio ($500 million). What is important in controlling interest rate risk with swaps is not the notional principal *per se* but the change in the swap's value when rates change.

the manager is to increase the duration instead, then a swap position that would increase in value when rates shift downward would be necessary. This would involve taking a position in a receive fixed swap. The procedure for determining the notional principal required is the same as explained above.

Third, while in our illustration we have used a 25 basis point change in value to determine what the swap position should be, approximately the same notional principal would have been determined for other small rate movements. The reasons for using small rate movements are (1) for large rate movements the change in value is not symmetric[5] and (2) most managers rebalance their portfolio position if market rates change by a large number of basis points.

The fourth point is that while we have used a plain vanilla swap with a constant notional principal in our illustration, the same procedure is followed for any swap structure. For example, consider the amortizing swap and accreting swap in Chapters 4 and 6. The change in the value of the amortizing swap with an initial $100 notional principal for a 25 basis point parallel shift in the term structure is as follows:

Amortizing Swap		
	Pay fixed swap	Receive fixed swap
downward shift	−$0.6036	$0.6036
upward shift	$0.5981	−$0.5981

Notice that these values are less than in the constant notional principal case. For the accreting swap the values are:

Accreting Swap		
	Pay fixed swap	Receive fixed swap
downward shift	−$1.4858	$1.4858
upward shift	$1.4652	−$1.4652

These values are greater than in the constant notional principal case.

Finally, the procedure can be extended to handle forward start swaps and swaptions. This procedure is described next.

---

[5] This is due to the convexity property of a swap.

Exhibit 10: Binomial Interest Rate Lattice for the Current Term Structure (Volatility = 10%)

	0.50	1.00	1.50	2.00	2.50	3.00	3.50	4.00	4.50
									13.4584%
								12.4902%	
							11.5207%		11.6836%
						10.7102%		10.8431%	
					9.9125%		10.0013%		10.1428%
				9.2477%		9.2977%		9.4131%	
			8.5798%		8.6053%		8.6824%		8.8052%
		8.0272%		8.0282%		8.0716%		8.1717%	
	7.4606%		7.4484%		7.4705%		7.5374%		7.6440%
6.9650%		6.9686%		6.9694%		7.0071%		7.0941%	
	6.4767%		6.4661%		6.4853%		6.5434%		6.6359%
		6.0496%		6.0503%		6.0831%		6.1585%	
			5.6134%		5.6300%		5.6805%		5.7608%
				5.2524%		5.2808%		5.3464%	
					4.8876%		4.9314%		5.0011%
						4.5844%		4.6413%	
							4.2810%		4.3416%
								4.0292%	
									3.7690%

Time in Years   0.50   1.00   1.50   2.00   2.50   3.00   3.50   4.00   4.50

DETERMINING THE CHANGE IN VALUE FOR COMPLEX SWAP STRUCTURES

In our discussion and illustrations thus far in this chapter our focus has been on plain vanilla swaps. The traditional approach as shown in Exhibits 6 and 8 was used to determine how the value of such swaps change if the term structure shifts. The general approach is the same for complex swap structures such as forward start swaps and swaptions. However, the valuation approach requires the use of an interest rate lattice.

The procedure for such swaps is as follows. We begin with the current term structure as shown in Exhibit 2. The binomial interest rate lattice based on these rates is shown in Exhibit 10. Now consider the term structure for a 25 basis point downward shift in the term structure as shown in Exhibit 2. Exhibit 3 shows the binomial interest rate lattice for that term structure. It is this interest rate lattice that is used to value the swap for a 25 basis point downward shift in the term structure. For the swap fixed rates shown in the second column, Exhibit 11 reports the change in value for several forward start swaps per $100 of notional principal. Exhibit 12 reports the change in value for several swaptions per $100 of notional principal.[6] Exhibit 4 shows the binomial interest rate lattice for a 25 basis point increase in the term structure and is the lattice used to obtain the values reported in Exhibits 11 and 12.

Exhibit 11: Change in Value of Several Forward Start Swap Values

Forward Start Swap	Swap Fixed Rate	Plus 25 bps	Minus 25 bps
(1,4)	7.0777%	0.8536	−0.8625
(2,3)	7.1157%	0.6634	−0.6688
(3,2)	7.1710%	0.4592	−0.4618
(4,1)	7.2443%	0.2389	−0.2397

Exhibit 12: Changes in Swaption Values for Shifts in the Term Structure

(a) Swaption values for shifts in the term structure

Type of Swaption	Pay Fixed Swaption (Strike Rate = 7%)			Receive Fixed Swaption (Strike Rate = 6.75%)		
	−25bps	Current	+25bps	−25bps	Current	+25bps
(4,1)	0.388293	0.483679	0.60249	0.3228	0.2651	0.2084
(3,2)	0.653494	0.834289	1.08781	0.5880	0.4740	0.3620
(2,3)	0.766996	1.020846	1.431449	0.7455	0.5828	0.4227
(1,4)	0.65852	0.962612	1.574425	0.6947	0.5124	0.3326

(b) Change in value

Type of Swaption	Pay Fixed Swaption (Strike Rate = 7%)		Receive Fixed Swaption (Strike Rate = 6.75%)	
	−25bps	+25bps	−25bps	+25bps
(4,1)	−0.09539	0.118811	0.0578	−0.0566
(3,2)	−0.18079	0.253521	0.1140	−0.1120
(2,3)	−0.25385	0.410602	0.1627	−0.1601
(1,4)	−0.30409	0.611813	0.1823	−0.1798

[6] The change in value for a swaption when rates shift is popularly referred to as the swaption's "delta."

QUESTIONS

1. A portfolio manager has a $250 million bond portfolio. The portfolio duration is 7. The portfolio manager would like to reduce the portfolio duration to 3 since he is bearish on interest rates. He wants to use a 5-year semiannual swap to achieve the reduction in portfolio duration. Assume that the appropriate term structure in this analysis is shown in Exhibit A. Exhibits B, C, and D are the corresponding interest rate lattices for the current term structure, the lattice for a +25 basis point shift, and the lattice for a −25 basis point shift, respectively.

Exhibit A – Current Term Structure

Term	Spot rate
0.5	6.5650%
1	6.6662%
1.5	6.7775%
2	6.8794%
2.5	6.9890%
3	7.0958%
3.5	7.2089%
4	7.3219%
4.5	7.4408%
5	7.5595%

a. Compute the dollar duration of the portfolio and the target dollar duration for a 25 basis point shift in rates.

b. Compute the swap fixed rate for the current term structure using the lattice in Exhibit B.

c. Compute the appropriate notional principal of the swap using the upward shift lattice, the downward shift lattice, and the average of the two lattices.

d. Explain which swap is the appropriate swap — a pay fixed or a receive fixed.

Exhibit B – Interest Rate Lattice for Current Term Structure

(The leftmost node, 6.5650%, is the initial rate shown to the left of the 0.50 time label.)

t = 0	0.50	1.00	1.50	2.00	2.50	3.00	3.50	4.00	4.50
									16.0856%
								14.5873%	
							13.1484%		13.9643%
						11.9237%		12.6635%	
					10.7610%		11.4144%		12.1227%
				9.7753%		10.3513%		10.9935%	
			8.8260%		9.3418%		9.9091%		10.5240%
		8.0274%		8.4862%		8.9862%		9.5437%	
	7.2465%		7.6620%		8.1099%		8.6023%		9.1361%
6.5650%		6.9688%		7.3670%		7.8011%		8.2851%	
	6.2908%		6.6516%		7.0404%		7.4679%		7.9313%
		6.0498%		6.3955%		6.7723%		7.1925%	
			5.7744%		6.1119%		6.4830%		6.8853%
				5.5521%		5.8792%		6.2440%	
					5.3059%		5.6281%		5.9773%
						5.1039%		5.4206%	
							4.8859%		5.1891%
								4.7057%	
									4.5047%

Time in Years: 0.50 1.00 1.50 2.00 2.50 3.00 3.50 4.00 4.50

Exhibit C – Interest Rate Lattice for Current Term Structure + 25bps

(The leftmost node, 6.8150%, is the initial rate shown to the left of the 0.50 time label.)

t = 0	0.50	1.00	1.50	2.00	2.50	3.00	3.50	4.00	4.50
									16.5558%
								15.0248%	
							13.5557%		14.3725%
						12.3031%		13.0434%	
					11.1145%		11.7680%		12.4771%
				10.1049%		10.6806%		11.3233%	
			9.1334%		9.6487%		10.2161%		10.8317%
		8.3142%		8.7723%		9.2721%		9.8300%	
	7.5142%		7.9289%		8.3763%		8.8688%		9.4032%
6.8150%		7.2178%		7.6154%		8.0493%		8.5336%	
	6.5233%		6.8833%		7.2717%		7.6992%		8.1632%
		6.2659%		6.6111%		6.9878%		7.4083%	
			5.9755%		6.3127%		6.6839%		7.0866%
				5.7393%		6.0663%		6.4313%	
					5.4802%		5.8024%		6.1521%
						5.2663%		5.5831%	
							5.0372%		5.3408%
								4.8469%	
									4.6364%

Time in Years: 0.50 1.00 1.50 2.00 2.50 3.00 3.50 4.00 4.50

Exhibit D – Interest Rate Lattice for Current Term Structure –25bps

	0.50	1.00	1.50	2.00	2.50	3.00	3.50	4.00	4.50
									15.6155%
								14.1499%	
							12.7412%		13.5562%
						11.5445%		12.2839%	
					10.4075%		11.0609%		11.7685%
				9.4458%		10.0220%		10.6639%	
			8.5186%		9.0350%		9.6022%		10.2165%
		7.7406%		8.2001%		8.7003%		9.2576%	
	6.9787%		7.3952%		7.8435%		8.3359%		8.8692%
6.3150%		6.7198%		7.1187%		7.5530%		8.0367%	
	6.0584%		6.4199%		6.8091%		7.2366%		7.6995%
		5.8336%		6.1799%		6.5569%		6.9769%	
			5.5733%		5.9112%		6.2823%		6.6841%
				5.3649%		5.6922%		6.0568%	
					5.1316%		5.4538%		5.8027%
						4.9415%		5.2580%	
							4.7346%		5.0374%
								4.5646%	
									4.3731%

Time in Years   0.50   1.00   1.50   2.00   2.50   3.00   3.50   4.00   4.50

2. Suppose that the portfolio manager in Question 1 had been bullish on interest rates rather than bearish. Based on this view, suppose that the he wants to increase the portfolio duration to 10.

a. Compute the appropriate notional principal of the swap using the upward shift lattice, the downward shift lattice, and the average of the two lattices.

b. Explain which swap is the appropriate swap — a pay fixed or a receive fixed.

3. Using the same information as in Question 1, compute the change in value of a (2,3) pay fixed swaption with a strike rate of 7%.

SOLUTIONS TO QUESTIONS

1. a. The dollar duration is found as follows for a 25 basis point increase in rates:

−value of portfolio × duration of the portfolio × 25bps shift
$$= -\$250,000,000 \times 7 \times 0.0025 = -\$4,375,000$$

Similarly the target dollar duration is

$$-\$250,000,000 \times 3 \times 0.0025 = -\$1,875,000$$

b. The swap fixed rate is found by first creating the cash flow lattice. Exhibit E illustrates the cash flow lattice that corresponds to Exhibit B. Exhibit F illustrates the corresponding value lattice. The SFR is 7.4898%. Both exhibits are created assuming a notional principal of $100.

Exhibit E – The Pay fixed cash flow lattice with an SFR of 7.4898%

	CF .5	CF 1	CF 1.5	CF 2	CF 2.5	CF 3.0	CF 3.5	CF 4	CF 4.5	CF 5
Notional==>	100.00	100.00	100.00	100.00	100.00	100.00	100.00	100.00	100.00	100.00
CF Lattice										4.2979
									3.5487	
								2.8293		3.2372
							2.2170		2.5869	
						1.6356		1.9623		2.3165
					1.1428		1.4307		1.7519	
				0.6681		0.9260		1.2097		1.5171
			0.2688		0.4982		0.7482		1.0270	
		-0.1217		0.0861		0.3100		0.5563		0.8232
	-0.4624		-0.2605		-0.0614		0.1557		0.3977	
		-0.5995		-0.4191		-0.2247		-0.0110		0.2207
			-0.7200		-0.5471		-0.3587		-0.1486	
				-0.8577		-0.6889		-0.5034		-0.3022
					-0.9689		-0.8053		-0.6229	
						-1.0920		-0.9309		-0.7562
							-1.1930		-1.0346	
								-1.3020		-1.1504
									-1.3920	
										-1.4925

Exhibit F – The Pay Fixed Cumulative Value Lattice with an SFR of 7.4898%

0	0.5	1	1.5	2	2.5	3	3.5	4	4.5
									3.9779
								6.5714	
							8.0285		3.0260
						8.6005		4.8827	
					8.4210		5.7641		2.1841
				7.6437		5.8765		3.3788	
			6.3350		5.3281		3.7358		1.4413
		4.5991		4.2492		3.4253		2.0437	
	2.4665		2.6948		2.5345		1.9261		0.7872
0.0000		0.7560		1.1746		1.2293		0.8617	
	-1.5417		-0.6092		0.0240		0.3171		0.2123
		-2.7374		-1.5953		-0.7301		-0.1820	
			-3.5912		-2.2223		-1.1093		-0.2922
				-4.0790		-2.4724		-1.1017	
					-4.2246		-2.3703		-0.7343
						-4.0169		-1.9106	
							-3.4826		-1.1213
								-2.6208	
									-1.4597

Time in Years   0.5   1   1.5   2   2.5   3   3.5   4   4.5

c. In order to compute the appropriate notional principal we first need to compute the value of the swap for each term structure shift while keeping the SFR at 7.4898%. Exhibits G and H illustrate the corresponding swap value lattices.

Exhibit G – The Pay Fixed Cumulative Value Lattice with an SFR of 7.4898% using the +25bps Term Structure

0	0.5	1	1.5	2	2.5	3	3.5	4	4.5
									4.1865
								6.9444	
							8.5345		3.2106
						9.2162		5.2156	
					9.1292		6.2184		2.3472
				8.4310		6.4321		3.6748	
			7.1912		5.9697		4.1421		1.5851
		5.5159		4.9647		3.9243		2.3062	
	3.4373		3.4748		3.1128		2.2881		0.9138
1.0189		1.5924		1.8212		1.6756		1.0939	
	-0.6552		0.0970		0.5427		0.6385		0.3235
		-1.9790		-1.0139		-0.3325		0.0228	
			-2.9552		-1.7590		-0.8247		-0.1947
				-3.5587		-2.1193		-0.9214	
					-3.8121		-2.1190		-0.6489
						-3.7043		-1.7521	
							-3.2611		-1.0466
								-2.4818	
									-1.3944

Time in Years   0.5   1   1.5   2   2.5   3   3.5   4   4.5

Exhibit H – The Pay Fixed Cumulative Value Lattice with an SFR of 7.4898% using the –25bps Term Structure

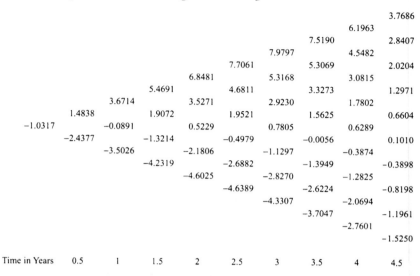

Time in Years	0.5	1	1.5	2	2.5	3	3.5	4	4.5

The swap value for the upward shift is $1.0189 per $100 notional principal and −$1.0317 for the downward shift. The respective percentage changes are then 1.0189% and −1.0317%.

We need the swap position to have a dollar duration of approximately the difference between the portfolio dollar duration and the target dollar duration which is $2,500,000. So the notional principal for the upward movement is

$$\$2,500,000/0.010189 = \$245,362,646$$

The notional principal for the downward movement is

$$\$2,500,000/0.010317 = \$242,318,503$$

The notional principal for the average is

$$\$2,500,000/[(0.010317 + 0.010189)/2] = \$243,831,073$$

d. The swap must have positive dollar duration so it must be a pay fixed swap.

2. a. The target dollar duration of the swap now needs to be

$$\$250,000,000 \times 10 \times 0.0025 = \$6,250,000$$

So the swap needs to add a dollar duration to the current position of −$1,875,000. Consequently, for the up move the notional principal of this swap is $184,021,985 and for the down move it is $181,738,878, and the average is $182,873,305.

b. The swap must have negative dollar duration so it must be a receive fixed swap

3. The first step is to produce the corresponding value lattices for the (2,3) swaption. Exhibits I, J, and K present the swap value lattices for a strike rate of 7% for each of the three term structures. Exhibits L, M, and N present the corresponding (2,3) pay fixed swaptions. So the change in swaption value for the 50 basis point shift is 0.86 (= 2.94 − 2.08) per $100 notional principal.

Exhibit I – Cumulative Swap Value Lattices for a Pay fixed Swap with an SFR of 7% using current Term Structure

0.5	1	1.5	2	2.5	3	3.5	4	4.5	
									4.2046
								7.0119	
							8.6745		3.2549
						9.4463		5.3293	
					9.4635		6.4207		2.4150
				8.8813		6.7382		3.8306	
			7.7678		6.3920		4.4019		1.6739
		6.2279		5.5140		4.3011		2.5002	
	4.2932		4.1605		3.6177		2.6006		1.0214
2.0270		2.4232		2.4638		2.1178		1.3224	
	0.3288		0.8860		1.1243		0.9990		0.4479
		−1.0356		−0.2844		0.1696		0.2823	
			−2.0697		−1.1068		−0.4208		−0.0554
				−2.7489		−1.5628		−0.6342	
					−3.0956		−1.6760		−0.4965
						−3.0986		−1.4402	
							−2.7832		−0.8826
								−2.1480	
									−1.2201

Time in Years   0.5   1   1.5   2   2.5   3   3.5   4   4.5

Exhibit J – Cumulative Swap Value Lattices for a Pay fixed Swap with an SFR of 7% using current Term Structure + 25bps

(0)	0.5	1	1.5	2	2.5	3	3.5	4	4.5
									4.4126
								7.3836	
							9.1780		3.4391
						10.0583		5.6609	
					10.1667		6.8729		2.5777
				9.6622		7.2905		4.1256	
			8.6161		7.0291		4.8062		1.8174
		7.1352		6.2237		4.7972		2.7618	
	5.2529		4.9333		4.1919		2.9609		1.1477
3.0333		3.2511		3.1051		2.5615		1.5537	
	1.2054		1.5858		1.6394		1.3189		0.5588
		−0.2849		0.2923		0.5649		0.4864	
			−1.4394		−0.6467		−0.1375		0.0418
				−2.2326		−1.2118		−0.4545	
					−2.6860		−1.4258		−0.4113
						−2.7877		−1.2823	
							−2.5627		−0.8080
								−2.0094	
									−1.1550

Time in Years   0.5   1   1.5   2   2.5   3   3.5   4   4.5

Exhibit K – Cumulative Swap Value Lattices for a Pay fixed Swap with an SFR of 7% using current Term Structure-25bps

(0)	0.5	1	1.5	2	2.5	3	3.5	4	4.5
									3.9958
								6.6382	
							8.1674		3.0700
						8.8291		4.9960	
					8.7537		5.9657		2.2517
				8.0923		6.1818		3.5344	
			6.9100		5.7496		3.9954		1.5301
		5.3098		4.7977		3.8018		2.2377	
	3.3218		3.3801		3.0393		2.2387		0.8949
1.0080		1.5868		1.8173		1.6716		1.0904	
	−0.5571		0.1802		0.6059		0.6778		0.3368
		−1.7931		−0.8651		−0.2277		0.0777	
			−2.7046		−1.5695		−0.7050		−0.1528
				−3.2682		−1.9153		−0.8143	
					−3.5071		−1.9269		−0.5818
						−3.4105		−1.5984	
							−3.0042		−0.9572
								−2.2868	
									−1.2853

Time in Years   0.5   1   1.5   2   2.5   3   3.5   4   4.5

Exhibit L – (3,2) Pay Fixed Swaption for the current term structure

				8.88
			6.89	
		5.16		5.51
	3.66		3.84	
2.48		2.43		2.46
	1.46		1.19	
		0.58		0.00
			0.00	
				0.00

| Time in Years | 0.50 | 1.00 | 1.50 | 2.00 |

Exhibit M – (3,2) Pay Fixed Swaption for the current term structure + 25bps

				9.66
			7.60	
		5.80		6.22
	4.22		4.49	
2.94		2.96		3.11
	1.85		1.64	
		0.86		0.29
			0.14	
				0.00

| Time in Years | 0.50 | 1.00 | 1.50 | 2.00 |

Exhibit N – (3,2) Pay Fixed Swaption for the current term structure-25bps

				8.09
			6.18	
		4.51		4.80
	3.13		3.19	
2.08		1.97		1.82
	1.16		0.88	
		0.43		0.00
			0.00	
				0.00

| Time in Years | 0.50 | 1.00 | 1.50 | 2.00 |

Appendix A
Theoretical Spot and Forward Rates

S pot rates and forward rates are critical inputs in the valuation of any financial instrument. Market participants often obtain these rates from the on-the-run yield curve for a particular issuer or market sector. In this appendix we will see how theoretical spot rates are obtained from the term structure of Treasury rates and how forward rates can be obtained from the theoretical spot rates. We will also see how the forward discount factor is obtained from the forward rates.

COMPUTING THE THEORETICAL SPOT RATES

The spot rate is a zero-coupon rate. The theoretical spot rates for Treasury securities represent the appropriate set of interest rates that should be used to value default-free cash flows. A default-free theoretical spot rate curve can be constructed from the observed Treasury yield curve. There are several methodologies that are used in practice. The particular methodology that we describe in this appendix is known as *bootstrapping*.

Bootstrapping begins with the yield curve for the on-the-run issues. In our illustration we will use the Treasury yield curve. In practice, the observed yields for the on-the-run Treasury coupon issues are not actually used. Instead, the coupon rate is adjusted so that the price of an issue would be par value. The adjusted on-the-run Treasury yield curve where the coupon issues are at par value and the coupon rate is therefore equal to the yield to maturity is called the *par yield curve*. For the 6-month and 1-year issues which are Treasury bills, the yields for these two issues are already spot rates.

Exhibit 1: Hypothetical Treasury Par Yield Curve

Period	Years	Annual Yield to Maturity (BEY) (%)*	Price	Spot Rate (BEY) (%)*
1	0.5	3.00	—	3.0000
2	1.0	3.30	—	3.3000
3	1.5	3.50	100.00	3.5053
4	2.0	3.90	100.00	3.9164
5	2.5	4.40	100.00	4.4376
6	3.0	4.70	100.00	4.7520
7	3.5	4.90	100.00	4.9622
8	4.0	5.00	100.00	5.0650
9	4.5	5.10	100.00	5.1701
10	5.0	5.20	100.00	5.2772
11	5.5	5.30	100.00	5.3864
12	6.0	5.40	100.00	5.4976
13	6.5	5.50	100.00	5.6108
14	7.0	5.55	100.00	5.6643
15	7.5	5.60	100.00	5.7193
16	8.0	5.65	100.00	5.7755
17	8.5	5.70	100.00	5.8331
18	9.0	5.80	100.00	5.9584
19	9.5	5.90	100.00	6.0863
20	10.0	6.00	100.00	6.2169

* The yield to maturity and the spot rate are annual rates. They are reported as bond-equivalent yields. To obtain the semiannual yield or rate, one half the annual yield or annual rate is used.

To illustrate bootstrapping, we will use the Treasury par yield curve shown in Exhibit 1. The par yield curve shown is for 20 Treasury securities and the longest maturity is 10 years. Our objective is to show how the values in the last column of the exhibit (labeled "Spot Rate") are obtained.

The basic principle underlying the methodology is that the value of a Treasury coupon security should be equal to the value of the package of zero-coupon Treasury securities that duplicates the coupon bond's cash flows. The resulting value will be an arbitrage-free value.

Consider the 6-month and 1-year Treasury securities in Exhibit 1. These two securities are Treasury bills and are issued as zero-coupon instruments. Therefore, the annualized yield (not the discount yield) of 3.00% for the 6-month Treasury security is equal to the 6-month spot rate. Similarly, for the 1-year Treasury security, the cited yield of 3.30% is the 1-year spot rate. Given these two spot rates, we can compute the spot rate for a theoretical 1.5-year zero-coupon Treasury. The value of a theoretical 1.5-year Treasury should equal the present value of the three cash flows from the 1.5-year coupon Treasury, where the yield used for discounting is the spot rate corresponding to the time of receipt of the cash flow. Using $100 as par, the cash flows for the 1.5-year coupon Treasury are:

$$
\begin{array}{llll}
0.5 \text{ year} & 0.035 \times \$100 \times 0.5 & = \$1.75 \\
1.0 \text{ year} & 0.035 \times \$100 \times 0.5 & = \$1.75 \\
1.5 \text{ years} & 0.035 \times \$100 \times 0.5 + 100 & = \$101.75
\end{array}
$$

The present value of the cash flows is then:

$$
\frac{1.75}{(1+z_1)^1} + \frac{1.75}{(1+z_2)^2} + \frac{101.75}{(1+z_3)^3}
$$

where

z_1 = one-half the annualized 6-month theoretical spot rate
z_2 = one-half the 1-year theoretical spot rate
z_3 = one-half the 1.5-year theoretical spot rate

Since the 6-month spot rate is 3% and the 1-year spot rate is 3.30%, we know that:

$$z_1 = 0.0150 \text{ and } z_2 = 0.0165$$

We can compute the present value of the 1.5-year coupon Treasury security as:

$$
\begin{aligned}
& \frac{1.75}{(1+z_1)^1} + \frac{1.75}{(1+z_2)^2} + \frac{101.75}{(1+z_3)^3} \\
& = \frac{1.75}{(1.015)^1} + \frac{1.75}{(1.0165)^2} + \frac{101.75}{(1+z_3)^3}
\end{aligned}
$$

Since the price of the 1.5-year coupon Treasury security is par value (see Exhibit 1), the following relationship must hold:[1]

---

[1] If we had not been working with a par yield curve, the equation would have been set equal to whatever the market price for the 1.5-year issue is.

$$\frac{1.75}{(1.015)^1} + \frac{1.75}{(1.0165)^2} + \frac{101.75}{(1+z_3)^3} = 100$$

We can solve for the theoretical 1.5-year spot rate as follows:

$$1.7241 + 1.6936 + \frac{101.75}{(1+z_3)^3} = 100$$

$$\frac{101.75}{(1+z_3)^3} = 96.5822$$

$$(1+z_3)^3 = \frac{101.75}{96.5822}$$

$$z_3 = 0.0175265 = 1.7527\%$$

Doubling this yield we obtain the bond-equivalent yield of 3.5053%, which is the theoretical 1.5-year spot rate. That rate is the rate that the market would apply to a 1.5-year zero-coupon Treasury security if, in fact, such a security existed. In other words, all Treasury cash flows to be received 1.5 years from now should be valued (i.e., discounted) at 3.5053%.

Given the theoretical 1.5-year spot rate, we can obtain the theoretical 2-year spot rate. The cash flows for the 2-year coupon Treasury in Exhibit 3 are:

0.5 year	$0.039 \times \$100 \times 0.5$	$= \$1.95$
1.0 year	$0.039 \times \$100 \times 0.5$	$= \$1.95$
1.5 years	$0.039 \times \$100 \times 0.5$	$= \$1.95$
2.0 years	$0.039 \times \$100 \times 0.5 + 100$	$= \$101.95$

The present value of the cash flows is then:

$$\frac{1.95}{(1+z_1)^1} + \frac{1.95}{(1+z_2)^2} + \frac{1.95}{(1+z_3)^3} + \frac{101.95}{(1+z_4)^4}$$

where z_4 = one-half the 2-year theoretical spot rate.

Since the 6-month spot rate, 1-year spot rate, and 1.5-year spot rate are 3.00%, 3.30%, and 3.5053%, respectively, then:

$$z_1 = 0.0150 \quad z_2 = 0.0165 \quad z_3 = 0.017527$$

Therefore, the present value of the 2-year coupon Treasury security is:

$$\frac{1.95}{(1.0150)^1} + \frac{1.95}{(1.0165)^2} + \frac{1.95}{(1.017527)^3} + \frac{101.95}{(1+z_4)^4}$$

Since the price of the 2-year coupon Treasury security is par, the following relationship must hold:

$$\frac{1.95}{(1.0150)^1} + \frac{1.95}{(1.0165)^2} + \frac{1.95}{(1.017527)^3} + \frac{101.95}{(1+z_4)^4} = 100$$

We can solve for the theoretical 2-year spot rate as follows:

$$\frac{101.95}{(1+z_4)^4} = 94.3407$$

$$(1+z_4)^4 = \frac{101.95}{94.3407}$$

$$z_4 = 0.019582 = 1.9582\%$$

Doubling this yield, we obtain the theoretical 2-year spot rate bond-equivalent yield of 3.9164%.

One can follow this approach sequentially to derive the theoretical 2.5-year spot rate from the calculated values of z_1, z_2, z_3, and z_4 (the 6-month-, 1-year-, 1.5-year-, and 2-year rates), and the price and coupon of the 2.5-year bond in Exhibit 1. Further, one could derive theoretical spot rates for the remaining 15 half-yearly rates.

The spot rates thus obtained are shown in the last column of Exhibit 1. They represent the term structure of default-free spot rates for maturities up to 10 years at the particular time to which the bond price quotations refer.

FORWARD RATES

From the theoretical spot rate curve, forward rates can be extrapolated. Examples of forward rates that can be calculated from the theoretical spot rate curve are the:

- 6-month forward rate six months from now
- 6-month forward rate three years from now
- 1-year forward rate one year from now
- 3-year forward rate two years from now
- 5-year forward rates three years from now

Since the forward rates are implicitly extrapolated from the theoretical spot rate curve, these rates are sometimes referred to as *implicit forward rates*. We begin by showing how to compute the 6-month forward rates. Then we explain how to compute any forward rate. Of course, the same framework is used in deriving 3-month forward rates from a yield curve that has yield each 0.25 years rather than each half year.

To illustrate the process of extrapolating 6-month forward rates, we will use the yield curve and corresponding spot rate curve from Exhibit 1. We will use a very simple arbitrage principle as we did to derive the spot rates. Specifically, if two investments have the same cash flows and have the same risk, they should have the same value.

Consider an investor who has a 1-year investment horizon and is faced with the following two alternatives:

- buy a 1-year Treasury bill, or
- buy a 6-month Treasury bill, and when it matures in six months buy another 6-month Treasury bill.

The investor will be indifferent toward the two alternatives if they produce the same return over the 1-year investment horizon. The investor knows the spot rate on the 6-month Treasury bill and the 1-year Treasury bill. However, he does not know what yield will be available on a 6-month Treasury bill that will be purchased six months from now. That is, he does not know the 6-month forward rate six months from now. Given the spot rates for the 6-month Treasury bill and the 1-year Treasury bill, the forward rate on a 6-month Treasury bill is the rate that equalizes the dollar return between the two alternatives.

To see how that rate can be determined, suppose that an investor purchased a 6-month Treasury bill for X. At the end of six months, the value of this investment would be:

$$X(1 + z_1)$$

Exhibit 2: Graphical Depiction of the Six-Month Forward Rate Six Months from Now

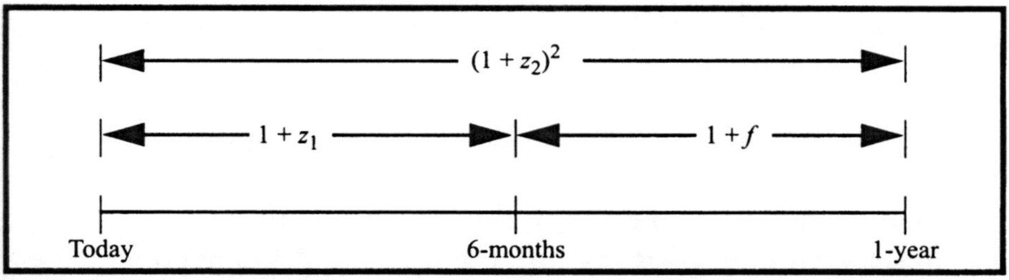

where z_1 is one-half the bond-equivalent yield (BEY) of the theoretical 6-month spot rate.

Let f represent one-half the forward rate (expressed as a BEY) on a 6-month Treasury bill available six months from now. If the investor were to rollover his investment by purchasing that bill at that time, then the future dollars available at the end of one year from the X investment would be:

$$X(1 + z_1)(1 + f)$$

Now consider the alternative of investing in a 1-year Treasury bill. If we let z_2 represent one-half the BEY of the theoretical 1-year spot rate, then the future dollars available at the end of one year from the X investment would be:

$$X(1 + z_2)^2$$

The reason that the squared term appears is that the amount invested is being compounded for two periods. (Recall that each period is six months.)

The two choices are depicted in Exhibit 2. Now we are prepared to analyze the investor's choices and what this says about forward rates. The investor will be indifferent toward the two alternatives confronting him if he makes the same dollar investment ($X) and receives the same future dollars from both alternatives at the end of one year. That is, the investor will be indifferent if:

$$X(1 + z_1)(1 + f) = X(1 + z_2)^2$$

Solving for f, we get:

$$f = \frac{(1 + z_2)^2}{(1 + z_1)} - 1$$

Doubling f gives the BEY for the 6-month forward rate six months from now.

We can illustrate the use of this formula with the theoretical spot rates shown in Exhibit 1. From that exhibit, we know that:

6-month bill spot rate = 0.030, therefore $z_1 = 0.0150$
1-year bill spot rate = 0.033, therefore $z_2 = 0.0165$

Substituting into the formula, we have:

$$f = \frac{(1.0165)^2}{(1.0150)} - 1 = 0.0180 = 1.8\%$$

Therefore, the 6-month forward rate six months from now is 3.6% (1.8% × 2) BEY.

Let's confirm our results. If $\$X$ is invested in the 6-month Treasury bill at 1.5% and the proceeds are then reinvested for six months at the 6-month forward rate of 1.8%, the total proceeds from this alternative would be:

$$X (1.015)(1.018) = 1.03327 \, X$$

Investment of $\$X$ in the 1-year Treasury bill at one-half the 1-year rate, 1.0165%, would produce the following proceeds at the end of one year:

$$X (1.0165)^2 = 1.03327 \, X$$

Both alternatives have the same payoff if the 6-month Treasury bill yield six months from now is 1.8% (3.6% on a BEY). This means that, if an investor is guaranteed a 1.8% yield (3.6% BEY) on a 6-month Treasury bill six months from now, he will be indifferent toward the two alternatives.

The same line of reasoning can be used to obtain the 6-month forward rate beginning at any time period in the future. For example, the following can be determined:

- the 6-month forward rate three years from now
- the 6-month forward rate five years from now

The notation that we use to indicate 6-month forward rates is $_1f_m$ where the subscript 1 indicates a 1-period (6-month) rate and the subscript m indicates the period beginning m periods from now. When m is equal to zero, this means the current rate. Thus, the first 6-month forward rate is simply the current 6-month spot rate. That is, $_1f_0 = z_1$.

The general formula for determining a 6-month forward rate is:

$$_1f_m = \frac{(1 + z_{m+1})^{m+1}}{(1 + z_m)^m} - 1$$

For example, suppose that the 6-month forward rate four years (eight 6-month periods) from now is sought. In terms of our notation, m is 8 and we seek $_1f_8$. The formula is then:

$$_1f_8 = \frac{(1 + z_9)^9}{(1 + z_8)^8} - 1$$

From Exhibit 1, since the 4-year spot rate is 5.065% and the 4.5-year spot rate is 5.1701%, z_8 is 2.5325% and z_9 is 2.58505%. Then,

$$_1f_8 = \frac{(1.0258505)^9}{(1.025325)^8} - 1 = 3.0064\%$$

Doubling this rate gives a 6-month forward rate four years from now of 6.01%

Exhibit 3 shows all of the 6-month forward rates for the Treasury yield curve and corresponding spot rate curve shown in Exhibit 1. The forward rates reported in Exhibit 3 are the annualized rates on a bond-equivalent basis. The set of these forward rates is called the *short-term forward-rate curve*.

Exhibit 3: Six-Month Forward Rates: The Short-Term Forward Rate Curve (Annualized Rates on a Bond-Equivalent Basis)

Notation	Forward Rate
$_1f_0$	3.00
$_1f_1$	3.60
$_1f_2$	3.92
$_1f_3$	5.15
$_1f_4$	6.54
$_1f_5$	6.33
$_1f_6$	6.23
$_1f_7$	5.79
$_1f_8$	6.01
$_1f_9$	6.24
$_1f_{10}$	6.48
$_1f_{11}$	6.72
$_1f_{12}$	6.97
$_1f_{13}$	6.36
$_1f_{14}$	6.49
$_1f_{15}$	6.62
$_1f_{16}$	6.76
$_1f_{17}$	8.10
$_1f_{18}$	8.40
$_1f_{19}$	8.72

Relationship between Spot Rates and Short-Term Forward Rates

Suppose an investor invests $\$X$ in a 3-year zero-coupon Treasury security. The total proceeds three years (six periods) from now would be:

$$X(1 + z_6)^6$$

The investor could instead buy a 6-month Treasury bill and reinvest the proceeds every six months for three years. The future dollars or dollar return will depend on the 6-month forward rates. Suppose that the investor can actually reinvest the proceeds maturing every six months at the calculated 6-month forward rates shown in Exhibit 3. At the end of three years, an investment of $\$X$ would generate the following proceeds:

$$X(1 + z_1)(1 + {}_1f_1)(1 + {}_1f_2)(1 + {}_1f_3)(1 + {}_1f_4(1 + {}_1f_5)$$

Since the two investments must generate the same proceeds at the end of four years, the two previous equations can be equated:

$$X(1 + z_6)^6 = X(1 + z_1)(1 + {}_1f_1)(1 + {}_1f_2)(1 + {}_1f_3)(1 + {}_1f_4)(1 + {}_1f_5)$$

Solving for the 3-year (6-period) spot rate, we have:

$$z_6 = [(1 + z_1)(1 + {}_1f_1)(1 + {}_1f_2)(1 + {}_1f_3)(1 + {}_1f_4)(1 + {}_1f_5)]^{1/6} - 1$$

This equation tells us that the 3-year spot rate depends on the current 6-month spot rate and the five 6-month forward rates. In fact, the right-hand side of this equation is a geometric average of the current 6-month spot rate and the five 6-month forward rates.

Let's use the values in Exhibits 1 and 3 to confirm this result. Since the 6-month spot rate in Exhibit 1 is 3%, z_1 is 1.5% and therefore[2]

$$z_6 = [(1.015)(1.018)(1.0196)(1.02577)(1.0327)(1.03165)]^{1/6} - 1$$
$$= 0.023761 = 2.3761\%$$

Doubling this rate gives 4.7522%. This agrees with the spot rate shown in Exhibit 1.

In general, the relationship between a T-period spot rate, the current 6-month spot rate, and the 6-month forward rates is as follows:

$$z_T = [(1 + z_1)(1 + {}_1f_1)(1 + {}_1f_2) ... (1 + {}_1f_{T-1})]^{1/T} - 1$$

Therefore, discounting at the forward rates will give the same present value as discounting at spot rates.

Valuation Using Forward Rates

Since a spot rate is simply a package of short-term forward rates, it will not make any difference whether we discount cash flows using spot rates or forward rates. That is, suppose that the cash flow in period T is $1. Then the present value of the cash flow can be found using the spot rate for period T as follows:

$$\text{PV of \$1 in } T \text{ periods } = \frac{1}{(1 + z_T)^T}$$

---

[2] Actually, the semiannual forward rates are based on annual rates calculated to more decimal places. For example, $f_{1,3}$ is 5.15% in Exhibit 3 but based on the more precise value, the semiannual rate is 2.577%.

Alternatively, since we know that

$$z_T = [(1+z_1)(1 + {}_1f_1)(1 + {}_1f_2) \cdots (1 + {}_1f_{T\text{-}1})]^{1/T} - 1$$

then, adding 1 to both sides of the equation,

$$(1 + z_T) = [(1+z_1)(1 + {}_1f_1)(1 + {}_1f_2) \cdots (1 + {}_1f_{T\text{-}1})]^{1/T}$$

Raising both sides of the equation to the T-th power we get:

$$(1 + z_T)^T = (1+z_1)(1 + {}_1f_1)(1 + {}_1f_2) \cdots (1 + {}_1f_{T\text{-}1})$$

Substituting the right-hand side of the above equation into the present value formula we get:

PV of $1 in T periods

$$= \frac{1}{(1 + z_1)(1 + {}_1f_1)(1 + {}_1f_2)\ldots(1 + {}_1f_{T-1})}$$

In practice, the present value of $1 in T periods is called the *forward discount factor for period T.*

For example, consider the forward rates shown in Exhibit 3. The forward discount rate for period 4 is found as follows:

$z_1 = 3\%/2 = 1.5\%$ ${}_1f_1 = 3.6\%/2 = 1.8\%$
${}_1f_2 = 3.92\%/2 = 1.958\%$ ${}_1f_3 = 5.15\%/2 = 2.577\%$

forward discount factor of $1 in 4 periods

$$= \frac{\$1}{(1.015)(1.018)(1.01958)(1.02577)} = 0.925369$$

To see that this is the same present value that would be obtained using the spot rates, note from Exhibit 1 that the 2-year spot rate is 3.9164%. Using that spot rate we find:

$$z_4 = 3.9164\%/2 = 1.9582\%$$

$$\text{PV of \$1 in 4 periods} = \frac{\$1}{(1.019582)^4} = 0.925361$$

Exhibit 4: Calculation of the Forward Discount Factor for Each Period

Periods	Years	Notation	Forward Rate*	0.5 × Forward Rate**	1 + Forward Rate	Forward Discount Factor
1	0.5	$_1f_0$	3.00%	1.5000%	1.01500	0.985222
2	1.0	$_1f_1$	3.60%	1.8002%	1.01800	0.967799
3	1.5	$_1f_2$	3.92%	1.9583%	1.01958	0.949211
4	2.0	$_1f_3$	5.15%	2.5773%	1.02577	0.925362
5	2.5	$_1f_4$	6.54%	3.2679%	1.03268	0.896079
6	3.0	$_1f_5$	6.33%	3.1658%	1.03166	0.868582
7	3.5	$_1f_6$	6.23%	3.1139%	1.03114	0.842352
8	4.0	$_1f_7$	5.79%	2.8930%	1.02893	0.818668
9	4.5	$_1f_8$	6.01%	3.0063%	1.03006	0.794775
10	5.0	$_1f_9$	6.24%	3.1221%	1.03122	0.770712
11	5.5	$_1f_{10}$	6.48%	3.2407%	1.03241	0.746520
12	6.0	$_1f_{11}$	6.72%	3.3622%	1.03362	0.722237
13	6.5	$_1f_{12}$	6.97%	3.4870%	1.03487	0.697901
14	7.0	$_1f_{13}$	6.36%	3.1810%	1.03181	0.676385
15	7.5	$_1f_{14}$	6.49%	3.2450%	1.03245	0.655126
16	8.0	$_1f_{15}$	6.62%	3.3106%	1.03311	0.634132
17	8.5	$_1f_{16}$	6.76%	3.3778%	1.03378	0.613412
18	9.0	$_1f_{17}$	8.10%	4.0504%	1.04050	0.589534
19	9.5	$_1f_{18}$	8.40%	4.2009%	1.04201	0.565767
20	10.0	$_1f_{19}$	8.72%	4.3576%	1.04358	0.542142

* The rates in this column are rounded to two decimal places.
** The rates in this column used the forward rates in the previous column carried to four decimal places.

The answer is the same as the forward discount factor (the slight difference is due to rounding).

Exhibit 4 shows the computation of the forward discount factor for each period based on the forward rates in Exhibit 3. Let's show how both the forward rates and the spot rates can be used to value a 2-year 6% coupon Treasury bond. The present value for each cash flow is found as follows using spot rates:

$$\frac{\text{cash flow for period } t}{(1 + z_t)^t}$$

The following table uses the spot rates in Exhibit 1 to value this bond:

Period	Spot rate BEY (%)	Semiannual spot rate (%)	Cash flow	PV of cash flow
1	3.0000	1.50000	3	2.955665
2	3.3000	1.65000	3	2.903397
3	3.5053	1.75266	3	2.847633
4	3.9164	1.95818	103	95.312278
			Total	104.018973

Based on the spot rates, the value of this bond is $104.0190.

Using forward rates and the forward discount factors the present value of the cash flow in period t is found as follows:

cash flow in period t × discount factor for period t

The following table uses the forward rates and the forward discount factors in Exhibit 4 to value this bond:

Period	Semiann. forward rate	Forward discount factor	Cash flow	PV of cash flow
1	1.5000%	0.985222	3	2.955665
2	1.8002%	0.967799	3	2.903397
3	1.9583%	0.949211	3	2.847633
4	2.5773%	0.925362	103	95.312278
			Total	104.018973

The present value of this bond using forward rates is $104.0190.

So, it does not matter whether one discounts cash flows by spot rates or forward rates, the value is the same.

Computing Any Forward Rate

Using spot rates, we can compute any forward rate. Using the same arbitrage arguments as used above to derive the 6-month forward rates, any forward rate can be obtained.

There are two elements to the forward rate. The first is when in the future the rate begins. The second is the length of time for the rate. For example, the 2-year forward rate 3 years from now means a rate three years from now for a length of two years. The notation used for a forward rate, f, will have two subscripts — one before f and one after f as shown below:

$$_tf_m$$

The subscript before f is t and is the length of time that the rate applies. The subscript after f is m and is when the forward rate begins. That is,

the length of time of the forward rate f when the forward rate begins

Remember our time periods are still 6-month periods. Given the above notation, here is what the following mean:

Notation	Interpretation for the forward rate
$_1f_{12}$	6-month (1-period) forward rate beginning 6 years (12 periods) from now
$_2f_8$	1-year (2-period) forward rate beginning 4 years (8 periods) from now
$_6f_4$	3-year (6-period) forward rate beginning 2 years (4 periods) from now
$_8f_{10}$	4-year (8-period) forward rate beginning 5 years (10 periods) from now

To see how the formula for the forward rate is derived, consider the following two alternatives for an investor who wants to invest for $m + t$ periods:

- buy a zero-coupon Treasury bond that matures in $m + t$ periods, or
- buy a zero-coupon Treasury bond that matures in m periods and invest the proceeds at the maturity date in a zero-coupon Treasury bond that matures in t periods.

The investor will be indifferent between the two alternatives if they produce the same return over the $m + t$ investment horizon.

For $100 invested in the first alternative, the proceeds for this investment at the horizon date assuming that the semiannual rate is z_{m+t} is

$$\$100 \left(1 + z_{m+t}\right)^{m+t}$$

For the second alternative, the proceeds for this investment at the end of m periods assuming that the semiannual rate is z_m is

$$\$100 \left(1 + z_m\right)^m$$

When the proceeds are received in m periods, they are reinvested at the forward rate, $_tf_m$, producing a value for the investment at the end of $m + t$ periods of

$$\$100 \, (1 + z_m)^m \, (1 + {}_t f_m)^t$$

For the investor to be indifferent to the two alternatives, the following relationship must hold:

$$\$100 \, (1 + z_{m+t})^{m+t} = \$100 \, (1 + z_m)^m \, (1 + {}_t f_m)^t$$

Solving for ${}_t f_m$ we get:

$$_t f_m = \left[\frac{(1 + z_{m+t})^{m+t}}{(1 + z_m)^m} \right]^{1/t} - 1$$

Notice that if t is equal to 1, the formula reduces to the 1-period (6-month) forward rate.

To illustrate, for the spot rates shown in Exhibit 1 suppose that an investor wants to know the 2-year forward rate three years from now. In terms of the notation, t is equal to 4 and m is equal to 6. Substituting for t and m into the equation for the forward rate we have:

$$_4 f_6 = \left[\frac{(1 + z_{10})^{10}}{(1 + z_6)^6} \right]^{1/4} - 1$$

This means that the following two spot rates are needed: z_6 (the 3-year spot rate) and z_{10} (the 5-year spot rate). From Exhibit 1 we know

z_6 (the 3-year spot rate) = 4.752%/2 = 0.02376
z_{10} (the 5-year spot rate) = 5.2772%/2 = 0.026386

then

$$_4 f_6 = \left[\frac{(1.026386)^{10}}{(1.02376)^6} \right]^{1/4} - 1 = 0.030338$$

Therefore, $_4 f_6$ is equal to 3.0338% and doubling this rate gives 6.0675% the forward rate on a bond-equivalent basis.

We can verify this result. Investing $100 for 10 periods at the spot rate of 2.6386% will produce the following value:

$$\$100\ (1.026386)^{10} = \$129.7499$$

By investing \$100 for 6 periods at 2.376% and reinvesting the proceeds for 4 periods at the forward rate of 3.030338% gives the same value

$$\$100\ (1.02376)^6\ (1.030338)^4 = \$129.75012$$

Interpretation of Forward Rates

The focus thus far was just on how to compute forward rates from spot rates based on arbitrage arguments. Now let's look at how forward rates should be interpreted. We will present two interpretations with a simple illustration.

Suppose that an investor has a 1-year investment horizon and has choice of investing in either a 1-year Treasury bill or a 6-month Treasury bill and rolling over the proceeds from the maturing 6-month issue in another 6-month Treasury bill. Since the Treasury bills are zero-coupon securities, the rates on them are spot rates and can be used to compute the 6-month forward rate six months from now. For example, if the 6-month Treasury bill rate is 5% and the 1-year Treasury bill rate is 5.6%, then the 6-month forward rate six months from now is 6.2%. To verify this, suppose an investor invests \$100 in a 1-year investment. The \$100 investment in a zero-coupon instrument will grow at a rate of 2.8% (one half 5.6%) for two 6-month periods to:

$$\$100\ (1.028)^2 = \$105.68$$

If \$100 is invested in a six month zero-coupon instrument at 2.5% (one-half 5%) and the proceeds reinvested at the 6-month forward rate of 3.1% (one-half 6.2%), the \$100 will grow to:

$$\$100\ (1.025)(1.031) = \$105.68$$

Thus, the 6-month forward rate generates the same future dollars for the \$100 investment at the end of 1 year.

One interpretation of the forward rate is that it is a "break-even rate." That is, a forward rate is the rate that will make an investor indifferent between investing for the full investment horizon and part of the investment horizon and rolling over the proceeds for the balance of the investment horizon. So, in our illustration, the forward rate of 6.2% can be interpreted as the break-even rate that will make an investment in a 6-month zero-coupon instrument with a yield of 5% rolled-over into another 6-month zero-coupon instrument equal to the yield on a 1-year zero-coupon instrument with a yield of 5.6%.

Similarly, a 2-year forward rate beginning four years from now can be interpreted as the break-even rate that will make an investor indifferent between investing in (1) a 4-year zero-coupon instrument at the 4-year spot rate and rolling over the investment for two more years in a zero-coupon instrument and (2) investing in a 6-year zero-coupon instrument at the 6-year spot rate.

A second interpretation of the forward rate is that it is a rate that allows the investor to lock in a rate for some future period. For example, consider once again our 1-year investment. If an investor purchases this instrument rather than the 6-month instrument, the investor has locked in a 6.2% rate six months from now regardless of how interest rates change six months from now. Similarly, in the case of a 6-year investment, by investing in a 6-year zero-coupon instrument rather than a 4-year zero-coupon instrument, the investor has locked in the 2-year zero-coupon rate four years from now. That locked in rate is the 2-year forward rate four years from now. The 1-year forward rate five years from now is the rate that is locked in by buying a 6-year zero-coupon instrument rather than investing in a 5-year zero-coupon instrument and reinvesting the proceeds at the end of five years in a 1-year zero-coupon instrument.

There is another interpretation of forward rates. Proponents of the pure expectations theory argue that forward rates reflect the "market's consensus" of future interest rates. They argue that forward rates can be used to predict future interest rates. A natural question about forward rates is then how well do they do at predicting future interest rates? Studies have demonstrated that forward rates do not do a good job at predicting future interest rates.[3] Then, why is it so important to understand forward rates? The reason is

[3] Eugene F. Fama, "Forward Rates as Predictors of Future Spot Rates," *Journal of Financial Economics* Vol. 3, No. 4, 1976, pp. 361-377.

that forward rates indicate how an investor's expectations must differ from the "break-even rate" or the "lock-in rate" when making an investment decision.

Thus, even if a forward rate may not be realized, forward rates can be highly relevant in deciding between two alternative investments. Specifically, if an investor's expectation about a rate in the future is less than the corresponding forward rate, then he would be better off investing now to lock in the forward rate.

Appendix B

Binomial Interest Rate Model

I n Chapter 5 we introduced the binomial interest rate lattice. As we explained, the construction of this lattice depends on the interest rate model used. In this appendix we will provide the technical details about the interest rate model used and how to construct the lattice.

The lattice construction begins with the following form for interest rate movements:

$$d\ln r = \theta dt + \sigma dz$$

where

θ = the drift rate of the short-term interest rate

σ = the volatility of $\ln r$

dz = a normally distributed random variable with a mean of zero and a variance of dt

This is a variation of the Kalotay, Williams, and Fabozzi model.[1] The objective is to create a lattice of interest rates such as in Exhibit 1 that produces the same prices as those in the market — hence no arbitrage exists between the model and the market.

It is easy to show that the discrete version of this model to match Exhibit 1 has the following form

$$r_{j, k+1} = r_{j, k} e^{\theta_k \tau + \sigma \sqrt{\tau}}$$

for an up move and

$$r_{j+1, k+1} = r_{j, k} e^{\theta_k \tau - \sigma \sqrt{\tau}}$$

for a down move. $\tau \ (= t_k - t_{k-1})$ is the time step in the lattice — in our case this is 0.5 years or 6 months. σ is the assumed volatility of $\ln r$, and θ_k is the drift rate of the short rate at t_k.

---

[1] Andrew J, Kalotay, George O. Williams, and Frank J. Fabozzi, "A Model for the Valuation of Bonds with Embedded Options," *Financial Analysts Journal* (May-June 1993), pp. 35-46.

Exhibit 1: A Binomial Short Rate Tree

$$
\begin{array}{ccccccc}
 & & & & & r_{1,3} & \\
 & & & & r_{1,2} & & \\
 & & & r_{1,1} & & r_{2,3} & \\
 & & r_{1,0} & & r_{2,2} & & \\
 & & & r_{2,1} & & r_{3,3} & \\
 & & & & r_{3,2} & & \\
 & & & & & r_{4,3} & \\
\end{array}
$$

$$t_0 \quad t_1 \quad t_2 \quad t_3$$

For example, suppose we have the term structure used throughout the book using rounded semiannual periods and $\sigma = 10\%$. We will assume that these semiannual rates are those obtained from the appropriate interest rate market (in this case the LIBOR market). We see that $r_{1,0} = 6.965\%$. We then need to compute the rates for $r_{1,1}$ and $r_{2,1}$. Using the relationship between forward rates and spot rates (see Appendix A for details), it is easy to show that the 1-year spot rate is 6.9662%. This spot rate produces a semiannual discount factor of 0.93382. The trick then is to find the values of $r_{1,1}$ and $r_{2,1}$ such that when combined with $r_{1,0}$ they give us the same discount factor.

Note that the ratio of the up move to the down move $(r_{1,1}/r_{2,1})$ is simply $\exp 2\sigma\sqrt{\tau}$. So the only unknown to solve for is θ_k. To compute $r_{1,1}$ and $r_{2,1}$ we must solve for θ_k.

To ensure no arbitrage we equate the price from the spot rate term structure (the discount factor) with the price from the binomial tree which gives us:

$$
P_2 = \frac{1}{(1 + R_2\tau)^2} = \frac{qp_{1,1} + (1-q)p_{2,1}}{1 + r_{1,0}\tau} = 0.93382
$$

Substituting in the forward discount factors $p_{1,1} = 1/(1 + r_{j,1}\tau)$ for $j = 1,2$ we obtain

$$
P_2(1 + r_{1,0}\tau)(1 + r_{1,1}\tau)(1 + r_{2,1}\tau) - q(1 + r_{2,1}\tau) \\
- (1-q)(1 + r_{1,1}\tau) = 0
$$

This is simply the previous equation rearranged. It is the no arbitrage equation that needs to be solved for θ_1. We let $r_{1,0} = R_1$. This equation can now be solved for θ_1. Using our values of $r_{1,0} = 6.965\%$, $\sigma = 10\%$, $R_2 = 6.9662\%$, and $q = 0.5$, we get $\theta_1 = -0.3938457\%$. Using this value (within rounding), we get $r_{1,1} = 7.461\%$ and $r_{2,1} = 6.477\%$. Moving beyond two periods produces an iterative process and demands a numerical search routine to compute the value of θ_k. However, the algorithm is relatively straightforward to create since there is only one unknown at each time step, θ_k.

Since θ_k is the only unknown and we know one of the rates at a given period, we can use that rate to compute all of the other rates. Typically, we compute the lowest rate at a given period and use that to compute the other rates. We denote the lowest rate at period t as $r_{t+1,t}$ as shown in Exhibit 1.

Appendix C

Valuation of Swaps Using the Trinomial Approach

I n this appendix we show how to use a trinomial interest rate lattice to value swap structures. We begin with a brief discussion of how a trinomial interest rate model is created. We then present the 5-year semiannual trinomial interest rate lattice using the same set of interest rates used throughout the book and explain how to use that lattice to value each structure introduced in the book. We will show that the values are all the same for those swap structures that are not dependent on the characteristics of the interest rate model (plain vanilla swaps with constant or varying notional principal). The complex swap structures (swaptions and forward start swaps) will have different values due to the different characteristics incorporated in the trinomial interest rate model compared to the binomial interest rate model discussed in Appendix B. This is a critical point. Since the value of some swap structures depends on the underlying interest rate model, users of these models need to be aware of the underlying interest rate model.

THE TRINOMIAL LATTICE

The trinomial model begins with a similar relationship as described for the binomial model:

$$d \ln r = (\theta - \phi \ln r)dt + \sigma dz \tag{1}$$

where

θ = the drift rate of the short-term interest rate

ϕ = the mean reversion term for the short-term interest rate

σ = the volatility of $\ln r$

dz = a normally distributed random variable with a mean of zero and a variance of dt

The mean reversion term allows the model to explicitly capture an important characteristic of interest rates. Many studies have shown that over time interest rates tend to increase when they are low and decrease when they are high. To better see this, equation (1) can be expressed as:

$$d \ln r = \phi(\mu - \ln r)dt + \sigma dz \tag{2}$$

where μ is equal to $\exp(\theta/\phi)$ and is interpreted as the *target rate of interest rates*.

Equation (2) allows us to more easily identify mean reversion. Notice as rates increase ($\ln r$ increases) above the target rate (μ), the first term in equation (2) is negative indicating that the change in rates will tend to be negative (decreasing rates) and when rates decrease below the target rate the change tends to be positive. When rates are equal to the target rate the average change in rates is zero. The ϕ term dictates the magnitude of these changes and is called *the speed of mean reversion factor*.

In order to use equation (1) within the trinomial framework, we first need to put it in a discretized form. That is, our time increments are not continuous as implied by equations (1) and (2), but rather in discrete increments. In our examples this has been either 0.25 or 0.5 years. Doing this results in the trinomial framework shown in Exhibit 1. The corresponding equations are:

$$r_{j, k+1} = r_{j, k} e^{(\theta_k - \phi \ln(r_{j, k}))\tau + \sigma\sqrt{\tau}} \tag{3a}$$

for an up move and

$$r_{j+2, k+1} = r_{j, k} e^{(\theta_k - \phi \ln(r_{j, k}))\tau - \sigma\sqrt{\tau}} \tag{3b}$$

for a down move and

$$r_{j+1, k+1} = r_{j, k} e^{(\theta_k - \phi \ln(r_{j, k}))\tau} \tag{3c}$$

for a middle move.[1]

---

[1] In more advanced versions of this model the mean reversion term and the volatility term can change throughout the lattice. For our purposes here we have used a simpler version since our objective is swap and swaption valuation and not term structure modeling. Regardless of the model used the valuation framework is the same.

Exhibit 1: A Trinomial Short Rate Tree with Recombination

$$
\begin{array}{ccccc}
 & & & & r_{1,4} \\
 & & & r_{1,2}\;\; r_{2,4} & \\
 & & r_{1,1}\;\; r_{2,2}\;\; r_{3,4} & & \\
 & r_{1,0}\;\; r_{2,1}\;\; r_{3,2}\;\; r_{4,4} & & & \\
 & r_{3,1}\;\; r_{4,2}\;\; r_{5,4} & & & \\
 & & r_{5,2}\;\; r_{6,4} & & \\
 & & & r_{7,4} & \\
\end{array}
$$

$$
\begin{array}{cccc}
t_0 & t_1 & t_2 & t_3
\end{array}
$$

As in the binomial model, the only unknown at each time step is θ_k since the ratio of the up and down move is a constant, exp $(2\sigma\sqrt{\tau})$. Also note that the notation is the same as used for the binomial interest rate model.

In order to compute the rates we proceed in the same manner as in the binomial model, except that we have one more branch to include in the first period no-arbitrage equation. This equation is:

$$
P_2 = \frac{1}{(1 + R_2\tau)^2} = \frac{q_1 P_{1,1} + q_2 P_{2,1} + q_3 P_{3,1}}{1 + r_{1,0}\tau} \tag{4}
$$

where the probabilities (q) must sum to one. In this model we set the up and down probabilities equal, $q_1 = q_3 = \frac{1}{6}$, and the middle move, $q_2 = \frac{2}{3}$. This ensures symmetry in our lattice. Again note that $p_{j,1} = 1/(1 + r_{j,1}\tau)$ for $j = 1, 2,$ and 3 (instead of 1 and 2 as in the binomial lattice). Equation (4) then becomes:

$$
\begin{aligned}
&P_2(1 + r_{1,0}\tau)(1 + r_{1,1}\tau)(1 + r_{2,1}\tau)(1 + r_{3,1}\tau) \\
&\quad - q_1(1 + r_{2,1}\tau)(1 + r_{3,1}\tau) - q_2(1 + r_{1,1}\tau)(1 + r_{3,1}\tau) \\
&\quad - q_3(1 + r_{1,1}\tau)(1 + r_{3,1}\tau) = 0
\end{aligned}
$$

Again, realizing that θ_1 is the only unknown. We let $r_{1,0} = R_1$. This equation can now be solved for θ_1. Using our values of $r_{1,0} = 6.965\%$, $\sigma = 10\%$, $R_2 = 6.9662\%$, $\phi = 5\%$, $\tau = 0.5$, $q_1 = q_3 = \frac{1}{6}$, and $q_2 = \frac{2}{3}$ we get a $\theta_1 = -12.9077\%.$[2] Using this value (within rounding) we get an $r_{1,2} = 7.491\%$, $r_{2,2} = 6.979\%$, and $r_{3,2} = 6.503\%$.

---

[2] Note that this is much larger than the term we computed in the binomial model. This is due to the mean reversion term. If we set the mean reversion term to zero, we get a much smaller value.

Exhibit 2: Semiannual No Arbitrage Trinomial Interest Rate Lattice

SFR==>	7.0513%								13.217%
								12.338%	12.315%
							11.441%	11.496%	11.474%
						10.677%	10.660%	10.711%	10.709%
					9.907%	9.948%	9.932%	9.998%	9.996%
				9.248%	9.231%	9.269%	9.271%	9.332%	9.346%
			8.591%	8.617%	8.601%	8.652%	8.653%	8.725%	8.739%
		8.042%	8.004%	8.029%	8.028%	8.075%	8.091%	8.158%	8.184%
	7.491%	7.493%	7.458%	7.494%	7.493%	7.550%	7.565%	7.640%	7.665%
6.965%	6.979%	6.981%	6.961%	6.995%	7.006%	7.059%	7.085%	7.156%	7.191%
	6.503%	6.516%	6.497%	6.540%	6.550%	6.612%	6.635%	6.713%	6.745%
		6.082%	6.075%	6.115%	6.135%	6.192%	6.225%	6.297%	6.338%
			5.680%	5.727%	5.746%	5.809%	5.839%	5.917%	5.955%
				5.364%	5.390%	5.449%	5.487%	5.559%	5.604%
					5.056%	5.120%	5.155%	5.232%	5.274%
						4.811%	4.851%	4.923%	4.971%
							4.565%	4.640%	4.685%
								4.373%	4.422%
									4.174%
Time in Years 0.5	1.0	1.5	2.0	2.5	3.0	3.5	4.0	4.5	

Moving beyond two periods demands a numerical algorithm. However, the algorithm is relatively straightforward to create since there is only one unknown at each time step, θ_k, since the ratios of each up and down rate are always constant. We suggest using the bisection method as the numerical search routine once the algorithm is developed.

Using the same term structure as in Chapter 2, a volatility of 10% and a mean reversion of 5%, we compute the 5-year semiannual trinomial lattice shown in Exhibit 2. Notice that the periods at 0.5 years match the rates computed earlier. Once the tree is created the valuation process is almost identical to that developed for the binomial interest rate lattice.

A PLAIN VANILLA SWAP USING THE TRINOMIAL FRAMEWORK

In this section we will explain how to value a plain vanilla swap using the trinomial lattice.

Computing the Swap Cash Flows Using a Trinomial Lattice

The swap cash flows in the trinomial framework are found in the same way as in the binomial framework. The only difference is that there are more interest rates to compute corresponding cash flows. Following the same procedure as in the binomial framework, the cash flows for a pay fixed swap are found as follows:

$$(F_{i,j-1} - \text{SFR}) \times \text{NP} \times 0.5$$

or for a receive fixed swap as follows:

$$(\text{SFR} - F_{i,j-1}) \times \text{NP} \times 0.5$$

For swap valuation either will work. $F_{i,j-1}$ is the rate corresponding to the floating rate at node $(i, j-1)$ that dictates the arrears payment at j, NP is the notional principal which can change to whatever value is necessary (they are all constant and equal to $100 for this plain vanilla swap), and the 0.5 is the day count (semiannual in this case, 0.25 for quarterly, and so on).

Using the lattice from Exhibit 2 and the swap fixed rate of 7.0513%, it is straightforward to compute the cash flows. For example, within rounding, the upper most cash flow at year 5 is found in the following manner:

$$(13.2170\% - 7.0513\%) \times \$100 \times 0.5 = \$3.083$$

Repeat this at each node in the lattice and we can create the corresponding cash flow lattice to Exhibit 2. Exhibit 3 illustrates the cash flow lattice.

COMPUTING THE CUMULATIVE SWAP VALUE LATTICE USING A TRINOMIAL LATTICE

Using the cash flow lattice (Exhibit 3), we now need to create the swap valuation lattice. Exhibit 4 presents the results. Just like in the binomial framework, each node presents the present value of all the nodes that take place after it. For example, let's consider the middle node at time 3.5, 0.135. This represents the cumulative present value of all the cash flows that feed into that node plus the cash flow that corresponds to that node. To clearly illustrate the point let's perform the following backward induction exercise to see how we obtain the value of 0.135.

Exhibit 3: Swap Cash Flow Lattice with a Swap Fixed Rate of 7.0513%

0.5	1.0	1.5	2.0	2.5	3.0	3.5	4.0	4.5	5.0
									3.083
								2.643	2.632
							2.195	2.222	2.211
						1.813	1.804	1.830	1.829
					1.428	1.448	1.441	1.473	1.472
				1.099	1.090	1.109	1.110	1.140	1.147
			0.770	0.783	0.775	0.800	0.801	0.837	0.844
		0.495	0.476	0.489	0.488	0.512	0.520	0.553	0.566
	0.220	0.221	0.203	0.221	0.221	0.249	0.257	0.294	0.307
-0.043	-0.036	-0.035	-0.045	-0.028	-0.023	0.004	0.017	0.052	0.070
	-0.274	-0.268	-0.277	-0.256	-0.250	-0.220	-0.208	-0.169	-0.153
		-0.485	-0.488	-0.468	-0.458	-0.430	-0.413	-0.377	-0.357
			-0.686	-0.662	-0.653	-0.621	-0.606	-0.567	-0.548
				-0.844	-0.831	-0.801	-0.782	-0.746	-0.724
					-0.998	-0.966	-0.948	-0.910	-0.889
						-1.120	-1.100	-1.064	-1.040
							-1.243	-1.206	-1.183
								-1.339	-1.315
									-1.439

Time in Years   0.5   1.0   1.5   2.0   2.5   3.0   3.5   4.0   4.5   5.0

Exhibit 4: Cumulative Swap Valuation Lattice with an SFR of 7.0513%

	0.5	1	1.5	2	2.5	3	3.5	4	4.5
									2.892
								4.829	2.479
							5.947	4.084	2.091
						6.419	4.938	3.388	1.736
					6.321	5.193	3.992	2.743	1.402
				5.765	4.919	4.043	3.112	2.140	1.096
			4.794	4.216	3.600	2.969	2.288	1.580	0.808
		3.494	3.124	2.757	2.366	1.962	1.521	1.057	0.544
	1.886	1.720	1.548	1.389	1.207	1.022	0.803	0.572	0.296
0.000	0.026	0.046	0.069	0.103	0.124	0.141	0.135	0.117	0.067
	-1.731	-1.528	-1.325	-1.103	-0.894	-0.682	-0.491	-0.304	-0.148
		-3.012	-2.632	-2.236	-1.846	-1.453	-1.074	-0.699	-0.346
			-3.862	-3.297	-2.739	-2.172	-1.620	-1.066	-0.532
				-4.294	-3.574	-2.847	-2.129	-1.409	-0.704
					-4.358	-3.477	-2.606	-1.728	-0.866
						-4.068	-3.050	-2.028	-1.015
							-3.467	-2.306	-1.156
								-2.568	-1.286
									-1.409

Time in Years   0.5   1   1.5   2   2.5   3   3.5   4   4.5

The values at year 4.5 are simply the discounted values of the cash flows at year 5.0:

$$0.566/(1+8.184\%/2) = 0.544$$
$$0.307/(1+7.665\%/2) = 0.296$$
$$-0.070/(1+7.191\%/2) = 0.067$$
$$-0.153/(1+6.745\%/2) = -0.148$$
$$-0.357/(1+6.338\%/2) = -0.346$$

The values at year 4.0 are going to be the discounted values of the values at year 4.5 plus the discounted value of arrears cash flows that take place at year 4.5. In other words, these are the cumulative swap values at year 4.0. Again using Exhibits 2 and 3, these values are found by using the following equation:

$$SV_j = \frac{q_u \times SV_{u,\,j+1} + q_m \times SV_{m,\,j+1} + q_d \times SV_{d,\,j+1} + CF_{j+1}}{\left(1 + \dfrac{r_j}{2}\right)} \quad (5)$$

where

$SV_{u,m,d}$ = swap values for the up, middle, and down states, respectively, relative to the node being evaluated

$q_{u,m,d}$ = corresponding probabilities for the up, middle, and down states, respectively

r_j = the interest rate that corresponds to the node being evaluated

CF_{j+1} = the arrears cash flow at the j+1 period due to the interest rate at j, r_j.

Applying equation (5) at year 4.0:

$$(0.1667 \times 0.544 + 0.667 \times 0.296 + 0.1667 \times 0.067 + 0.294)/$$
$$(1 + 7.640\%/2) = 0.572$$

$$(0.1667 \times 0.296 + 0.667 \times 0.067 - 0.1667 \times 148 + 0.052)/$$
$$(1 + 7.156\%/2) = 0.117$$

$$(0.1667 \times 0.067 - 0.667 \times 0.148 - 0.1667 \times 0.346 - 0.169)/$$
$$(1 + 6.713\%/2) = -0.304$$

These are then the $S_{u,m,d}$ feeding into the middle node at year 3.5. We substitute these into equation (5) along with the arrears cash flow to get:

$$(0.1667 \times 0.572 + 0.667 \times 0.117 - 0.1667 \times 0.304 + 0.017)/$$
$$(1 + 7.085\%/2) = 0.135$$

It is easy to see that the trinomial lattice approach is identical to the binomial lattice approach except for the number of branches and their respective probabilities. Iterating on the swap fixed rate results in a swap fixed rate of 7.0513% just like in the binomial lattice approach. This can be seen in Exhibit 3 where the incipient node has a value of zero, indicating that the net present value of the swap is zero.

AMORTIZING AND ACCRETING SWAPS USING THE TRINOMIAL FRAMEWORK

Exhibits 5 through 8 represent the cash flow and swap value lattices for amortizing and accreting swaps, respectively. The process here is the same as for the plain vanilla swap just presented except that when creating the cash flow lattice we allow for the notional principal to vary at each time step, j. The procedure here is no different than in the binomial framework.

Specifically, the cash flows are now based on the interest rate lattice in Exhibit 2, the varying notional principal (NP_j) shown in the top row of Exhibits 5 and 7, and the swap fixed rate (SFR). The cash flow equations are the same as for the plain vanilla swap and are

$$(F_{i,j-1} - SFR) \times NP_j \times 0.5 \text{ for a pay fixed swap}$$

$$\text{or } (SFR - F_{i,j-1}) \times NP_j \times 0.5 \text{ for a receive fixed swap}$$

For swap valuation either will work. $F_{i,j-1}$ is the rate corresponding to the floating rate at node $(i, j-1)$ that dictates the arrears payment at j, NP_j is the notional principal at time j that corresponds the cash flow at time j (the top rows in Exhibits 5 and 7), and the 0.5 is the daycount (semiannual in this case, 0.25 for quarterly, and so on) approximation. Of course, the varying notional principal can be based on anything — perhaps a PSA based prepayment formula or a varying notional principal as in a roller coaster swap.

Exhibit 5: Trinomial Pay Fixed Swap Cash Flow Lattice for an Amortizing Swap with an SFR = 7.011%

100.00	90.00	80.00	70.00	60.00	50.00	40.00	30.00	20.00	10.00
0.5	1	1.5	2	2.5	3	3.5	4	4.5	5
									0.310
								0.533	0.265
							0.664	0.448	0.223
						0.733	0.547	0.370	0.185
					0.724	0.587	0.438	0.299	0.149
				0.671	0.555	0.452	0.339	0.232	0.117
			0.553	0.482	0.397	0.328	0.246	0.171	0.086
		0.412	0.347	0.305	0.254	0.213	0.162	0.115	0.059
	0.216	0.192	0.156	0.145	0.120	0.108	0.083	0.063	0.033
-0.023	-0.015	-0.012	-0.018	-0.005	-0.001	0.010	0.011	0.014	0.009
	-0.229	-0.198	-0.180	-0.142	-0.115	-0.080	-0.056	-0.030	-0.013
		-0.372	-0.328	-0.269	-0.219	-0.164	-0.118	-0.071	-0.034
			-0.466	-0.385	-0.317	-0.241	-0.176	-0.109	-0.053
				-0.494	-0.405	-0.312	-0.229	-0.145	-0.070
					-0.489	-0.378	-0.278	-0.178	-0.087
						-0.440	-0.324	-0.209	-0.102
							-0.367	-0.237	-0.116
								-0.264	-0.129
									-0.142

Exhibit 6: Trinomial Cumulative Swap Valuation Lattice for a Pay Fixed Amortizing Swap with an SFR = 7.011%

Time in Years	0.5	1	1.5	2	2.5	3	3.5	4	4.5
									0.291
								0.737	0.250
							1.220	0.624	0.211
						1.659	1.013	0.518	0.175
					1.971	1.342	0.819	0.420	0.142
				2.110	1.532	1.044	0.639	0.328	0.112
			2.012	1.540	1.119	0.767	0.471	0.244	0.083
		1.659	1.306	1.005	0.736	0.508	0.315	0.164	0.056
	1.000	0.813	0.644	0.507	0.377	0.268	0.168	0.091	0.031
0.000	0.013	0.020	0.026	0.039	0.042	0.043	0.033	0.022	0.009
	-0.913	-0.722	-0.553	-0.396	-0.271	-0.167	-0.094	-0.041	-0.013
		-1.417	-1.094	-0.804	-0.563	-0.363	-0.211	-0.101	-0.033
			-1.601	-1.184	-0.836	-0.545	-0.322	-0.156	-0.051
				-1.541	-1.090	-0.716	-0.424	-0.208	-0.068
					-1.329	-0.875	-0.520	-0.256	-0.085
						-1.024	-0.610	-0.301	-0.100
							-0.693	-0.343	-0.114
								-0.382	-0.127
									-0.139

Exhibit 7: Trinomial Swap Cash Flow Lattice for a Pay Fixed Accreting Swap with an SFR = 7.067%

100.00	110.00	120.00	130.00	140.00	150.00	160.00	170.00	180.00	190.00
0.5	1	1.5	2	2.5	3	3.5	4	4.5	5
									5.842
								4.744	4.985
							3.718	3.986	4.186
						2.888	3.054	3.279	3.460
					2.130	2.305	2.435	2.637	2.782
				1.527	1.622	1.761	1.873	2.038	2.165
			0.990	1.085	1.150	1.267	1.348	1.492	1.587
		0.584	0.609	0.673	0.720	0.806	0.869	0.981	1.061
	0.233	0.255	0.254	0.298	0.319	0.386	0.422	0.515	0.568
-0.051	-0.048	-0.052	-0.069	-0.051	-0.046	-0.007	0.015	0.079	0.117
	-0.311	-0.331	-0.371	-0.369	-0.388	-0.365	-0.367	-0.320	-0.306
		-0.591	-0.645	-0.667	-0.700	-0.700	-0.717	-0.693	-0.693
			-0.902	-0.939	-0.991	-1.007	-1.044	-1.036	-1.057
				-1.193	-1.258	-1.295	-1.344	-1.357	-1.390
					-1.508	-1.558	-1.626	-1.652	-1.704
						-1.805	-1.884	-1.930	-1.992
							-2.127	-2.185	-2.264
								-2.425	-2.513
									-2.749

Exhibit 8: Trinomial Cumulative Swap Valuation Lattice an Accreting Swap with an SFR = 7.067%

	0.5	1	1.5	2	2.5	3	3.5	4	4.5
									5.480
								8.898	4.696
							10.646	7.522	3.959
						11.146	8.835	6.236	3.284
					10.638	9.013	7.137	5.043	2.650
				9.388	8.273	7.010	5.557	3.928	2.068
			7.550	6.860	6.048	5.139	4.077	2.894	1.521
		5.310	4.914	4.477	3.963	3.383	2.699	1.927	1.019
	2.761	2.607	2.425	2.240	2.004	1.743	1.408	1.029	0.547
0.000	0.027	0.052	0.083	0.133	0.171	0.206	0.207	0.189	0.113
	-2.561	-2.357	-2.125	-1.843	-1.552	-1.230	-0.919	-0.590	-0.296
		-4.630	-4.199	-3.701	-3.164	-2.576	-1.967	-1.320	-0.672
			-6.153	-5.443	-4.677	-3.833	-2.949	-1.998	-1.026
				-7.082	-6.093	-5.012	-3.864	-2.633	-1.352
					-7.423	-6.113	-4.722	-3.224	-1.660
						-7.146	-5.521	-3.778	-1.944
							-6.272	-4.293	-2.212
								-4.777	-2.459
									-2.693
Time in Years	0.5	1	1.5	2	2.5	3	3.5	4	4.5

The corresponding swap values are shown in Exhibits 6 and 8. Notice that with a SFR of 7.011% the value of the amortizing swap is zero per $100 of notional for a pay fixed swap. We iterated on SFR to find that the correct SFR is 7.011%. Similarly, the SFR for the accreting swap turns out to be 7.067%. Both of these values are the same as those obtained using the binomial and traditional methods. Only the mechanics have changed moving from a binomial lattice to a trinomial lattice.

As with the other approaches note that for the amortizing swap the SFR decreased and for the accreting swap it increased relative to the plain vanilla swap. This is a result of both the time value of money and how cash flows are weighted. In a plain vanilla swap the SFR will be the geometric average of the forward rates or the rate that produces a zero value for the swap. With increasing notional principal (accreting) the SFR must increase relative to the plain vanilla swap to retain a zero value for the swap; conversely for the decreasing notional principal (amortizing) swap relative to the plain vanilla swap. Simple net present value analysis shows this result.

VALUING FORWARD START SWAPS USING THE TRINOMIAL FRAMEWORK

We now present how the trinomial method can be used to value and evaluate the forward start swap. The procedure is directly analogous to the binomial development. The difference lies in how to probability weight each node in the lattice. Remember that in the binomial framework computing the probabilities was a relatively easy task. Here it is not so easy. However, once the probabilities are computed, the process is the same as in the binomial framework.

The Trinomial Probability Lattice

Exhibit 9 shows the probability tree associated with computing the forward start swaps. In this section we present how to compute the probabilities of each node. Unlike the binomial lattice where we gave a simple formula, here we spare the reader the algebra and outline the simple procedure used. The transition probabilities for our simple form of the trinomial tree are ⅙ for the up state, ⅔ for the middle state, and ⅙ for the down state throughout the trinomial tree. In order to illustrate how the probability of each node in the tree is computed we use the same convention used in the binomial lattice. Each node in the tree will be identified by two indices: i and j; i stands for the number of vertical down steps from the top node at each time step in the tree and j stands for the number of periods (time steps) from the current time. As with the binomial, both indices start at zero. By doing it this way each node in the tree is uniquely defined.

The following example illustrates this convention for a 3-step tree using our (i,j) notation:

$$
\begin{array}{cccc}
 & & & (0,3) \\
 & & (0,2) & (1,3) \\
 & (0,1) & (1,2) & (2,3) \\
(0,0) & (1,1) & (2,2) & (3,3) \\
 & (2,1) & (3,2) & (4,3) \\
 & & (4,2) & (5,3) \\
 & & & (6,3)
\end{array}
$$

The probabilities for the first step of the tree are therefore:

$$
1 \quad
\begin{array}{c}
⅙ \\
⅔ \\
⅙
\end{array}
$$

The probabilities for all successive nodes can be obtained from the immediately preceding nodes using the following formula:

$$
\text{Prob}(i,j) = q_d(i-2, j-1) \times \text{Prob}(i-2, j-1) + q_m(i-1, j-1) \\
\times \text{Prob}(i-1, j-1) + q_u(i, j-1) \times \text{Prob}(i, j-1)
$$

where q_u represents the up move from the previous period to the current node, q_m represents the middle move from the previous period to the current node, and q_d represents the down move from the previous period to the current node. Note that these probabilities do not have to be the same throughout the tree. Alternative models allow the probabilities to change with both i and j. In our trinomial lattice, however, they are the same throughout the tree so this equation becomes:

$$
\text{Prob}(i,j) = ⅙ \times \text{Prob}(i-2, j-1) + ⅔ \times \text{Prob}(i-1, j-1) \\
+ ⅙ \times \text{Prob}(i, j-1)
$$

Exhibit 9: Trinomial Probability Lattice

n=0	n=1	n=2	n=3	n=4	n=5	n=6	n=7	n=8	n=9
									0.0000001
								0.0000006	0.0000036
							0.0000036	0.0000191	0.0000580
						0.0000214	0.0001000	0.0002715	0.0005620
					0.0001286	0.0005144	0.0012253	0.0022672	0.0036044
				0.0007716	0.0025720	0.0052726	0.0086020	0.0122861	0.0161037
			0.0046296	0.0123457	0.0212191	0.0300069	0.0380837	0.0452103	0.0513534
		0.0277778	0.0555556	0.0771605	0.0925926	0.1032022	0.1103252	0.1149930	0.1179412
	0.1666667	0.2222222	0.2361111	0.2345679	0.2276235	0.2191358	0.2105731	0.2024653	0.1949714
1.0000000	0.6666667	0.5000000	0.4074074	0.3503086	0.3117284	0.2836934	0.2621742	0.2449739	0.2308043
	0.1666667	0.2222222	0.2361111	0.2345679	0.2276235	0.2191358	0.2105731	0.2024653	0.1949714
		0.0277778	0.0555556	0.0771605	0.0925926	0.1032022	0.1103252	0.1149930	0.1179412
			0.0046296	0.0123457	0.0212191	0.0300069	0.0380837	0.0452103	0.0513534
				0.0007716	0.0025720	0.0052726	0.0086020	0.0122861	0.0161037
					0.0001286	0.0005144	0.0012253	0.0022672	0.0036044
						0.0000214	0.0001000	0.0002715	0.0005620
							0.0000036	0.0000191	0.0000580
								0.0000006	0.0000036
									0.0000001

For example, Prob(1,2), i.e., the probability of reaching node (1,2), can be computed in the following way:

$$\text{Prob}(1,2) = \tfrac{1}{6} \times \text{Prob}(-1, 1) + \tfrac{2}{3} \times \text{Prob}(0, 1) + \tfrac{1}{6} \times \text{Prob}(1, 1)$$
$$= \tfrac{1}{6} \times 0 + \tfrac{2}{3} \times \tfrac{1}{6} + \tfrac{1}{6} \times \tfrac{2}{3} = \tfrac{2}{9}$$

It is essential that whenever the formula refers to a node that is not in the tree (i.e., $i < 0$), its probability is zero (this is the case for Prob(-1,1) in the above example).

Using this procedure the probability of all the nodes in the tree can be computed by successively rolling forward in the tree. By adding the previous nodes together in this manner we are implicitly counting the number of paths to each node and weighting each by its likelihood of occurring.

So for a 3-step trinomial tree the node-probabilities are as follows:

			0.46%
		2.78%	5.56%
	16.67%	22.22%	23.61%
100.00%	66.67%	50.00%	40.74%
	16.67%	22.22%	23.61%
		2.78%	5.56%
			0.46%

Notice that this matches Exhibit 9. Also note that the sum of the probabilities at any period (summing vertically) is 1.

Determining the Value of a Forward Start Swap

Exhibit 10 presents the probability weighted cumulative swap values using Exhibits 4 and 9. The added row on the bottom corresponds to swaps that start anywhere from 0.5 years to 4.5 years and are pay fixed swaps. This is the same as in the binomial forward start swap except we do not include the receive swaps since they are simply the mirror image of the pay fixed swaps.

The tenor of each of these swaps is simply the difference between the five years and the start time. For example, the forward swap that starts in one year has a tenor of 4 years, denoted a (1,4) forward start swap. The value of each of these swaps is found by summing the probability weighted nodes vertically at each point in time. We will show how this is done below.

Exhibit 10: Probability Weighted Cumulative Trinomial Swap Valuation Lattice for Forward Start Swaps at an SFR of 7.110%

```
                                                                          0.0000
                                                                  0.0000  0.0000
                                                          0.0000  0.0001  0.0001
                                                  0.0001  0.0005  0.0009  0.0010
                                          0.0008  0.0026  0.0048  0.0061  0.0050
                                  0.0043  0.0123  0.0208  0.0261  0.0256  0.0172
                          0.0214  0.0502  0.0737  0.0859  0.0841  0.0690  0.0401
                  0.0916  0.1638  0.2009  0.2071  0.1915  0.1589  0.1152  0.0609
          0.2777  0.3381  0.3237  0.2896  0.2450  0.2006  0.1519  0.1045  0.0521
 -0.2434 -0.1311 -0.0774 -0.0449 -0.0186 -0.0027  0.0095  0.0138  0.0151  0.0090
         -0.3260 -0.3847 -0.3554 -0.2955 -0.2338 -0.1730 -0.1208 -0.0729 -0.0344
                 -0.0894 -0.1563 -0.1847 -0.1833 -0.1611 -0.1276 -0.0868 -0.0441
                         -0.0187 -0.0427 -0.0610 -0.0685 -0.0649 -0.0507 -0.0288
                                 -0.0034 -0.0095 -0.0156 -0.0190 -0.0180 -0.0118
                                         -0.0006 -0.0018 -0.0033 -0.0040 -0.0032
                                                 -0.0001 -0.0003 -0.0006 -0.0006
                                                          0.0000  0.0000 -0.0001
                                                                  0.0000  0.0000
                                                                          0.0000
```

Pay Fixed Forward Start Swap Value

```
Time      0.5      1.0      1.5      2.0      2.5     3.0     3.5     4.0     4.5
       -0.2434  -0.1794  -0.1219  -0.0665 | 0.0000 | 0.0480  0.0909  0.1041  0.1034  0.0623
```

To find the corresponding SFR that makes the forward swap zero we simply iterate on SFR until this sum is zero. This is the same procedure we use to compute the SFR for a plain vanilla swap. Notice that at an SFR of 7.110% all of the forward start swaps are off market except for the (2,3) forward start swap. We have computed the SFR for a 3-year pay fixed forward start swap that starts in two years.

Also note that the 7.110% is slightly lower than the 7.116% found using the binomial method. This is due to the different interest rate properties incorporated within the trinomial framework that are not included in the binomial model. The trinomial model includes an explicit modeling of the mean reversion and so the drift rate within the trinomial model will be lower than in the binomial model, thus resulting in slightly lower forward rates. This will result in lower swap fixed rates for all forward start swaps when compared with the binomial model. This is an important aspect of the derivative valuation procedure within the fixed income area. The user should always be aware of the term structure model before using it for valuation or risk analysis. Different term structure models will cause very different values as well as other metrics such as OAS, effective duration, and effective convexity.

VALUING SWAPTIONS USING THE TRINOMIAL FRAMEWORK

We now present the trinomial framework for swaptions. We follow the same procedure as in the binomial method. Exhibit 11 corresponds to the cash flow lattice we presented earlier in the appendix except that we have changed the swap fixed rate to 7%. The swap fixed rate is now acting as the strike price for the swaption. For swaptions we will see that the methodology introduced for the plain vanilla swap remains the same. The only difference is that instead of iterating on the swap fixed rate, the swap fixed rate becomes the strike rate for the swaption. In other words, we follow the same procedure except the cash flows, and corresponding swap values, are computed using a strike rate for the swaption. The lattice in Exhibit 11 represents the cash flows resulting from the swap with a swap fixed rate of 7%.

Exhibit 11: Trinomial Pay Fixed Swap Cash Flow Lattice for Plain Vanilla Swap with a Strike or SFR of 7%

0.5	1.0	1.5	2.0	2.5	3.0	3.5	4.0	4.5	5.0
									3.108
								2.669	2.657
							2.221	2.248	2.237
						1.839	1.830	1.856	1.855
					1.454	1.474	1.466	1.499	1.498
				1.124	1.115	1.135	1.135	1.166	1.173
			0.795	0.809	0.800	0.826	0.827	0.862	0.869
		0.521	0.502	0.514	0.514	0.538	0.545	0.579	0.592
	0.245	0.246	0.229	0.247	0.246	0.275	0.282	0.320	0.333
−0.018	−0.010	−0.009	−0.019	−0.003	0.003	0.030	0.042	0.078	0.095
	−0.249	−0.242	−0.251	−0.230	−0.225	−0.194	−0.182	−0.144	−0.127
		−0.459	−0.463	−0.443	−0.433	−0.404	−0.388	−0.351	−0.331
			−0.660	−0.637	−0.627	−0.596	−0.580	−0.542	−0.522
				−0.818	−0.805	−0.775	−0.757	−0.720	−0.698
					−0.972	−0.940	−0.922	−0.884	−0.863
						−1.095	−1.074	−1.038	−1.015
							−1.217	−1.180	−1.158
								−1.313	−1.289
									−1.413

Exhibit 12: Trinomial Pay Fixed Swap Values for a Plain Vanilla Swap with a Strike or SFR of 7%

	0.5	1.0	1.5	2.0	2.5	3.0	3.5	4.0	4.5
									2.916
								4.876	2.503
							6.016	4.131	2.116
						6.509	5.007	3.436	1.760
					6.432	5.284	4.062	2.791	1.427
				5.896	5.031	4.135	3.183	2.187	1.121
			4.947	4.349	3.713	3.062	2.359	1.628	0.833
		3.667	3.277	2.891	2.481	2.055	1.592	1.105	0.569
	2.079	1.895	1.704	1.525	1.322	1.116	0.874	0.620	0.320
0.213	0.221	0.223	0.225	0.239	0.239	0.235	0.206	0.166	0.092
	−1.534	−1.350	−1.167	−0.965	−0.778	−0.587	−0.419	−0.255	−0.123
		−2.833	−2.473	−2.097	−1.729	−1.358	−1.002	−0.650	−0.321
			−3.702	−3.158	−2.621	−2.077	−1.548	−1.016	−0.507
				−4.154	−3.456	−2.751	−2.056	−1.360	−0.679
					−4.239	−3.381	−2.533	−1.679	−0.841
						−3.971	−2.977	−1.978	−0.990
							−3.394	−2.257	−1.131
								−2.518	−1.261
									−1.384

Exhibit 12 is the same lattice as that presented in Exhibit 4, but using a swap fixed rate of 7% and is found in the same way. The difference here is that no iteration is necessary since we are not trying to compute to the swap fixed rate. Notice that the value of the 5-year pay fixed swap is 0.213. This is because the swap fixed rate that produces a zero swap value is 7.0513% and this lattice corresponds to the lower swap fixed rate resulting in lower cash flows for the fixed rate payer — hence, the positive swap value. This lattice will be the basis for all pay fixed swaption valuation. We will see that all permutations of swaptions are simply an exercise of backward induction — a technique frequently used throughout all contingent claim valuation frameworks and illustrated in Chapter 8 within the binomial framework.

Following the same development as in Chapter 8, we will use Exhibit 12 to produce corresponding swaption lattices. We value different pay fixed swaptions — an (i,j) swaption represents a swaption that expires at time i on a swap with a tenor of j. We will illustrate this process for swaptions with expirations of 1, 2, 3, and 4 years. The corresponding swap tenors are 4, 3, 2, and 1 year(s). This is the same notation as in the binomial framework.

Exhibit 13 illustrates the swaption valuation lattice for a (4,1) pay fixed swaption. Since this is a swaption that expires in four years, the appropriate expiration values occur at year 4. Consequently, notice that the last column of this lattice represents the maximum of either the swap value or zero, max(Swap Value, 0). Since the swaption represents the right to enter into the 1-year swap at the end of four years, it will only be exercised in the event that the swap value is greater than zero. The swap values less than zero correspond to swaps with a swap fixed rate less than 7% and therefore the swaption holder would be better off not exercising the swaption. Once the expiration values are computed at year 4, it is then simply an exercise of backward induction using the interest rate lattice (Exhibit 2) to compute the discount factors. So the equation is similar to equation (5) as shown below:

Exhibit 13: (4,1) Trinomial Pay fixed Swaption with a Strike of 7%

0.5	1.0	1.5	2.0	2.5	3.0	3.5	4.0
							4.876
						3.916	4.131
					3.111	3.270	3.436
				2.430	2.545	2.665	2.791
			1.846	1.927	2.010	2.098	2.187
		1.340	1.394	1.449	1.507	1.567	1.628
	0.905	0.934	0.965	0.998	1.032	1.068	1.105
	0.552	0.561	0.569	0.576	0.584	0.592	0.602	0.620
0.300	0.295	0.289	0.281	0.269	0.254	0.234	0.207	0.166
	0.128	0.117	0.104	0.089	0.071	0.051	0.027	0.000
	0.035	0.027	0.019	0.011	0.004	0.000	0.000
	0.005	0.002	0.001	0.000	0.000	0.000
	0.000	0.000	0.000	0.000	0.000
	0.000	0.000	0.000	0.000
	0.000	0.000	0.000
	0.000	0.000
	0.000

$$\text{Swaption}_j = \frac{q_u \times \text{Swaption}_{u,\,j+1} + q_m \times \text{Swaption}_{m,\,j+1}}{\left(1 + \dfrac{r_j}{2}\right)}$$

$$+ \frac{q_d \times \text{Swaption}_{d,\,j+1}}{\left(1 + \dfrac{r_j}{2}\right)} \tag{6}$$

where Swaption$_{u,m,d}$ are the swaption values that feed into the node (j) being evaluated and the other variables are the same as in equation (5).

For example, the upper most node at year 3.5 for the (4,1) pay fixed swaption is found by applying equation (6) in the following manner:

$$\frac{0.16667 \times 4.876 + 0.66667 \times 4.131 + 0.16667 \times 3.436 + 3.581393}{\left(1 + \dfrac{0.11441}{2}\right)}$$

$$= 3.916$$

This approach is identical to the binomial approach except that the probabilities reflect the trinomial lattice weights.

Repeating this process throughout the lattice results in a (4,1) pay fixed swaption value of $0.300 per $100 notional principal. This value is significantly less than the (4,1) swaption value obtained from using the binomial framework. Why? This is again an example of the point emphasized at the beginning of this appendix. To repeat, different term structure models will give very different option values due to the embedded interest rate characteristics and the probabilities used throughout the lattice. Recall that the binomial model equally weighted all states while the trinomial model weights the upper and lower states much less than the middle state. This causes the binomial model to produce option values that will be much larger than the trinomial model. Since the binomial model implicitly weights extreme interest rates much higher than the trinomial model, the corresponding options will have larger values.

The problem is exacerbated when the volatility increases. This may seem odd since all the models are no arbitrage models, meaning that they will all give the same results for plain vanilla swaps (as well as option-free bonds). This is by design, however. The interest rates in the lattice are computed precisely to give the market prices of the plain vanilla swaps (as well as an option-free bond) but they are based on very different dynamics. It is the dynamics that affect the option valuation process.[3] This phenomenon will hold true for all of the swaption values that follow.

Before presenting a similar lattice for the other pay fixed swaptions, let's comment on this valuation framework. Notice that the swaption lattice relies completely on the interest rate and the swap value lattices. Therefore, computing swaption values as the inputs to the model change is easy. It becomes obvious then that we can further extend the swaption valuation to swaptions on exotic swap structures such as swaps with a varying notional principal. To do this we simply base the swaption lattice on the corresponding exotic swap value lattice. It is this kind of flexibility that makes our systematic approach so attractive.

Exhibits 14, 15, and 16 correspond to the (3,2), (2,3), and (1,4) pay fixed swaptions, respectively. The lattices are computed in the same manner as the (4,1) lattice except that the expiration values take place at different times within the swap value lattice. The behavior of swaptions within this framework is the same as in the binomial model shown in Chapter 9. Receiver swaptions are also valued in an analogous manner but are not presented here.

---

[3] For extended coverage of this phenomenon, see Gerald W. Buetow, Jr., James Sochacki, Frank J. Fabozzi, and Bernd Hanke, "The Effects of Different Term Structure Models on Interest Rate Risk Metrics," working paper (2000).

Exhibit 14: (3,2) Trinomial Pay fixed Swaption with a Strike of 7%

	0.5	1.0	1.5	2.0	2.5	3.0
						6.509
					5.047	5.284
				3.800	3.965	4.135
			2.725	2.834	2.946	3.062
		1.796	1.856	1.919	1.987	2.055
	1.038	1.049	1.059	1.069	1.085	1.116
0.516	0.497	0.472	0.439	0.394	0.331	0.235
	0.176	0.148	0.115	0.078	0.038	0.000
		0.029	0.017	0.006	0.000	0.000
			0.001	0.000	0.000	0.000
				0.000	0.000	0.000
					0.000	0.000
						0.000

Exhibit 15: (2,3) Trinomial Pay Fixed Swaption with a Strike of 7%

	0.5	1.0	1.5	2.0
				5.896
			4.184	4.349
		2.699	2.795	2.891
	1.456	1.466	1.483	1.525
0.627	0.574	0.503	0.400	0.239
	0.140	0.089	0.039	0.000
		0.006	0.000	0.000
			0.000	0.000
				0.000

Exhibit 16: (1,4) Trinomial Pay Fixed Swaption with a Strike of 7%

	0.5	1.0
		3.667
	1.843	1.895
0.592	0.449	0.223
	0.036	0.000
		0.000

Index

A

Accreting swaps, 10, 24, 53
Actual/360 day count convention, 17
American style swaption, 111
Amortizing swaps, 10, 24, 39, 53
Annualized rates on a bond-equivalent basis, 203
Arbitrage value, 65
Arbitrage-free values, 65

B

Backward induction, 70, 78, 116
Basis swaps, 10, 145
Binomial interest rate lattice, 68, 215
Binomial model, 66
Bond-equivalent yield (BEY), 201
Bootstrapping, 195

C

Calculating the dollar duration of a swap, 174
Calculating the fixed payments, 22
Calculating the floating payments, 17
Calculating the present value of the floating payments, 33
Cash flow for the pay LIBOR TED swap, 147
Cash flow for the swap, 2
Cash flows associated with a pay LIBOR swap, 150
Change in value for complex swap structures, 183
Changes in the term structure on a forward start swap's value, 101
Changes in the term structure, 136
Changing the strike rate, 131
CMS, 148
CMT swap, 148
Computing the swap cash flows using a trinomial lattice, 223
Constant maturity swaps (CMS), 10
Constant Maturity Treasury (CMT) swaps, 10, 148
Constant Maturity Treasury, 145
Constructing the binomial interest rate lattice, 71
Convexity bias, 106
Counterparty risk, 4
Cumulative swap valuation lattice, 77, 96, 112, 114

D

Determining future floating payments 20
Determining the dollar amount of the fixed payment for the period, 22
Discount rate, 79
Discounting of swap payment streams, 51
Dollar duration of a swap, 171
    calculation of, 174
Dollar price exposure, 170
Dollar value of an 01 (DV01), 169
Drift rate, 104
Duration, 169

E

Effect of changes in the term structure on a swap's value, 86
Effect of interest rate volatility on the swap fixed rate, 104

E

Effective duration, 169
Eurodollar certificates of deposit (CDs), 18
European style swaption, 111
Expiration of the swaption, 129
Expiration values, 114, 115

F

Fixed-rate payer, 1, 9
Fixed-rate receiver, 1, 9
Floating payment, 18, 36
Floating-rate payer, 1
Floating-rate receiver, 1
Forward discount factor, 34, 37, 195
Forward rates, 34, 69, 195, 199
    interpretation of, 211
Forward start swap, 10, 95
Forward swap fixed rate, 95

I

Implicit forward rates, 200
Implied drift rate, 104
Interest payments, 1
Interest rate models, 66
Interest rate options, 65
Interest rate volatility, 68, 104, 136
International Monetary Market of the Chicago Mercantile Exchange, 18
Interpretation of a swap
    package of cash flows, 5
    package of cash market instruments, 7
    package of futures (forward) contracts, 5, 6
Inverted term structure, 139

L

Lattice approach, 11, 65
    to value a basis swap, 150
Lattice construction, 68
Lattice model, 65
London interbank offered rate (LIBOR), 2
London International Financial Futures Exchange, 18

M

Modified duration, 169

N

Notional amount, 1
Notional principal, 1
Number of paths that arrive at a given node, 98

O

Obtaining the cash flow at each node of the lattice, 72
Off market swaps, 80
One-factor models, 66
Options embedded in bond structures, 65
Over-the-counter (OTC) instruments, 4

P

Par yield curve, 195

241

Pay fixed swaption, 111
Pay LIBOR TED swap, 145
Payer's swaption, 10, 111
Period forward rate, 34
Plain vanilla swap, 1
   and interest rate volatility, 90
Portfolio's dollar duration, 171
Present value of swap values, 71
Present value of the fixed payments, 49
Present value of the floating payments, 49
Price value of a basis point (PVBP), 169
Principles of interest rate risk control with swaps, 169
Probability of getting to a node, 100
Probability of reaching a node can be computed, 99

Q

Quoting a swap fixed rate, 4

R

Receive fixed swaption, 111, 118
Receiver's swaption, 10, 111
Roller coaster swaps, 24, 53

S

Shifting term structure, 136
Short-term forward-rate curve, 203
Speed of mean reversion factor, 220
Spot rate, 34
Steeper term structure, 139
Strike rate, 131
Swap dealer, 4
Swap fixed rate (SFR), 1, 22, 37
Swap floating payments when rates change, 49
Swap payments adjusted for the notional principal for the
   period, 23
Swap rate, 1
Swap value
   changes when the term structure steepens and shifts
      from its original position, 88
   for both counterparties as the term structure changes,
      89
   traditional approach, 11
Swaps to control interest rate risk, 165
Swaption lattice, 116
Swaption valuation, 116, 129
   effect of shape of the term structure, 138
   effect of the strike rate, 131
Swaptions, 10, 111

T

Target dollar duration, 170
Target rate of interest rates, 220
TED spread, 145
Tenor of the underlying swap, 129
Term structure of interest rates, 86
Term structure of Treasury rates, 195
Theoretical spot rates, 195
Traditional approach, 11
Treasury-eurodollar CD spread, 145
Trinomial interest rate model, 219
Trinomial models, 66
Trinomial probability lattice 229
Two-factor model, 66

V

Valuation model, 65
Valuation of an interest rate swap using the traditional
   approach, 55
Valuation using forward rates, 205
Valuation using the lattice approach, 150
Valuing a swap, 49, 69
   after rates change, 51
   complex swap structures, 95
   forward start swap, 101
   plain vanilla swap, 11
   to the fixed-rate payer, 52
   with varying notional principal, 82
Value bonds with embedded options, 65
Value of a Treasury coupon security, 196
Value of the future cash flows at a node, 70
Value options on bonds, 65
Valuing swaptions with a varying notional principal, 116
Valuing varying notional principal forward start swaps,
   101
Valuing forward start swaps using the trinomial frame-
   work, 229
Valuing swaptions using the trinomial framework, 234
Volatility of interest rates, 129
Volatility, 131

W

Weighted by the probability of realizing its value, 96

Z

Zero-coupon rate, 195

Printed in the United States
117994LV00001B/8/A